VILLAGES
of the
WHITE HORSE

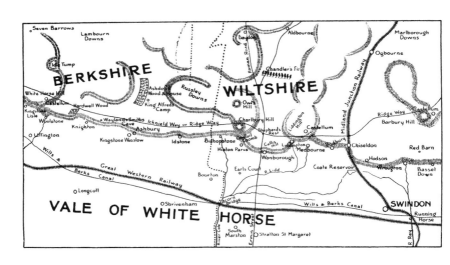

ALFRED WILLIAMS

VILLAGES
of the
WHITE HORSE

NONSUCH

To
Mrs Story Maskelyne,
Lover of the Down-Side,
Basset Down, Wroughton, Wilts

First published 1913
Copyright © in this edition Nonsuch Publishing, 2007

Nonsuch Publishing Limited
The Mill, Brimscombe Port, Stroud, Gloucestershire, GL5 2QG, UK
www.nonsuch-publishing.com

Nonsuch Publishing is an imprint of NPI Media Group

British Library Cataloguing in Publication Data
A catalogue record for this book is available from the British Library

ISBN 978 1 84588 061 3

Typesetting and origination by Nonsuch Publishing Limited
Printed and bound in Great Britain by Oaklands Book Services Limited

Contents

Introduction to the Modern Edition

STRETCHING FROM THE EDGE OF Oxford to the outskirts of the Cotswolds, the 'Vale of White Horse' is one of the few areas in England to have retained its original prehistoric landscape, its scenery having altered very little since the Neolithic era. The valley takes its name from the ancient and majestic hill figure found there: the mysterious white horse carved into the chalk hillside above the village of Uffington. The area is also home to several other sites which have long been the subject of legend and folklore: Dragon Hill is a flat-topped mound where it is said St George slew the dragon, the blood of which prevents grass from growing there; the Manger, an unusual, steep-sided valley, is said to be the feeding place of the White Horse on moonlit nights; and the Iron Age hill-fort of Uffington Castle crowning White Horse Hill. The countryside around the White Horse fascinates due to the mystery surrounding these ancient sites, and in his account of rural life during the early years of the twentieth century Alfred Williams offers a valuable historical record of the customs, traditions and beliefs held by local people at that time, often touching upon the superstitions that were then so common in rural communities.

The White Horse which overlooked this locality, and gave it its name, is perhaps the most famous hill figure in Britain, and probably the oldest. It has rarely fallen into disrepair, but has been maintained and re-cut many times throughout its long existence, largely voluntarily by the people from the local villages. The reasons behind the creation of the Horse, which would explain why this tradition has been so adhered to, have been much discussed. Its exact origin remains unknown, although it is so steeped in mystery that it has long evoked fascination and speculation, giving rise to many theories. Local tradition held that the carving was not intended to be a horse at all, but instead a representation of the dragon killed by St George on nearby Dragon Hill. By the late seventeenth century, however, people began to look for more plausible explanations for its existence. Some believed it may have been cut into the hillside by Hengist of Kent, the Saxon king whose symbol was said to be a white horse. A later, and long-enduring, theory was that it was carved by King Alfred to commemorate his victory over the Danes at the Battle of Ashdown in A.D. 871, a connection which was celebrated in a song composed by G.K. Chesterton for the scouring and cleaning of the horse. However, it has become clear from recent archaeological evidence that it can be identified from an era long before that of King Alfred, probably as early as the late Bronze Age, placing the figure at around 3,000 years old.

Despite much conjecture, the reason behind its creation remains a mystery. It may have been the emblem or badge of a local tribe, as a means of marking out their territory. It is possible that it had some religious significance or purpose, perhaps created to represent the Celtic symbol of the goddess Epona, the protector of horses, or was even cut by worshippers of the sun god Belinos, who had associations with horses. Horse-worship is certainly recognised as common during the Bronze and Iron Ages, and the location of the carving, at an angle where the best vantage point is looking down on it from above, enabling it to be seen by the god himself, would further support this type of theory. Whichever of these hypotheses might be correct, it is clear that the effort required to create the figure in the first place must have been considerable, and its preservation for 3,000 years indicates a reverence implying religious significance of some nature.

The tradition of cleaning the site, known as the 'scouring' of the Horse, is believed to have been a religious festival in later times, particularly during the eighteenth century, adding further credibility to the figure having religious origins. This event traditionally took place roughly every seven years, with all the villages in the area participating. The scourings were celebrated amidst an atmosphere of fairground revelry, under the jurisdiction of the local lord, who funded the event. The celebrations consisted of pastimes such as cheese-rolling, wrestling, backsword play, horse-racing and climbing the greasy pole for a leg of mutton. Food stalls, musicians and acrobats all added to the festivities, which could last for over three days. Williams remarks on the 'boundless enthusiasm' that the local people he encountered had for this tradition, despite the fact that the revelry of it had by that time long since declined, as had village festivals in general, with the last scouring of its kind taking place in 1857. It was, however, such a famous event that, amongst all the other significant happenings of the day, he notes how 'there is none that is so well and fondly remembered for miles about the Vale as are the great "Revels" of 1857'. By the time he wrote *Villages of White Horse*, maintenance was undertaken by workmen from a local estate, but the decline of the accompanying festivities was regretted by many. The Horse's significance today is seen in terms of its place as part of English heritage, and the discovery that its existence can be traced back much further than originally thought has only added to the importance of maintaining its condition, work which is now undertaken by the National Trust.

Preface

IN A PREVIOUS WORK I endeavoured to sketch out a single village; here I have attempted to present a whole locality, as I see it, and as I have known it; to give an idea of its general scenic and detailed beauty; to show the villages in their natural setting and geographical order, touching lightly on their origin, history, and industries; and, most of all, to give them animation, to depict as much characteristic life as possible, and to have the whole faithful, actual, real, and recognizable. I was unable, in the compass of one small book, to enter into a very minute description of things of minor importance scattered throughout the district, since the ground covered is twenty miles in extent, and the villages themselves number a score; the most I could do was to flit from place to place, loitering longest in those I love best, and gathering additional chips of information by the way. The range of country, down-land throughout, is sweetly and chastely beautiful, and unsurpassed in interest, while the villages are some of the most ancient in the world, having been first of all inhabited by remote prehistoric peoples, then by the early Britons in their fortified camps, next they were Roman stations, afterwards Saxon villages, then Danish settlements, and, finally, as we know them here, strongly and typically English, second to none in the land.

As to the persons and "characters" that figure in the pages, I have made a point of introducing them exactly as I found them, rough and plain, frank and hearty, honest and homely; there was no need to dissemble in their case, to metamorphose them into different beings, or to dress them up in fictitious finery; I am proud of every single one of them. Some of the dialect and narrative may appear a little barbarous to those of refined tastes, but I can assure them it is all accurate and characteristic, typical of the countryside still, while the bits of anecdote, and clownish fun—usually not honoured with a place in serious literature—are of that kind which delights the simple-hearted peasant people, and so are in keeping with the object of the volume.

Whoever reads the pages will form his own opinion as to the economic conditions obtaining in the locality, which I shall confess I have not been at any great pains to set forth, since that was not altogether a part of my design; but this much I will say, wherever I have gone I have found the villagers industrious, sturdy in principle, breezily optimistic, cheerful, philosophic, and exceedingly kind-hearted, but poor, much poorer, in fact, than they ought to be in this wonder-working age of ours.

If anything I have written is able to enlist the smallest sympathy in their behalf, I shall be happy: they are deserving of the best that can be given them for their patience, courage, simplicity, and modesty.

A.W.

Villages and Hamlets included in this Book in their General Order

I

The carter of Woolstone—Sketch of the downs—
Villages of the down-side—Cock-fighting—"Barley-
bangers"—Weird beliefs

WILLIAM BREAKSPEAR, THE STURDY OLD carter of Woolstone,
with corduroy suit, billycock hat, and leather gaiters reaching above the knees, stumped into the stable carrying a chalk-soiled
overcoat under his arm, with broad flag-basket and brass-handled
whip in the hand, which he first of all deposited on top of the big
wooden corn-bin, and then proceeded to harness black "Diamond,"
who stood grinding her food in the manger and blowing out her
nose now and then, making the chaff fly. He pushed the big collar
over her eyes and ears—she thrusting her head forward to assist the
operation—turned it right side up, clapped on the hames, fitted the
blind halter, pad, and breeching-tackle, and buckled up the belly-
band, with a snatch of song that old Farmer Brooks, of Stanford-
in-the-Vale, used to sing every year at harvest-home:

> A sack o' wild oats in our youthful days,
> And we're happier when they're gone.

Then he turned the mare's head round to the door, and addressed
the youngster in the next stall:

"Come an, ther, an' fetch thaay two along to tha drill. We be
gwain to put thaay black cyarter's wuts in to-daay. Breng thi cwut
along wi tha. I warn thee't want un a dinner-time. 'Tis a main

percin' blaw ayant tha owl' White 'Oss tha smarnin'. We could do wi tha owl' shepherd's leather britches very well."

"What sart o' britches be thaay, then?" the youth inquires, with a grin.

"Why, essent a never yerd tell o' owl' Joby Cark an' 'is leather britches? A got 'em wet-droo, an' tha missis put 'em in tha o-ven to dry, thas know'st, an' a couldn't get 'em an tha nex' marnin'. Zo a started blerin' a bit. Then tha owl' dooman begun an to 'n. 'Thee must thenk o' thi namesake, dost know, Job, an' hae patience, like 'e did.' 'Aa, begad mun,' Job zed, 'but 'e was never fooast to wer baked britches, like I got to.' Jest put thi nammet down, an' 'elp I wi that owl' graay a minute, oot. Now then, ther, stan' awver. Tha bist too fat to mauve. Tha oostn't draa a sprat off a gridiron. Tha's moore at it! Now we be awright. Gee up, ther!" And off they go singing:

> Tha owl' black 'oss is no longer in tha stall,
>   Drat tha owl' toss! I'm jolly glad a's gone;
> For a oodn't do na work, an' a was no good at all;
>   Drat tha owl' 'oss! I'm jolly glad a's gone.
>   Hi-i-o,
>   Tha stall in tha stable's empty;
>   Hi-i-o,
>   For tha owl' black 'oss is gone.

That is a fair sample of the spirit of the north Berkshire and Wiltshire Downs, and the language and characteristic of the hardy, cheerful race, who for centuries have toiled and dwelled there, in the fresh, strong breezes and clear, bright sunlight. Where would you find a more robust type of villager than that portrayed in "The Scouring of the White Horse," those frequenters of the feast and revel, the heroes of numerous battles and contests, of wrestling, back-swording, and other vigorous games and exercises? But this type was not confined to the locality of the White Horse alone; it was common to the whole expanse of country from the Blowing

Stone to Wroughton, and right on to Devizes. The same boisterous nature and spirit prevailed; the same—or nearly the same—language was spoken; work was the same; play was the same; life was the same in its general aspects and relations; there was a common tone and feeling throughout the villages. Here were the ballad-singers and comic actors, who attended the festivals and fairs, tramping from place to place; there were the fiddlers and dancers, the "wras'lers," "back-zoorters," and cock-fighters, from end to end of the chain. There were a few local features and characteristics. The dialect of Broad Hinton and Wroughton differs a little from that of Woolstone and Uffington, and the humour is gentler and finer at the Berkshire end. But let us first sketch out the ground.

Whoever has journeyed from London west of Didcot has caught a glimpse of the famous Berkshire Downs, and the old White Horse stretching his huge length upon the western side of the towering chalk hill that overlooks Uffington and the valley there. These downs first take the eye of the traveller at Streatley, and again above the town of Wantage, the reputed birthplace of Alfred the Great. There they are low, and generally unconspicuous, sometimes dropping almost out of view, and now again rising and projecting to the north-west by Kingstone Lisle, mounting higher and higher, till they reach their topmost point in the noble hill of White Horse, 900 feet above sea-level. West of the White Horse, towards Wayland Smith's Cave, the contour line falls considerably, and continues fairly even for five miles, when it rises again, up, up, up, with a series of wavelike sweeps and curves, and shows a beautiful round hill, sweet in its simplicity, garmented with delicious soft turf, and golden with rock rose, bird's-foot trefoil, and quaint kidney vetch, enthroned above the plateau, and with skirts reaching down into the valley. This is Charlbury, or Hinton Hill. Following this is a high ridge, which ends abruptly at Totterdown, by the Shepherd's Rest Inn, and lands you on Wanborough Plain, the scene of two fierce battles, in A.D. 591 and A.D. 717, between Ceolric and Ceawlin, and Ceolred and Ine. Across the plain Liddington Hill rises with a stately slope, and opposes its broad front of half a mile in length to sundown, and receives the flood of gold full on the breast, while the purple shadows creep slowly up the sides, and steal over the rugged earthworks, obliterating the high clump of beeches at the other end. Once more the outline drops rapidly to the south-west, and continues, this time, beyond Wroughton to Barbury Castle—the highest point at the western end—after which it declines again, and soon after fades quite away. The downs fall back, rolling on to Devizes, and the valley of the Avon begins. This stretch of downs, which seem continually to rise out of nothing and fade again into the skyline, dropping down behind you, is about thirty-five miles in length.

The actual ground of our observations is about half this distance, and comprises the western portion, part of which is in Wiltshire and part in Berkshire—that is, beginning near Wroughton, and ending with the Blowing Stone at Kingstone Lisle. Roughly speaking, the field lies between Barbury Castle and Uffington Castle; if we take these two historic camps as landmarks, we shall easily identify our position, and grasp the locality. The other landmarks are Charlbury Hill and Liddington Hill, a mile or so apart, and about half-way from either end.

To view the hills face to face from the valley, opposite Charlbury, four or five miles away, you would think them to run in a perfectly even and continuous line, at an equivalent distance from you, so completely are the subservient lines and detail blended up and concealed with the blue of the atmosphere; but if you shift your position to the Ashbury Road, or to Swindon Parish Church, they assume quite another shape—they now appear to have turned quite round, and face you from a different direction.

The view from the Uffington end, whether taken from the vale or the downs themselves, is irregular and confusing. It is something like looking along a huge flight of stairs turned sideways. The reason of this is that when the valley was carved by the mighty stream that flowed through it, the motion was from west to east, consequently the declivities and slopes are in that direction, as may be seen from either of the eminences, and which is especially visible in the Giants' Stairs, at the end of the Horse's Manger, where a series of channels were washed out of the hillside.

The light also interferes with the view from the eastern end, for the simple reason that it is always in front of you; you are looking against it all the while, and the disposition of the slopes being towards you, you do not obtain a sight of the surface, but are always confronted with more or less of shadow. But from the western end the view is always soft and pleasing; the gentle slopes and terraces, trailing away, are clothed with lovely light, and tints of warm green or gold, crimson, brown, or purple. There could be nothing more tenderly sweet and soothing than the view of Charlbury Hill and the Bishopstone and Ashbury slopes from the top of the road that brings you up from Wanborough to the Shepherd's Rest. The still, calm beauty, the charming interfusion of colour, the soft radiance of light—especially in the afternoon—and the overpowering sense of rest, hold you spellbound; you seem to melt and dissolve into it, to feel the beautiful within you, and when you go forward through the fresh, pure air, you are like another being, a thing new created.

The hills, except the high parts of Liddington, Hinton, and the White Horse, are fully cultivated. The colours of the chalk ground and crops in the summer and autumn are very striking. The fallowland, after a few days of sunshine, gleams like snow in the distance; at one time there is the bright green of the young corn and the patches of vivid yellow charlock; at another the crimson and purple of the clover and sanfoin, or the rich red and gold of the cornfields. Here and there, along the skyline, is a cluster of farm buildings or a solitary barn, showing like a speck against the blue heavens or steel grey clouds. The white roads up the hills look as steep as walls, while farther back are a few stunted trees, usually of hawthorn, and a thin plantation or hedge of beech, looking exactly like a broken line of cavalry on the march.

There are in all twenty villages and hamlets nestling composedly along the slopes and under the hills, some entirely concealed among the dense trees, and others scattered about, more plainly visible. Beginning at the western end there are: Basset Down, Wroughton, Hodson, Chiseldon, Badbury, Medbourne, Liddington, Wanborough, Aldbourne, Baydon, Hinton Parva, Bourton, Bishopstone, Idstone, Ashbury, Kingstone Winslow, Knighton, Woolstone, Uffington, and Kingstone Lisle, all ancient and interesting, the scene of generations of hearty and vigorous life, and inhabited by a strong and sturdy race, of which any country in the world might justly be proud, equal to the ancient Spartans in simplicity, and to the Dorians in wit and humour.

These villages are some of the oldest in the land, dating from a very remote age, long before the Romans came to the island; and there is every reason for believing that they were in existence before those of the valley. In the first place, in early times the valley was no more than forest and swamp, an unwholesome waste, and beset with all kinds of wild beasts, so that living there, from a human point of view, was impossible; but by reason of the fine facilities it afforded for hunting on the one hand, and the comparative bareness of the downs on the other, the people would naturally wish to dwell as near to it as possible. There is evidence of this in the so-called remains of the ancient pit-dwellings, and in the prehistoric camps or villages of Blunsdon, Binknoll, Wroughton, and possibly Wanborough, all which were built upon considerable eminences, overlooking the level ground. At a later date the hill-slopes were found most convenient for pasturing cattle, and, later still, for tillage and corn-growing, and for building, too—with chalk from the downs—and, furthermore, in civilized times, because the elevation of the springs enabled the inhabitants to construct mills easily for grinding the corn, while the situation was always dry and healthy.

Diodorus Siculus, the ancient Greek historian, tells us a little of these early peoples. He says they built themselves houses of timber and clay, and thatched them with reeds. They busied themselves with agriculture, kept much cattle, made cheese, and lived upon the produce of the land. In reaping their corn they cut off the ears from the stalks, and stored them up in repositories under the ground. The grain they threshed out every day as required, and, after bruising it with stones, made it into bread. They were people of just character and sound principle; to use Diodorus's own words: "They are of much sincerity and integrity, far from the craft and knavery of men among us, contented with plain and homely fare, strangers to the excess and luxury of rich men." This latter part sounds very well, but I do not know what Diodorus would have thought of the modern gentleman who lived on the Wiltshire Downs, and earned for himself the title of Bacon Jack. This hearty son of the soil made a wager that he would eat a pound of raw bacon and suck thirteen duck's eggs, which he did, in fact, to the huge delight of a crowd of villagers, and the fun was intensified when it was discovered that the old carter had cut the front of his new white waistcoat into shreds, where he had held the bacon against it to slice it up.

Another historian, Julius Cæsar, who, by the way, is said to have ridden a wonderful horse with prehistoric feet of five toes, tells us that there were "infinite multitudes" of men, very many houses, a great number of cattle, and all kinds of timber, except silver fir and sweet chestnut, in South Britain. The men were shaven, except on the top lip, and had wives in common, and they used copper or iron tallies in place of money. They considered it impious to eat hares, geese, and cocks, but they kept the last-named for sport. The ancient Britons revelled in cock-fighting, so it is no wonder it was indulged in throughout all the villages here so enthusiastically till half a century ago.

The old road-mender has told me of the cock-fighting as he sat grinning in the chair, gripping his ground-ash stick tightly with both hands and leaning hard upon it, looking at me with his grey head a little on one side and his eyes brimful of mischief.

"S'pose thees yerd tell o' tha cock-fightin'?"

"I've heard you old folks speak of it, before now,

"Thees't a laaf't if thees't a bin ther, I can tell tha."

"What do you know about it?"

"Bin at it miseif, mun, many a time."

"You been a cock-fighting!"

"Ha-a!"

"Tell me about it."

"Ust to brade 'em a purpose, dost know. Ther was two or dree sarts an 'em. Ust to gie 'em port wine; veed 'em wi port-wine sops. My hi! that made 'em upstrapalous. Couldn' owld 'em, you. Never let 'em zeed one another, thas know'st. Ust to cut ther spers off when tha was little, and clip ther wings. Didn' thaay croww! Ther ust to be reg'ler clubs fer cock-fightin' all round, mun—Stratton, an' Wanborough, an' Bushipstone. Ust to challenge one another, an' put tha money down—vive pown' a side, an' sometimes moore. Someb'dy watched fer tha cunstable, an' at it we ust to go, mi lads."

"Used to have a ring, I suppose."

"Aw aa, a cooass; us ed a reng. Then ther was tha two 'owlders. Tha ust to stan' in tha reng, one aache side, an' 'owld tha cocks. Didn' thaay struggle! Tha'ed tha piccid steel spers strapped an ther vit, dost know. Bymby tha lets loose an 'em. Off thaay goes, mi lads, straight at one another, an' the feathers did flee. Sometimes tha killed one another the fust go; tha 'ed to kip an till one an 'em was done for. I calls to mind one day, when tha was at it, one cock fled at t'other an' bowled un awver flat on 'is back, an' ther a led, kickin' 'is death-kick. As soon as a fell down, mun, up jumped tothern a top an in, an' begun a shoutin' 'Er-er-er-er-err-r' as proud as a paacock. But 'e was a bit afoore 'is time. While a was a-crowin' ther, bagger if tother didn't kick 'is sper right droo ees 'ed, an' 'ee died fust aater all. An' it didn' allus end wi cock-fightin' neither, you. Us often 'ed to pick em up an' run awaay wi tothers aater us. Tha ust to saay: 'We byet e a cock fightin', an' now ya got to 'ev summat else;' an' at it tha went, else tha cut off as hard as tha was able. Ther was some gwains on at that time, thee medst depend upon't."

William Breakspear belongs to the eastern extremity of the field, the old road-mender represents the middle, and Matty Matthews hails from the other end, going towards Devizes.

"Now thee nawtice, if ever thee bist beyand Broad 'Inton, aal the yawk got girt yuds down thick woy."

"How do you account for that, Matty?"

"Aw, livin' an the chaak, e spwause, snaa. Tha's what tha ses. Tha's wher tha myeks the barley-bangers."

"Barley-bangers?"

"B*arr*ley-bangers."

"What's a barley-banger?"

"Why, a cyuk theng, made out o' barley-maal, a sure."

"What is it—round, square, or what?"

"Squer naw. 'Tis jest a bit o' barley-maal mexed up wi' water an' byeked in the pot awver the vire, chocked in anyhow."

"Baked in the pot?"

"Pot, aa! Code struth, essent thee never seed narn o' thaay owl' dree-legged pot thengs? Tha's what tha byeks barley-bangers in. I've yerd my mother tell a tale many a time, as a wur zot bi tha vire, 'bout ole Bob Cooper the cowman. They wur devulish 'ard times mind, they wur. The ole chap 'ad a hawl zwarm o' kids, an' awni aaight shillin' a wik comin' in to kip 'em. A allus 'ad zum pegs in tha sty, an' varty lug o' Ian' bi tha zide o' tha 'owse. Ust to graw taties an' a leetle patch o' barley every year. When 'twur dreshed out a used to zend it to tha mill, an' ae't ground inta maal, zee. Ust to zell tha pegs to buy claws an' paay tha rent. When a wur gone to work, tha ole dooman ust to zift the peg's maal an' myek zum barley-bangers an' gie to the nippers. One day ole Bob come whum yarly an' cotched 'er at it. Didn' 'e caal 'er! I've yerd my mother zaay't times: 'Thee't starve my pegs to veed thay blasted young uns. Let 'em go awver that 'edge yander an' yet zwedes, same as I got to, yels let 'em die.' Tha ole dooman zot an' cried an' thawt a bit. At last a thawt a'd get zum snayuls. Ther was one gyel a didn't like out o' tha lot, zo a thawt ef ar a one was to die it shud be thick un. Zo a gied 'er tha snayuls vust, thenkin' tha might pizen 'er; but 'er snapped 'em up sa quick, an' liked 'em sa well, that aal tothern wanted 'em, too. Zo tha ole dooman gied out myekin' tha barley-bangers an' ved tha kids wi' zwedes an' snayuls, an' my mother ull tell e tha same, look, if you dwunt-belave it."

Then old Tommy Whale, the sweeper, spoke up:

"Le's see, tha's wher tha dunged tha monniment, to make 'e grow, down Churl woy, yun it?"

"Naw tha didn't, neether. Tha dunged tha staple, tha did, at B'kampton, to make un graw as 'igh as tha tower."

"An' wher was it as tha whiteweshed tha owl' rawn bool?"

"Aw, that was Lavinton woy. Didn' we ust to tarment ole Jakey 'bout 'e! Us got un as wi-yuld."

"An' that yent so bad as gettin' in tha pond to save the owl' duck from drownin'. Tha's right anuf, yun it?"

"Aw aa, cos I wur ther. An' the best o't wur a put 'is best claws an to do't wi'. Tha ole chap wur terr'ble frade tha duck ood be drownded, an' 'gun gettin' in aater 'n. Then Billy 'Edges, the ole cyarter, comes up an' ses: 'I should go an' put mi best claws un vust, Willum, if I was in thy place.' An' baggar if a didn't go an' do't, too, an' zaved tha ole duck. But thee mus'n't saay nothin' about it ther now, yels thee't soon get chocked out on't."

Though the dialect differs, from the White Horse to Barbury, and the humour is broader at the Wiltshire end, there is nevertheless the same picturesqueness of imagination and romanticism evident throughout the whole region, recalling something of the medieval spirit, and tinctured with the old superstition. At Woolstone and Ashbury there are the legends of Wayland Smith and St. George and the Dragon; at Wroughton and Broad Hinton the old folks still relate the belief that on Christmas Eve the oxen and all cloven-hoofed beasts kneel down in the stalls to worship the infant Saviour. Another weirdly imaginative belief, local here, was to the effect that if one waited in the church porch on Christmas Eve, and peered through the keyhole, he would see a phantasm of every wedding and funeral to be conducted in the church the following year. One night, at Broad Hinton, a pair of villagers set out for the church and waited in the porch as usual. By-and-by one dropped off to sleep, while the other continued the watch. At last the interior of the building grew light; shadowy forms moved about. There was the parson in his surplice, and the old sexton setting the trestles before the choir-stalls within. He heard the deep toll of the bell in the tower, and quaked with fear, yet continued crouching at the keyhole, like one transfixed. Presently the bell stopped, and the cortège entered. There were the bearers with the coffin, and the mourners, all in ghostly silence, but in terrible reality. But the tragic part was that the corpse was the watcher's own, and the mourners were his friends and kindred; he had been viewing his own funeral. Horrified, he ran off, and left his companion fast asleep in the porch, to be awakened by the bell-ringers soon afterwards. Such a relation, coming from a simple village, is worthy of "Faust," or the "Magico Prodigioso" of Calderon.

II

Barbury Castle—Hay Lane—"Word Ale"—Basset
Down—The gardener's cottage—Granny Ferris—Bees
and badgers—The woodman—The wrong pig—
Election riots

B ASSET DOWN, WHERE WE TAKE the field, is about a mile west
of Wroughton, and a short way from Broad Hinton, on the
one hand, and the busy industrial town of Swindon on the other.
The road leads from Lydiard Tregoze over the railway by Hay Lane,
shoots up the steep hill, dense with beech and fir, holly, privet, and
laurel, and lands you on the open downs near Red Barn, exactly
opposite the huge hill of Barbury, crowned at one end with exten-
sive earthworks, at the other with a high clump of beeches, visible
for many miles over the valley to the north and east. "Her Cynric
and Ceawling fuhton with Bryttas æt Beran Byrg."—"Now Cynric
and Ceawlin fought with the Britons at Barbury," the old Saxon
Chronicle tersely tells us. This was in A.D. 556. Here the Britons,
burning to avenge their defeat of a few years earlier, assembled a
mighty host of their bravest warriors to oppose the Saxons. But
neither choice of ground, nor the tradition of Roman tactics, nor
heroic Celtic valour, could withstand the terrible impetuosity of
the West Saxon foot, and when the sun set, after a stout hand-to-
hand fight that had lasted all day, Ceawlin was victor; the kingdom
of Wessex was firmly established.

All that is past now. The huge, whale-backed downs roll away—
looking suddenly at them you seem to catch their motion visibly,
like that of a sleek, round-bellied monster turning in the deep green

waters; line after line and curve after curve run into each other, and are intermingled. To the east is the impregnable fortress of Liddington; here are the mysterious-looking woods and hangars that mock and tantalize you with their deeply felt silence; there the frowning, rigid earthworks, overlooking the wide red and gold cornfields stretching to the north east: there is little that is reminiscent of the bloody battle-ground.

The road through Hay Lane—formerly an ancient British cattle-track—is bordered with hedges of blackthorn, interspersed with briars of the sweetly delicate field-rose, distinguishable from the dog-rose by the sparseness of thorn and the charming clusters of creamy-white bloom, while along the roadside are tufts of strong, spearlike grass, uncommon in the valley, a remnant of the time when all was marsh, swamp, and quagmire, the home of the ichthyosaurus, the hippopotamus, and the beaver. Here and there, in the angles of the fields, are small, waste patches of bushes, rushes, and reeds, with stagnant pools, half-concealed under the boughs and thickets, or a copse of elm, birch, and poplar. A short way from the hill a tiny spring flows beneath the road, and near by stands a broken milestone whose record is rendered undecipherable by the lapse of years, lichens, and tempest. The banks of the hedgerows are strewn with primrose and violet in the spring; higher up strong-smelling garlic escapes from the plantations, and half covers the greensward by the roadside.

Lower down from the hill the canal and railway pass along, though the first-named is in disuse now, and the wharf and buildings are dilapidated; the silent barges no longer glide between the deep banks underneath the stone arch out towards the Bristol Avon, and the channel is overgrown with rushes, weeds, and flowering-plants. Near the wharf an inn formerly stood, a noted rendezvous of poachers and gamesters, and the scene of much back-swording, wrestling, and cock-fighting; but the poachers brought the place into ill-repute, and after an affair with firearms at the inn, in which the grandfather's clock was shot full in the face—though the contents of the piece were intended for another—the licence was withdrawn and the house closed. It was in a field near Hay Lane that the famous Rob Roy was run to earth. This happened some sixty years ago, the Rob Roy being one of the huge broad-gauge engines, which ran off the track, and leapt over the fence into the field, with a train of carriages behind it. The accident befel at the week-end; everyone, from far and near, came to see the sight on the Sabbath—there were none to ring the bells or worship at the churches round about.

Running alongside Hay Lane is a strip of land called Midgehall, that has been exempt from the payment of tithes for seven centuries, the freedom from which has depended, it was supposed, upon the annual observation of a curious custom known as "Word Ale." The tithing was given by Henry II to the Cistercian Abbey of Stanley, and all the Cistercian land had been declared tithe-free by Pope Innocent in 1139. One consequence of the gift was that the worthy Rector of Lydiard Tregoze, deprived of his revenues, appealed to the rich Abbot of Stanley for redress, who, "having a holy respect unto charity," allowed him the munificent sum of eight shillings per annum with which to provide for the needs of the church.

There were formerly no written records of "Word Ale." The only evidence of the court was the White Rod, a hazel wand in which one notch was cut annually to denote a session or meeting. The court was attended by the tenants holding the lands, and the steward of the estate. The rod was in the custody of the tenant at whose house the court was next to be held—it was held at all the farmhouses in turn. Tenants and steward alike were bound by a solemn oath never to divulge any of the proceedings, which were of a sacred character. After the dissolution of the monasteries, when the property had passed out of the control of the abbot into lay hands, secrecy was of the utmost importance; many efforts were made to prevent the holding of the court, man-traps being frequently set to catch the steward, to hinder his attendance on the day stipulated.

At the farmhouse where the court was held there was first of all prepared a loaf of bread, into which a small white wand, 3 feet long, had been thrust, together with a thin cheese, and a small barrel of ale, provided by the farmer at whose house the session took place. When all had arrived, they proceeded to the attic, where a Bible was placed on the table. There the minutes of the last meeting were muttered over, and a fresh holder of the wand sworn in, according to the oath. After this followed chants and prayers, the Master of the White Rod addressing each one and saying: "You are now to pray for the soul of the Abbot of Stanley, and all the monks of the Cistercian Order, by whom we are tithe-free, tithe-free, tithe-free." This was formerly sung by a chorus, while one quaffed the ale from a bowl, holding the white wand in his hand, and so on all round.

After the prayers and ritual all went downstairs and partook of a feast, primitive in its simplicity, of bread, cheese, and ale, and there was afterwards a toast to be drunk in a mixture of cheese, beer, and onions, flavoured with spices, which recalls the μνττωτὸυ—a mess of cheese, honey, and garlick, a favourite dish of the Asiatic Greeks, and an object of the satire of the poet Hipponax. In later times the monkish chants have been discarded, and the Lord's Prayer substituted, while the feast is on a more liberal scale: the custom is still observed by the farmers. A statute of Henry VIII provided that lands which had been tithe-free under the great monasteries should continue to be so; but the tenants of Midgehall still believe that it is only by their yearly observance of "Word Ale" that they are exempt from paying the impost.

Perched upon a slope of the hill and surrounded with magnifi-cent elms, spruces, and cedars, is Basset Down House, the home of the old squire, whose grandfather was Astronomer-Royal, and obtained world-wide renown as the inventor of the Nautical Almanac, which, by a mathematical calculation, enables the wave-tossed mariner to find his bearings in any quarter of the globe, and in any weather, while the other was a famous mineralogist, and the greatest authority on diamonds of his time; but, by a peculiar irony, characteristic of a man's locality, their learned qualities were quite unknown to the countryside round about them; they were merely "the owl' squire," and nothing else there. The outstanding feature of the country squire and landowner are his politics; all else is ignored by the people at large.

There are beautiful terraces and walks along the hillside, between the beeches and towering fir plantations, and rare specimens of wild flowers grow there, and on the open downs above. Here, among others, may be found the mountain crane's-bill, the sweet wild pea, and the curious little pink and brown bee orchis, which is seldom found away from the clean short turf of the downs. In classic times the Roman dames used a preparation of this dainty plant to darken their eyebrows. The bee-orchis even strays on to the lawns of the mansion at Basset Down, but there it must not be plucked even, much less roasted or boiled; the good genius of the garden would never tolerate such treatment of her gold-laden, fairy-like visitors.

The gardener's cottage is situated in the corner of the orchard at the foot of the slope, the way down to which, through the shrubs and rockeries, is called "the crooked walk." Here he dwells with his two sons, who help him with the work, and his aged mother, Granny Ferris; his wife has been some time dead. At the bottom of the orchard, in white-painted hives, are twenty lots of bees, which discover the gardener's hobby and recreation—a perfectly natural one for him—first to grow and tend the sweets, and afterwards to send forth his myriads of winged marauders to rifle them and bring home the golden honey.

It was five o'clock—the gardener's teatime at the cottage; he came up the path wearing his green apron, the badge of his profession, and almost dragged me inside. Here I was immediately presented to Granny and the boys. She was busy filling the tea pot, and wiped her hand in her print apron before offering it to me for the salutation. The kitchen was bright and cheerful; everything was tastefully arranged, and the table was set.

"Come an' 'ev e a cup o' tea," Granny exclaimed.

"Thanks, Granny, but I've had one tea."

"Don' matter. Breng the cheer up an' 'ev another. I don' know who you be though."

"I've just called to see you, Granny, and have a chat, you know."

"To see I? Ther's some 'oney, look. Jes' try that. You'll like that."

"Is this your own honey?"

"Why, yes, to be sure 'tis, out of our bees."

Granny is tall and stoutish, with a chubby, cheery face, grey eyes, strong features, a little masculine, hardy and healthy looking, wearing a white sun-bonnet on her head, and as active and nimble as many a young woman of forty. Her son, the gardener, inherits the chief of her physical characteristics. He, too, is tall and sturdily built, with a squarish face, arched eyebrows, thickish nose, bronzed cheeks, and a square bit of grey beard of the Brother Jonathan type.

"The fust swarm o' bees I can remember was when I was a little gel," Granny went on. "My dad bought 'em off a farmer at Broad Town, an' I went along wi'n. A gied aaf a suverin far 'em. I was too little to know what money was then, an' I said: 'Oh, dad! you oni gied 'e a farden for thaay.' Then I 'ad to stop at 'ome an' look aater 'em."

It was amusing to listen to Granny's account of her girlhood days. She would not go to school, but always wanted to be with her dad, who was woodman, gamekeeper, and village constable combined. So she wore breeches and a little coat like a boy, and helped her dad cutting the underwood at 2d. a pole or faggoting at 5s. the hundred, or worked the heavy cross-cut saw, to which her dad had affixed a small rope for her tiny hands, and climbed the trees and drew up the rope with twine to attach to the top, with which to pull the tree over when it was sawn through. Later on, at the age of fifteen, she had a set of ferrets and terrier, and went about dressed in a white smock like the farm boys, and was the official local ratcatcher. The price for a rat—paid on production of the tail—was 2d. She presented her bill on St. Thomas's Day, as the children went "gooding" at the farms. At one time she had a whole sovereign to draw in a lump.

The conversation concerning bees brought to light several curious customs and superstitions which survive in the locality, and in which Granny believes, though the gardener several times intervened and declared we had "done wi' they old times now, an' was goin' in for something more modern and up to date." One of the old customs was that of telling the bees of the death of the owner, or of a near relation of the same. As soon as the death occurred it was imperative to "tell the bees" forthwith, otherwise it was confidently believed they would all die in the hives. Again, on the death of the squire, it was the custom to "tell the bees" immediately, and to affix a little black crape to the hives just above the entrance. When the King died it was usual to tell the bees of the fact. This time it was thought they would scatter the news broadcast as they flew about, and make all Nature acquainted with it.

If a swarm of bees settled on dry wood, that was a certain sign of death in the owner's family. A short while ago, at Basset Down, a labourer's daughter was lying ill, and a swarm of bees happening to alight on some dry wood, nothing could dissuade the mother from believing it was a sign of the girl's death. When a visitor called to inquire after the patient, the mother declared she would die, adding: "An' 'er knows it as well as I do, for the bees bin an' settled on dry 'ood." Strange to say, the young girl died the day following. Another curious custom is that of visiting the hive on Christmas Eve to hear the bees talking. Questioned as to this, the gardener was sceptical; but Granny believes they talk that night, and she is certain the two queen bees hold a conversation just before the swarming. Then, she says, if you listen at the hive, you may hear the old queen saying, "Out, out, out, out," and the new one responding, "M-m-m-m."

When the queen bee is ready to leave the hive, she arranges with a certain number of males for a flight, and the first male that comes up with the queen fertilizes her and then drops dead, as the belief is. Fertilization only takes place once; that is sufficient for the queen's lifetime. If she laid 100,000 eggs they would all be fertile. A queen bee is said to lay 2,000 eggs a day in the season. The old queen and the new one are very jealous each other; it is said that they even go mad with the passion; but the period of jealousy is of brief duration, for as soon as the new queen is fit, the old one is destroyed. The ancients supposed the ruler of the hive to be a male, and called it *rex*, and curiously thought that honey settled like dew from the heavens; it was always *aërium mel* among the Latins.

"Isn't it marvellous!" I exclaimed.

"Aw, 'tis terrable!" Granny replied from her arm chair by the fireplace.

The old habit of ringing the bees, so as to call them home, still continues. The gardener keeps a small tin for the purpose; but Granny, anxious to give a practical demonstration, seized up the shovel and poker from over the fender, and beat them noisily together, saying: "This is my bell, look!"

If a swarm of bees had settled on another person's premises, you could not claim them under the old law, unless you had first "rung" them.

Presently Granny rose from her arm-chair to refill the teapot, and I discovered a dark object spread over the back of the seat.

"Why, Granny, you've got a badger's skin?" I cried.

"Yes. Yen 'e a beauty! I bin offered ten shillings for 'e," Granny answered.

Then the gardener chimed in: "Who was it as killed the dead badger? You tell 'e 'ow you killed the dead badger."

"No e didn't kill the dead badger, neether."

"Yes you did."

"No e didn't."

"Yes you did, now."

"Knows e didn't. A wasn' dead no more than I be. You brought un 'ome in a sack one Sunday marnin'"

"You was main frightened an in, wasn' e?"

"Well! a was gwain to bite ma, wasn' a."

"Bite, no. A was oni gaspin' for breath."

"But did you really kill the poor badger, Granny?" I inquired.

"Ha-a. 'E put a coord round 'is neck, an' then slipped un droo the chink o' the door, an' draad un right up, an' I 'it un wi' a girt stick. When I was along o' my dad I killed 'em many a time."

Badgers used to be eaten for food by labourers and gamekeepers, and were thought highly of, and especially badger's hams, which were counted a delicacy. Granny had oft-times cooked them. The fat of badgers is still considered of great value by reason of its softening qualities; there is nothing so penetrating as that, according to the rustics. It is even claimed that if you place it in the palm of the hand it will go right through, and come out at the back. It was especially in demand for anointing the ears of deaf people, and for use in cases of acute bronchitis, swellings, and inflammation. Granny's last pot of badger's fat is just exhausted; people come from far off to beg a little of it.

If a badger bites you it will not loose its hold, but will gradually work its teeth into the flesh till they meet. Once when a man found a badger asleep on a bank and tried to take it, the badger seized his arm and held it so firmly that its mouth had to be cut clean away from the man's flesh. The badger is possessed of an extraordinary sense of smell and hearing, and is gifted with great intelligence. To prove how keen its scent is, it will smell a nest of young rabbits *through* the earth, and dig its way straight down to them, even though the hole be open a few feet away. When the men had been all round the farm putting potassium before the entrances to the wasps' nests, the badgers followed them round by night, and dug out all the nests from the rear side. If gins are set to catch them, they artfully lie on their backs and continue to roll up to the gin till they have thrown it, and then pass along their track in safety. They are exceptionally clean in their habits, and will touch nothing that is greasy.

Once the gardeners and farm-staff paraded no less than sixteen badgers before a party of visitors at the house, for their inspection. Cords were put about their necks, and they ran along like dogs on the lawn. Each leader was furnished with a forked stick with which to keep them from his legs; as long as he kept a sharp eye on the animal it did not attempt to bite him. The badger, if taken when young, may be tamed and taught to fraternize with the domestic pets; it is amusing to see it playing with the young puppies. The badger is the largest of our carnivora, and has been known to turn the scale at twenty-nine pounds. Besides young rabbits and wasp-grubs, it is fond of eggs, fruits, beetles, frogs, and mice. Like the otter, it is being continually hunted down; but if our legislators did their duty, both these would be protected, seeing they do not upset the balance of Nature, nor live to the prejudice of mankind.

The ballad-singers came regularly to the village; every Christmas, when Granny was a girl. There was a band of minstrels, and one preceded the others, carrying a great wooden bowl for the ale upon his head. As they walked they sang an ancient piece beginning:

> Wassail, wassail, all over the town,
> Our toast is white, and our ale is brown;
> Our bowl it is made of a sycamore-tree,
> And a wassailing bowl I will drink unto thee.

The bowl was replenished at every farmhouse; all the company quaffed from it, and wished good health to the farmer and his wife.

At this time Granny picked up her sewing from the small table and began to stitch away.

"What are you making, Granny?" said I.

"A shirt for 'e, look," pointing to the gardener.

"But can you see to do it?" I continued.

"See? Of course I can see. Jest you zamin that."

Then the gardener interposed again: "Bless tha, 'er's as mischifful now as ever a was. A sawed a tree down t'other day, an' a's agwain to 'elp fetch thaay elms down in the spring."

"Aa, if I be alive, awhever, I be gwain to 'ev a cut at 'em. E med as well wer out as rust out," she declared.

The woodman's cottage stands in a little hollow place immediately under the hill. It is overshaded with dense beech-trees that shut out the sun till the evening part. He was filling his pipe and preparing to go for a walk, but put it back in his pocket, and sat down in the arm-chair. I made some remark about country-people.

"Well, the country-people thaay *is* the people, byen 'em," the woodman replied.

I readily assented to this, and the more heartily perceiving the splendid specimen before me. He is of middle height, bronzed, and well-seasoned with out-of-doors work, with iron-grey hair, strong, kindly eyes, firm and erect, as hard as the oak to look at, and possessed of a manly spirit, agreeing with the freedom of his occupation. The room was large and spacious, and everything was spotlessly clean; the faint sweet scent of the leaves was borne in from outside. A big log burned in the fireplace; it was a typically rustic interior. On the table was a pile of books.

"Even you find time to read, then," I observed.

"Yes, thenk God. I can read, an' I can see, an' I can thenk. Ah! ther's a lot as yent right bi a long way it. Ther yent the right spirit in people. Tha be all for downin' a man as dwunt come up to thaay, or as 'ev done a bit o' wrong. Let a man be as bad as 'e ull, ther as bin some time in 'is life when 'e 'ev done good."

"Are you always engaged with the trees?" I asked.

"Well, chafely, you know," he replied, "eether cuttin' or trimmin'. Besides that, I mows the outer lawns, feeds the swans, mends the roofs wi' thatch er tiles, an' does anything tha's wanted an ma."

"Did you ever eat a badger?" I ventured.

"No, but I knowed thaay as did, an' squirrels, too," he answered. "Plenty o' people 'ev ate thaay. An' why not? Tha lives on the best an't, an' be as clane as a noo pin."

According to the woodman's account, squirrels do not store their winter's food in the nest, nor in a hollow tree, but bury it in the earth. He has watched them many a time burying nuts—walnut, hazel, and beech. These they deposit in the ground—having first scratched a tiny hole, about an inch deep—and never more than one by itself. When they require one they smell it out, dig it up, and carry it off to eat in the trees. They are constantly searching the trees for any chance nut that may have become lodged in the fork or in the crevices of the bark. When a squirrel mounts a tree, it usually climbs all round it, ascending in a spiral. This is both to lighten the ascent and to search the tree for nuts also. The wood-man described the squirrel's nest as being like that of the "nanny fodger," which he explained to be the "nanny wren," better known as the "jenny wren."

There are many goldfinches and linnets, with numerous black-birds, thrushes, and blackcaps, about the wood. The little blackcaps are very mischievous in the garden, and much given to pea-stealing. The large green woodpecker is a common resident at Basset Down. This bird may be known by its uneven flight, its rising and falling, and by the peculiar cry it utters—a kind of "Ya, ha, ha, ha!" which has earned it the name of the "Ya, ha" in the neighbourhood. Another local name for this, from the peculiarity of its cry, is the "eke-aw."

The woodman's early days were hard and stern. "My father was eighty-eight when a died, an' a worked seventy years out on't. I've bin for a year an' not tasted nothin' wi' mi bread, an' very often not much o' that, wi' flour £5 5s. a bag; yet I'll lay we was stronger an' hardier than the young uns to-day."

"That was the barley-bangers," I said.

"Aa, barley-scawters, barley-dampers, and pot cyeks, we called 'em," he continued. "My owl' mother made some 'underds o' thaay. Most thengs was terrabul dear, but bacon an' cheese was chep, an' we could get dree pounds o' whey butter for a shillin'. I minds the owl' carter very well at Broad Town. A was comin' 'ome from church one marnin', an' maaster stopped un an' said: 'I thenks t'ood be chepper for you to bake yer own bread, John.' 'Aa, zo do I, maaster,' John said. ''E got it aal but the flour an' the 'ood.'" Here the wood-man's eyes sparkled; he was touched with the finger of fun and gaiety.

"Did 'e yer about Gargey Narton? Gargey was carter, too, an' 'ad bin out somewhere, an' got lost one night down Broad Town way, an' yerd the owld owl a hollain' up in the trees aboove 'is 'ed 'Whoo-oo-oo!' so a shouted out: 'Garge Narton, sir, the honestest man as ever lived.'"

"Then ther was Mark Drew the cowman. Maaster sent 'e to the next farm wi' a sow, an' when a went to fetch un back a brought the wrong un.

"'Why, Mark, you brought back the wrong un,' maaster said.

"'No I hent,' said Mark.

"'Yes you hev. This yent the right peg.'

"'Eece 'tis, maaster.'

"'But I tells tha chent.'

"'Aw tis, bless e, maaster.'

"'But this yent my peg.'

"'Eece 'tis, bless e.'

"'Well, I *knows* chent, then.'

"'Daal if I didn' thenk, comin' along the road, a was a bit too 'eavy in the yer, maaster,' Mark answered.

"Then ther was Jimmy Mower, the owld carpenter, as cut the corner off. Jimmy was gwain to Devizes, an' went terrin' acraas a carner ground o' young woats. When a got aaf waay awver a was skeered a bit, an' a said to 'isself: 'Well, I can back-zoord, an' I can kick legs, but daal if I can run a mossel if anybody comes.' Then a yerd a gallopin' behind, an' up come the farmer on 'is owld nag.

"'Hey!' he shouted, 'ther's no road yer, mun.'

"'I knows chent, maaster, an' I byent agwain to stop to make narn, neether,' Jimmy answered un."

Wootton Basset, from which Basset Down derives its name, has been famous for its perfervid election enthusiasm and riots, though there are none living at this time who took part in them; but Jesse Giles, a big, burly labourer, with strong features, little goatee beard, and pronounced nasal twang, can tell of the Cricklade riots, in which he took part, over half a century ago. All voting was in the open then; the voter merely shouted out the name of his favourite candidate before a pigeon-hole in the wall of a house. There was a small, narrow way, fenced off with a low rail, along which the voters passed. The crowd was tightly packed all along the rail, and close to the voters, the most of whom wore the old-fashioned top-hat. As the voter called out the name of his candidate the crowd cheered or yelled; the tall hats were seized off the voters' heads, and tossed into the air, or knocked off, or bashed down over their eyes, amid convulsive shrieks and laughter, and the wild din of the onlookers. The next day—the day of the declaration of the poll—huge crowds were sent down from Swindon in barges, armed with sticks and cudgels, hammer-shafts, stones, and bottles, intent on a disturbance, while all the countryside, chiefly democratic, had flocked in, too. Each party had its band of musicians, who paraded the streets, followed by a long train of supporters, fully armed, cheering and shouting. The poll was declared about noon, and then the fighting began, to the discomfiture of the invaders, who were driven off pell-mell, through mud and water, in all directions, and often ducked in the Thames. The old women of the town ransacked the faggot-piles for cudgels; there they stood, with their arms full of great sticks, and sold them at a penny each to the rioters. Blood was freely shed; there was no quarter given, and none expected, and the few constables present were powerless to quell the uproar, which was continued till midnight and the early hours of the next morning, though the wardens of the law managed to arrest a few of the ringleaders, several of whom were transported, and worked in the mines, and came back with their pockets full of golden sovereigns, to the envy of the local farm-labourers and folks.

III

Carter Leighfield—Saltrop—Ellendune—Ancient
charges—The sporting farmer

Fʀᴏᴍ Bᴀssᴇᴛ Dᴏᴡɴ ᴛʜᴇ ᴡᴀʏ leads along the hill to Red Barn,
where it joins the highroad a short distance from Barbury
Castle, and runs steeply down to Wroughton. Away back on the
hill is a farm house, with ricks and buildings, and, near by, a large
beech plantation and a cottage, where, for forty years, has dwelled
the carter, Robert Leighfield, and grown tough and strong in the
bracing air and robust surroundings of the downs. His little daughter, a bright, pretty girl of fourteen, with laughing eyes and cheeks
as fresh as an apple, tastefully dressed in black, with spotless white
pinafore, keeps house for him, since his wife died some time back;
there they live, strongly bound together, each dependent on the
other, pathetically tender and trustful, sharing a common sorrow,
yet smiling and cheerful in spite of it.

"Olive is young to be your daughter," I said to the carter.

"Yes," he replied. "Ther is but two an 'em, both gels, an' they
be seventeen years apert. The oldest, 'er's married, an' lives a way
off, an' this un looks aater I. I don' know what I should do wi'out
'er. I allus said, when a was borned, 'er was send for a purpose; an'
sure enough 'er was, as you can see, look!"

The carter is tall and square, well knit together, a picture of
health, as strong as a lion to look at, the very type and feature of
his profession, one of the old sort—as we sometimes say—and a

credit to the countryside that bore him. His face is broad, with even nose, strong, clear eyes, stubbled chin, and cheeks of a ruddy hue, painted by those master artists, the sun and wind. He was dressed in a corduroy suit, and wore the usual leather gaiters reaching up the thighs.

"Were you always with the horses, carter?" I inquired.

"No, by golly, no," he replied. "I worked wi' the cows fust of all. Then I said to guv'nor: 'Ef you don' gie I more money I shane stop.' But a oodn't; so I left, an' got a job in the factory, an' was allus bad, an' my owl' mother bagged ma to chock out ont, so I left it, an' come up yer, an' I can safely zaay I've never 'ad a day's illness since."

"And you look well enough now, doesn't he, Olive?" I said.

She blushed and replied, with a merry laugh, while the carter's face lit up with an ineffable smile as he looked proudly and fondly at her.

The carter's day begins about 5 a.m., and ends soon after 4 p.m., with breakfast and dinner-time out. The horses require feeding for two or three hours before taking the field; you must not send them out with bellies half-filled, or you would never get the work done, and horses, like human beings, will not eat stale food; they want it served fresh, at regular hours of the day, otherwise their appetites fail, and they suffer in health.

"And how about the carter boys?" I asked.

"Bless you," he replied, "we caan't get no bwoys. Us got to plough wi' two 'osses instead o' dree, 'cause us caan't get no drivers to lade 'em. Bwoys now stops a-schoolin' till tha be fourteen, an' tha be no good for nothin' aater that; tha wunt dreeve plough then, but off tha goes into the factory."

It was formerly a custom with carters, when the boy had been guilty of any offence, to take him by the ears and throw him over the horse on to the ground; but Leighfield did not believe in "sich geamms as that." He had heard about "one owld bwoy," who, when the carter had given him a severe beating, came to work the next day with a sack over his shoulders, whistling unconcernedly. When he entered the stable the carter eyed him up and down sternly, and said: "Wha's got that theng awver thi back var?" "Aw," the boy answered, "tha's byet ma a main bit isterday, an' I thawt tha's might kill ma to-day, so I brought a bag so tha's med pick mi bwuns up an' carr 'em whoam to mother, for 'er to bury 'em."

Saltrop Farm is but a short way from the carter's cottage, and is situated by the roadside. Here are stacks upon stacks of wheat, oats, meadow-hay, clover and sanfoin, with stables and stalls, the cart house and barn in the rear, and the dwelling-house beyond, partly surrounded with tall beech-trees, but open to the south. Here, for nigh half a century, Farmer Ferris has lived, and gathered up the produce of the bounteous old earth year after year, and trafficked in cattle and sheep on a large scale into the bargain. "If you wants to know anything about farmin', Ferris is the man to go to," you are told, all round the neighbourhood.

The old farmer is very tall, with silver grey hair and beard, a cultured appearance, a kind face, and a musical voice. His manner is that of one well bred, and of wide experience with the world. The first thing he required of me was a catalogue of names of all the old people I knew in the locality, so that he could refresh his memory with them, and tell me of this and that one, so far as he was acquainted with them. After that, I spoke of his success as a farmer; but he shook his head and laughingly interposed with: "Never made much money at it;" and "Just made a living, you know, and nothing more;" while his eyes twinkled merrily, telling of the inward delight and satisfaction.

"This chalk is heavy and cold," he went on. "Two or three showery days a year is enough wet in these parts."

"Oh, father!" the daughter cried. "We want more than that, or however should we have enough water for the cattle to drink?"

"Well, we could do with more, perhaps, but we don't want much," he continued. "Last year, in that very dry season, we had double the corn we've got this time. A lot of wet is no good on this soil. Kind, light land yields a bigger corn crop. Sheep farming is the most profitable on cold chalk. If a man wants to be a good farmer he must keep a big flock of sheep, but you can't do that on sixty or seventy acres. You can't afford to pay a shepherd, for one thing, because the flock is not big enough; but, on the other hand, you can't farm three or four hundred acres without a big flock. I lends mine out to my neighbours in the summer-time; they manure the land, and clean the rubbish off, too. A good shepherd and a good carter are a treasure to any man; they are the principal managers of the farm, and I am happy in both of mine. As for the talk of going back to the land, that is all bosh. Small holdings could only succeed in chosen situations; half the land that the farmers hold in the country would starve 'em to death; they'd have to work their eyes out to get a living. If they could have all the best land, and a favoured market for their produce, they might do very well; but you can't have everything you wants in this world; you've got to take it as it comes, good and bad together."

Questioned as to the "good old times," he replied: "People did more work then, and were better satisfied. My father went with his own teams, and drove plough, and I did the same; and all my sisters went milking. Labour was quite 30 per cent cheaper fifty years ago than it is now. Flour was £4 4s. a sack, and bread 2s. a gallon. At the time of the Crimean War wheat was 90s. a quarter, and 60s. a quarter during the Franco-German War. In my opinion every class of people is better off now, except landlords and parsons. They don't work so hard, and they live better, and have more enjoyment, but they are not so hardy and healthy as they used to be. As for young men and boys, you can't get them for love nor money; they won't give their minds to farm work, what with the schooling and that. Education is all right, but knowledge is not all for good, you know. A good deal of it makes men cunning, and, after all, we can't live on pride and high notions; some must do a bit, or we should soon starve."

"And what is your amusement?" I inquired.

"Work, and allus has been," he replied. "I can't put it better than that; and I shall keep on wi't as long as I'm able."

Hereupon food and ale were brought, and we continued chatting, while the south-west wind whistled and moaned like the low voice of the sea in the boughs of the beech-trees, and the great downs without gradually faded from view, till the round red moon rose up over Barbury Castle and discovered them again to us, pale and ghostly, in the dim weird light, just as they appeared to the fierce, chalk-stained, blood-dyed, battle-scarred warriors after the terrific onslaught of A.D. 556.

From Red Barn the road glides down the steep hill alongside a great coomb, one slope of which is cultivated, and the other richly draped with a mass of trees and vegetation, called Clout's Wood, and then lands you on a small plateau overlooking the vale to the north and east, where the village, half concealed with luxuriant elms, is extended. The village of Wroughton—the Ellendune of old times—is very ancient, and rich in historical associations and traditions, though by reason of a careless slip made by the historian Leland, it has been for centuries deprived of its chief renown—viz., as being the site of the famous battle between Egbert of Wessex and Beornwulf of Mercia, A.D. 823.

The Battle of Ellendune was fought 267 years later than that at Barbury Hill; and the story is told in the Anglo-Saxon Chronicle of 823, and in the Winchester Annals. Here we learn: "There was a challenge and the two Kings—Egbert and Beornwulf—chose the time and place. Beornwulf, deriding the ambition of Egbert, was the first to try whether the taught or the untaught does the better when the game is played with the dice of Mars." The chronicler had evidently read Sallust's "Catiline": "Certamen fuit vine corporis an virtute animi res militaris magis procederet." Then he continues: "Egbert's lords, being consulted, thought it more honourable to have their heads cut off than to lay their free necks beneath the yoke." Again: "The time pleased them in the summer, the place at Ellendune." Beornwulf is said to have had thousands to Egbert's hundreds, but his defeat was crushing and final. "Egbert's men were pale and lean, Beornwulf's well-fed and ruddy, but inexperienced and rash." "When Beornwulf fled he would not for three pence have lost his spurs." Then it was that, in the words of an unknown and long-forgotten West Saxon poet: "The Brook of Ellendune ran red with gore; it was choked with slain, and became foul with the carnage." The Brook of Ellendune was the modern River Rey, a tiny stream that issues from the hill and winds round the valley to the distant Thames near Cricklade. Six of the seven mills recorded in the Domesday survey—though they are in disuse now—still remain, a pathetic but crumbling monument to a once flourishing local industry.

The Manor of Elcombe was the property of the Lovels, the last of whom, Lord Lovel, was a follower of Richard III, and fought with him at Bosworth Field, and afterwards incurred the hatred meted out to his royal master, as is shown by the political skit:

> The Cat, the Rat, and Lovel the Dog,
> Ruled all England under the Hogg.

A description of the revenues of the Manor, taken from a document dated 1310, is interesting. There was: "The capital messuage, with the garden, worth 13s. 4d., with 140 acres of arable land, price of acre 4d., sum, 46s. 8d. Also 16 acres of meadow, price of acre, 12d., sum 16s. There is there pasture in Common for 50 Oxen, price per head 4d., sum 16s. 8d. There is a Windmill, and it is worth 6s. 8d. per annum. The rent of the freemen by the year is 10s. 1d. at the four principal terms of the year in equal proportions. Also 1lb. of Cummin, at the feast of St. Michael, price 1d. The rent of the Customars and nineteen Cottars who hold 13 virgates of land is 23s. by the year. The rent of the hens is by the year 8s. 4d. The pannage of the pigs is 6d. The rent of the eggs at Easter, 4d. The work and customs of the said Customars are worth by the year £9 6s."

So the rent of the hens and pigs' pannage together was almost equivalent to that of the freemen, and the windmill earned less than either; though there were the long summer calms to be taken into account, which kept the huge fans motionless, and the workmen idle. The pannage of pigs was the charge for allowing them to roam the woods to gather up the acorns and beechmast. Some of the rents for meadowland in the locality, near Wanborough, have risen, since the compilation of the document, from 12d. to £4 an acre, and the land is profitable at that; it would almost seem that the higher the rent of a farm is, the more applicants there will be for it when it is evacuated by the tenant.

The sporting farmer's occupation is over two miles in extent, and reaches from Red Barn far down into the valley. All the arable land is upon the downs, while all below is pasture. The farmstead is immediately underneath the hill; a steep road brings you up to the downs above. A large dairy is kept, and the milk is despatched off to the metropolis daily. To reach the railway-station, four miles north, the milkcart must first proceed up the long, steep hill for a mile, due south to Red Barn, then traverse the ground back again: a tremendous waste of time, material, and energy, which is so often a characteristic of the countryside, and which, in this case, might easily be obviated; the construction of half a mile of rough track would cut off a big portion from the daily journey of the farm-carts.

The men, clad in clean white smocks, had just brought in their last pails full of the fragrant, foaming milk from the stalls. Some were attending to the refrigerator, some were cleaning out the milk-pails and strainers, and others were washing their hands at the tap in the corner of the shed, preparing to go home. The old farmer was shuffling about within, seeing to this and to that; by-and-by he came out and requested me to go inside. I followed him into a great room, half full of harness of all kinds, suspended from the walls and massive wooden beams, and destitute of furniture, beyond a rough bench or two. On one side was an old-fashioned fireplace, three yards wide, where a heaped-up pile of logs was burning, the flames from which rose and fell languidly, now lighting up the interior with a cheerful, ruddy glow, and now leaving it in deep shadow; it was twilight out of doors and on the downs.

The old farmer is of moderate stature, grey-headed, with bushy grey eyebrows, clean-shaven face, horsey looking, with features expressing keenness, strength, and character. He was wearing a short dust-coat, cap, and breeches and gaiters. The saddles and bridles, top-boots and spurs, signified the old man's mode of recreation; hunting had been his one and only hobby outside the farm; he was known far and near as "The Hunting Farmer." He thrust both hands into his coat pockets, and stood with his back close up to the fire.

"Ah! this farmin' nowadays is about as bad a sight as ever I seed. Chent wuth nothin' at all. Yer I be, a owld man, aater all these years, wuss off now than ever e was, an' I tells you, mister, if it wasn't for my son yer an' the childern, I'd sooner be in the workus, or else in Devizes jail, yes, begad if I oodn't. There's nothin' got at farmin' nowadays, you can take my word for that."

"But you have had *some* good luck," I said.

"Yes, and some most infernally bad luck, too," he replied. "Jest look at things to-day! You caan't get a decent man, nor a bwoy, nor nothin' else no good on. You caan't ship-shape 'em a mossel. Tha gets this heducation an' tha be as useless as a log. Tha caan't cut a 'edge, ner thatch a rick, ner milk a cow, dreeve plough, ner nothin' else. Ther's the County Council fawks, they be a 'evin' claasses, but you caan't kip the people an the land. 'Tis no good to saay as thaay'll stop, cause thaay wunt. There's no bwoys to be 'ad. Tha kips 'em at school an' stuffs 'em up wi' a lot o' oonderment; thaay wunt 'it a stroke for you. Then ther's my rates! Jest look at 'em. Thirty-five years ago I paid £15 an' now e pays £40 for the same land. Years ago, in a bad saason, I've ed £50 back out o' the rent, but ya gets nothin' now. Yer's this year. One girt field o' whate e never cut at all, an' yander's a patch o' sin fine, wuth £20, a rottin' an the ground now. Then along comes thaay Government Specter fellas an' noses round e. Bless you, mister, it costs I double an' traable to fodder my cattle an' kip 'em, to what it used to, an' if ya don't do't tha 'evs e that waay; 'tis all extra 'spence, whichever way you turns, and for all I be a tellin' you, if I was to gie this farm out tomorra, ther'd be a 'undred applications for'n afore the wik was out."

After the foregoing, delivered with an earnestness amounting almost to vehemence, the talk was of sport.

"Yes, I allus 'unted two days a wik in the time, till last year. I allus said if I could'nt 'unt, I oodn't work; na' moore I oodn't, neether. One day, when I was out in the field wi' King Edward at Sherbourne, I was a'ed wi' the 'ounds, an' the King was be'ind. So one o' the top uns come gallopin' up be'ind I an' shouted: 'Get out o' the road for the King,' an' I said to 'n: 'I shan't get out for nobody. Ketch ma if you can. You can ride be'ind ma, or azide an ma, but you'll never go afore ma wi' this yer mount.' Nar a couldn't. One day mi lard comes an' wants to barra 'n. 'No,' says I, 'I never lends my mount to nobody. When I lends anytheng, I lends mi wife;' an' 'e could see from that as I wasn't agwain to lend 'e nothin'."

IV

Wroughton—The church and clerk—The old
shepherd—"Sawyer John"—The mill carter.—
The cowman—The innkeeper

THE PRINCIPAL PART OF WROUGHTON lies underneath the hill,
with Overtown on the summit, near to the downs. On the
slope, at the mouth of a coomb, are important waterworks, supplying the adjacent town, which tapped the spring at its source,
and emptied its banks of the pure limpid stream, settling the fate
of the six mills, whose rights to the water were purchased out; the
trade of grinding was already doomed. Here also is Brimble Hill,
which leads away to Burderop and Chiseldon. The story is told
that Queen Elizabeth, who was on her way from Ramsbury to
Down Ampney, had passed the night at Burderop House, and, on
resuming her journey, experienced the rush of cold air driving up
the steep roadway, whereupon she cried out: "Od-zooks! but the
wind shot shrewdly on my cheek;" and the cottages at the foot of
the hill have been known as Windshot Cottages ever since.

The ancient ramparts and ditches of the hill fort—now almost
obliterated—are on a jutting spur of the chalk, precipitous on the
western side, and running steeply down towards sunrise. The interior of the fortress is level, and contains a small field, the church,
vicarage, and schools. Near by is a large yew-tree, with spreading
branches, underneath which stood the whipping-stocks, which
Granny Hunt, the 96 years old dame, has seen many times occupied.
The stone walls by the roadside, and leading to the churchyard, are

covered with the beautiful ivy-leaved toadflax, with its sweet lilac and yellow blossoms; this even flourishes hanging halfway up the walls of the chancel, and continues in bloom till after Christmas, if the weather is mild. Seeing a carter boy eyeing me with great curiosity as I was examining the plants, I held out a bunch to him, and asked him if he knew what it was. He looked at the posy, and answered immediately: "Clover, yen it?" I smiled, and corrected him, and made him view the little blooms more closely.

"I zeed 'em on the wall plenty o' times, an' allus thawt 'twas clover," he said. He was off home to Broad Hinton, and was soon out of sight, wending his way up the hill towards Red Barn.

The church is a great stone building, with a massive, high tower, built to withstand the storms of centuries. The interior is spacious and austere; there is little sculpture or ornamentation to take the eye of the visitor. The entrance to the tower is outside; there is a second door opening from this thirty feet above the ground. On one side the churchyard ends abruptly, sheer on the edge of the rampart; the hollow beneath is full of elms and beech, the tops of which are level with the fence and mounds. The enclosure is packed full of graves and tombs, containing the bones and dust of those long departed this life. Here the dead are heaped together in unspeakable confusion; high and low, rich and poor, proud and humble, have been gathered together for ages, housed and unhoused by turns, first duly installed and afterwards disinherited to make room for others, pitiable in their weakness, at the utter mercy of the pick and shovel of the sexton, who continues to break open the calm retreat, and intrude upon the sacred peace of the grave.

A large yew stands before the porch. Here the tombs are thickest, reaching right inside under the low branches, and around the trunk, packed so closely together that there is scarcely room to admit the hand between the stones, leaning some this way, and some that, this one propped against the other, that one gaping open, as though its inmate had fled hurriedly forth, others sunken and hollow, or stooping and tottering, ready to touch the ground, the whole in a state of topsy-turvydom, like a little silent city, dilapidated, and tumbling to ruins. Beautiful ivy, green, brown, and golden, with exquisite leaves and tendrils, creeps and twines, and clings to the stones, or hangs down in festoons to the ground, as the poet tells us it did around the tomb of ancient Sophocles, which the present picture brings to mind.

> Gently, where lies our Sophocles in sleep,
> Gently, green ivy, with light tendrils creep;
> There may the roseleaf and clustering vine
> Clamber, and nestle, and lovingly twine.

Out in the open, amid the sombre surroundings, is a gleam of colour which proves to be that of a rose-tree in full bloom, growing out of a small mound, evidently that of an infant. Loving hands had planted the bush; there it stood, blooming beautifully in mid-winter, as though the soul of the child still dwelled there, and had been incarnated with the rose, spreading abroad its lovely light, and breathing its soft fragrance around in the sunless air.

"Dicky" Austin, the old church clerk, nearly ninety years of age, lives in a small cottage halfway down the hill, together with a middle-aged daughter, who tends him in his infirmity. He is tall and upright, silver haired, with large kind eyes, prominent nose, and thin side-beard, but his old hand trembles, and his head shakes visibly; he cannot converse much since he had the seizure last fall. The little room is packed full of furniture, and the walls are hung with pictures, works of art, some of them, including a painting of Richard himself, done by the vicar's wife, and given to the clerk sixty years ago, or more. Upon a chest of drawers stands a stuffed brown owl, looking as wise as Athene herself, and a pile of books containing records of weddings and funerals, dating back nearly two centuries. Old Dicky has been clerk, gravedigger, and undertaker combined all his life, as were his people before him for the last 300 years, and the records certify that during Richard's tenure of the office he buried no less than 3,000 dead in that moderate-sized churchyard. How he found room for so many graves is a mystery; he must have dug out the old bones time after time; it is no wonder the tombstones are all packed and piled up together in heaps confusedly.

The old clerk has many quaint stories to tell, of the coal merchant, who, coming to be married, frequently interrupted the clergyman with unlooked for questions and remarks, and tried to sell him "aaf a ton" in the midst of the ceremony; of the wayward villager who came home late from the inn, and fell into the open grave, and had to be rescued the next morning; of the sporting parson, who, time after time, went a-hunting, and forgot the weddings and funerals, and how they used to leave the corpse in the church porch all night till the next day, while the mourners went back home again, and how he used to disappoint the bride and bridegroom, and cause the wedding to be postponed for a week or a fortnight, until the Bishop was apprised of the facts, and severely admonished the defaulting vicar. Such are the tales old Dicky has to tell, with many smiles, and a few tears coursing down his poor old cheeks, but it all seems so very long ago, and no one comes to talk with him about it, and refresh his memory, especially since he has not been able to get out to see his old neighbour, Granny Hunt, who lives a stone's throw adown the hill.

Granny is aged ninety-six; she would shame many a one at sixty. Her cottage door was wide open in the afternoon; she was busy scouring her candlesticks. "I doos this every day o' mi life," she declares. "The candles as e gets nowadays tha do guttur so. 'Tis nothin' so good as it used to be." She is tallish and stoutish, stooping a little, though not much, with fine features, face deeply wrinkled, but with fresh, ruddy cheeks, robust and healthy looking; if outward indications are at all trustworthy, she should easily complete her centenary. Her cottage is small, consisting of one tiny room and a pantry downstairs, and two small bedrooms above. The walls are pasted over with illustrated papers of sixty and seventy years ago, which give an antiquated air to the interior. Here and there are photographs of soldier and sailor sons, taken when the art was in its infancy, and one or two fine old coloured engravings. In her young days Granny did spinning and weaving, and also straw-plaiting, which were regular industries in the village; every cottage had a loom or a wheel in those days, which enabled the poor folks to obtain a livelihood.

"Have you lived in the cottage long, Granny?" I asked.

"Lived yer, yes. Never lived nowhere else, as e knows on," she answered. Then she went on to talk about her father who was carter, her husband who was carter, and her son who was carter, of feasting and revelling, back-swording and leg-kicking, working for Id a day in the fields, whipping-stocks, wind mills, watermills, and other old-fashioned paraphernalia, until I felt to be whirled back a whole century, and to be lost to the present time altogether. By-and-by I found time to question her again.

"Do you enjoy good health, Granny?"

"Good 'ealth? Lar bless tha, no 'E caant' walk no distance wi'out a stick, that e caant."

"But have you never had any severe illness?" I ventured.

"Ye-es, severe illness, ye-es; but nothin' saarious, awhever," she answered. "My 'usband, look, 'e drapped down dead at the table yer, one Sunday a dinner-time. I was jest gone into the panterny, an' the vittals was on the table, an' I yerd a naise, an I sed: 'Lar, Willum, whatever be at? You bin an' knocked the leaff o' the table down;' but a niver answered ma, an' ther a was, crooched up dead, jest wher you be now, look."

Hereupon Granny began to apologize for the small fire, and then she piled on the lumps of coal, picking them up with her fingers, while I blew the fire with the bellows, and brought it to a flame. Presently I fished out a small coin and a package for Granny, which raised her up to the seventh heaven. "Lark a massy! Why, 'tis a sixpunce, yun it? Is 'e fer I now? Lar now, dwun e distrust yerseif. You be the best friend I sid for many a day."

"I've got something else besides," I said, rummaging forth a second package from underneath my coat, and undoing it. "Do you know what this is, Granny?"

"Why, 'tis holly! No, chunt. 'Tis mistletoe, to be sure 'tis. Jes' thenk o' that now. 'Tis Christmas to-morrow, yun it?" she exclaimed.

So I held the mistletoe over Granny's head and kissed her cheek once or twice, and she kissed mine, and insisted on getting me a cup of hot milk, after drinking which I went outside and ran straight into the old shepherd, who had just come from his sheep upon the downs, and was going home to tea.

Abraham Ashton is a witty old fellow of seventy-five years, whose whole life has been spent with the sheep about the downs between Wroughton and Andover. He is of moderate height, with merry, sparkling eyes, a prominent nose, ruddy, healthy cheeks, clean-shaven face, a fringe of beard under the chin, and billy-cock hat on the head. He wore a thick sack, fastened with a buttonhook in front, around his shoulders, another tied round his waist, and carried a third, containing a heavy load, at his back. On seeing me he plumped this down by the roadside, and put on a broad smile.

"I got summat yer to show e, look; summat as you never seed afore," he began, as he fumbled at the sack on the ground, and presently brought to view a monster turnip, certainly the biggest I had seen, and which he handled with great pride. Then he went on:

"Yelleky, look! Did e ever zee am like that afore? No, that you never did. What d'e think 'e, then? An' as sound as a bell right droo, look!" Here he flicked it with his thumb to prove its solidity. "Tha hallus ses as ya caant grow turmuts in a garden, tha do, but this un was growed in one. The howl' carter jest gin in to I. This is one o' the 'Amshur turmuts, ya know, one o' thaay as the owl' yeow nibbles out an' then draps a lamb aside on it, an the lamb crapes into 'n fer shelter. Tha never wants no shelters up ther aside the turmut uds. Tha gets ship as beg as donkeys, yelleky. I got some an 'em up a top ther, now, look."

"And how do you manage that, shepherd?" I inquired.

"Feeds 'em, mun; feeds 'em. Gies 'em some grub for ther bellies, tha's the oni way to do't. But tha wants a lot o' lookin' aater, else ya'd soon lose one haaf an 'em. Tha suicides therselves, ya know."

"Sheep commit suicide? But how?" I asked.

"Why, tha gorges therselves to death, an' lays an' rowls over an to their backs, an' does all sarts o' comical thengs," he continued.

"Tha be jest like ladies an' gennulmen gwain to a beg dinner, or like little childern at a taa-party; tha yets an' yets, an' stuffs therselves up till tha caan' do nothin', an' ther tha be, blowed out like barrels. Tha dwun' know when tha've 'ed enuf, de zee."

Here I offered the shepherd a smoke, but he refused it. "No thenkee. God bless tha, never smawked in mi life. 'Tis oni a 'abit, the same as drenkin' an' swerin'."

Then he proceeded to talk of the fold again: "Sometimes us haes 1,000 yeows, an thaay'll gie us 1,200 lambs, 200 per an moore, but chent all plaain saailin' wi' um. Back in '79 purty nigh every ship an thase downs died, aa, an' hers an' rabbuts, too. Tha 'ed the flooks, tha's summat in the liver, 'an ther was no stoppin' on't. I wur down Amesbury way, then. Tha's wher tha feels fur daylight. Tha never haes nar a clock upstairs, yelleky, but tha jest puts ther 'and out a winder, and feels for daylight, then tha knows 'tis time to get up in the marnin'. But yer's owl' Saayer John a-comin, thees better go along o' 'e, an see what tha cast make on in, for 'e's too dry fer we chaps. Dost yer what I be a-tellin' on in, John?"[1]

"Aw, aa. I can yer, mun; but I knowed what thy oondermentin' was afoore to-day," he replies.

Sawyer John is a slight-made man, pleasant and witty, full of cheerful gossip, and of varied experience. He is dressed in a corduroy suit, with billycock hat, and wears a white kerchief, tied in a bow, and with the ends artfully arranged, around the neck, which gives him a swagger appearance. His old head is frosty white; his eyes are nearly closed with continual smiling; the cares of life sit lightly on his shoulders.

"I looked for you at the Fox and Hounds, but your corner was empty," I said.

"Aw did e, now! Was any o' the bwoys up ther?" he replied.

"About half a dozen, all telling yarns of foxes, one against the other," I answered.

"Aa, thaay owl' foxes! Us used to hae some games wi'thaay, ketchin' 'em in the pits, and sendin' em into Wales for the huntin'. 'Ev e seed the owl' gamester?"

"Why, you are all old gamesters. Which do you mean?" I replied.

"Aw, Fightin' Jack, o' Broad 'Inton."

"That's Theobald, isn't it?" I said.

"Tha's 'im," he continued. "Mi lard was ridin' acrass 'is bit o' land one daay, an' up comes the owl' chap an shouts: 'Wher b'e gwain to yer, then?' So mi lard pops up 'is dooks, an ses: 'Dost thee want a bit o' this?' 'Aa, get off that 'oss, an thee cast hae as much ant as thees wants, an' a bit moore, too,' t'other said, but mi lard chocked un down aaf a suverin' an telled un to come round tomarra, a was too busy to stop then."

The business of hand-sawyering, like every other trade of the countryside, has almost ceased to be now. The steam saw has crept into favour everywhere. All those with big estates, and very many of the farmers, too, keep a set of the tackle. The old pits have fallen in, or have been filled in, and are seldom met with. The occupation of a sawyer is distinct from that of a woodman. The woodman merely fells the timber, and trims it; the other cuts it up ready for use. The price paid for hand-sawing is usually 2s. 6d. per 100 ft. for spruce and deal, and 2s. 9d. for ash, elm, and oak. Nothing is cut, at this rate, under 6 inches in thickness; the men can get through the soft woods at about 1 ft. a minute. The hard woods do not pay as well, but the difficulty is overcome by "putting two and two together," as the sawyer says. The sawyers are very clever at their work, and are capable of many creditable feats. All kinds of uses, and even door-panels, were cut with perfect accuracy, over the pit, though no one would pretend that the process was cheaper or better than the modern method. Years ago the sawyer and his wife used to leave home during the summer and harvest, and roam all over the downs, at mowing and reaping, and return again in the fall, but that has long since come to an end, there is no work to be had now, outside the ordinary everyday duties on the farms.

King's Mill, the fifth on the stream, is about five minutes' walk from Sawyer John's cottage. The old building is of three stories, and is much dilapidated. The huge water-wheel is within, enclosed in a kind of closet, like a dungeon. The water flowed over the top of this, and fell below into a deep, pit-like place, and ran out into the open, and underneath the road to the meadows again. The mill-pound is situated behind the house, but that is empty and dry now. The stream is turned off by a hatch, above the pound; then it leaps down some stone steps with a loud plashing noise, underneath a spreading maple-tree, and converges round the building. The old house is full of machinery from roof to base. There are three sets of stones on the second floor, with several lots of "silks," cleaners, and refiners. The huge, wooden spindles, that communicated the power from the wheel, and turned the mill-stones, are as big as the trunks of trees, and as hard as iron still, but the beams and floors, and bins for the flour are all rotting and crumbling away; it is dangerous to climb up the crazy ladder-like stairs and venture among the worn-out tackle. Magnificent elms grow above the mill-pound, and on the banks of the stream; a large walnut-tree, centuries old, stands near the house. The old stable has been turned into a motor-shed now, and the ground-floor of the mill is piled up with lumber. A deathlike silence fills the whole place; the musical gushing of water and the rumble of the machinery is heard no more.

The old mill carter is still living, in a cottage on the hill-side, tended by his son and daughter, and surrounded by a merry troop of grand-children. He is of moderate stature, stiffly built, with shortish nose, clean-shaven face, and robust complexion.

"Ah! I've hed some thousands o' sacks o' flour an my owl' back, all an 'em two 'underd an' a quarter," he tells you. "Us used to carr' 'em up the steps as ef tha was bags o' wool; us was as 'ardy as ground twuds in them times. The men grows taller an' begger, nowadays, but they byent so strong by a purty deal, an' us didn't hae none too much to eat, neether. I've bin from one Christmas to another wiout tastin' a bit o' bif. Us used to cut off a slish o' bacon an aat it raw, wi' a bit o' bread, as sweet as a nut. We carred flour into Wales when 'twas five pounds a bag, an' hed the owl' mill 'ouse stocked wi' whate from top to bottom, an' piled up in the yard covered wi' tarpaulins, an' dree or vower teamms a-waitin' to come in, an' no room to turn round. Ther was 'leven on us implied, besides millwrights, carpenters, blacksmiths, an' odd men an' wimmen for sortin' the bones for grindin' into manure. These went through a special cylinder, an' come out a'most like flour. We ground they sixty years ago an' moore."

The carter had had many experiences on the road, when the countryside was infested with thieves, who waylaid the waggons, and stole what they could from the vehicles. At one spot, going for Salisbury, where trees overhung the road, the thieves used to fasten hooks to the branches, and when the waggons passed underneath, these caught in the bags and took them off the load. Corn was also conveyed loose in barges along the canal, and the boatmen, by a crafty device, used regularly to steal it. The plan was to stand small sticks amongst the corn and trickle water down them, which caused the grain to swell. When they came to their destination the corn was measured out; all that remained belonged to the boatmen.

Presently the carter turned his head aside and called my attention to a livid patch behind his ear, and running down the neck. "This is black currant jam," he exclaimed. I understood the allusion immediately; he meant it was a birthmark. Then he continued: "'Twas as simple as anything. My mother jest put her hand up to brush her hair back, an' this is the result on't. I got a strawberry on mi breast, besides that."

Country-people still firmly believe in birthmarks. Some bear the mark of port wine, some of an apple, a blackberry, or a strawberry. They imagine that whatever the mother strongly desires, if she be not immediately satisfied with it, and chances to touch any part of her body, that part of the child's body, when it is born, will bear the mark of the object. Only last year, while I was in my garden, gathering strawberries, a poor woman sent to beg a few, the messenger whispering apologetically in my ear that she was expecting a baby, and I picked her a handful of the biggest berries I could find.

The majority of the cottages, underneath the hill, are very old, made of chalk or stone, with thatched roofs, and whitewashed on the outside. Here dwell the farm labourers, the agricultural part of the population; nearly all those who are engaged at the neighbouring town live lower down, in houses of brick and tile. These are really not villagers at all, since they merely come home to sleep, and spend the week-end; there is a great difference between them and the agricultural folk proper. One would imagine that work in the town, and at the factory, with a crowd, would make the men more keen, intelligent, and interesting, but that is far from being the actual case; as a matter of fact, though occupying a slightly higher level as regards work and wages, they do not possess as many individual features and outstanding characteristics as do the true rustic labourers; they have lost all charm and picturesqueness of habit and language.

Meeting with one of the town toilers recently on the way home to the village, and chancing to remark on the mildness of the winter, he proceeded to enlighten me on the subject.

"Do you naw why we be 'evin' these yer mild winters, cause if you dwunt I can soon tell e," he began.

I told him I thought it might be due to local accident, or something of the kind.

"Chent no sich theng," he retorted. "We be further south than we used to be."

"Further south?" I said, with a little surprise.

"Yes, further south. We be turned round, ya flaw. This earth o' ourn reciles."

"Reciles!" I answered.

"Yes, reciles. Tell ya 'ow that is. I bin thenkin' an't over this long time. It puzzled I for a bit, but I got it now, awright."

"And what is your conclusion?" I asked.

"I'll tell e, look. For years an' years tha bin deggin' coal down in Wales, ane 'em?"

"Yes," I said.

"An' tha bin cartin' an't away to London bi the trainload, ane 'em?"

Again I acquiesced.

"Well now, it stands to raason, as they can't do that wiout upsettin' summat or nother. If you takes a apple an cuts a piece off one side an in, you makes un 'eavier a one side than a is a t'other, don' e?"

"I suppose so," I said.

"Well then, tha's jest what they bin a doin' wi' our earth. Tha bin deggin' an' deggin', an' cartin' an't away, an' made un overbalance, an' that 'ev brought us round more to the south look, an' tha's tha raason of these yer mild winters we be 'evin'. 'Twas never like it when I was a bwoy. Us never haes a good owl'-fashioned winter now, an' never shaant no moore."

The cowman lives at the Lower Mill, the last of the half-dozen on the stream, and which is in dilapidation, though the pond is kept full of water, not to turn the wheel, however, but to provide a swimming place for the ducks. The cowman is a man of about forty years, small of stature and feature, but great in courage, perseverance, and energy. He was feeding the pullets and ducks with meal when I came into the paddock. Two young sows were following him everywhere from point to point, whining and squealing in a subdued tone, begging for their supper, as well as they knew how. He set the little troughs for the ducks, filled them with meal, thickly mixed up, keeping the sows from it with his foot and leg, and stood by a moment, then went to a big tub, full of pot liquor and barley-meal, and stirred it up vigorously with a short stick, while the pigs set up an increased squealing. Hereupon he addressed them kindly: "You hold on a minute, an' hey patience. You shall hey yer supper directly. You byent so hungry as all that, now, I know;" whereat they stopped a moment, and looked up at him knowingly, then continued the supplication. Now he dipped a bucket into the tub and filled the long trough near by, then stood and patted the pigs, and rubbed them fondly, while they made haste to devour the sweet meal and liquor, sucking it through the teeth into their mouths. "The purtiest little hilt in Wroughton, her is," he went on, "an her ther is the best little mother as ever lived. Jest look at the shape o' that little un, an' mark her hind-quarters; her's a perfect beauty." And she was really a well-shaped creature, and extraordinarily sociable, follow ing us everywhere, and pushing against our legs, or rubbing her nose against them like a dog.

Besides his pullets, ducks, and pigs, the cowman has a yearling, which runs loose with the master's herd, and which the farmer maintains for him at a slight cost. By-and-by he hopes to take a small farm for himself, and realize his heart's desire; his whole happiness consists in his work about the fields and in the farmyard.

Remembering that the landlord of the Three Tuns was an old acquaintance, and formerly a smith, I stepped in to take a glass of ale and to see how things were going with him. I found him in the bar, greatly changed, in appearance and manner, too, from what he had been when he came to work in the forge. At that time he was tall, square, and sprightly, sound in health, quick and witty in conversation, genial and affable. Now he looked seedy, dyspeptic, gloomy and care-stricken; the brightness was gone, both from his mien and speech.

"I miss the tools," he explained, "the moving about, and the habits of the forge. There is not enough exercise here to keep you well. I often wish I was back at the fires again; there's nothing like the old times. Depend upon it, you're better off when you've got manual work to do."

As to the philosophy of his remarks, there is no doubt of the wisdom of that. I have known many who have left active work to go inn-keeping, but I do not remember one who really benefited by the change finally. The mere "easy life," without intellectual pursuits, will never make up for the joys of vigorous toil; and if there are troubles and trials to be borne at work, there are compensations in other ways, as the poet testifies:

> S'il est des jours amers il en est de si doux.
> (If there are bitter days, there are some that are so sweet.)

1. As I was preparing these pages for the printer word was brought that the old shepherd had been found dead in the fold, surrounded by his sheep, with his head pillowed on the grassy bank, in a lonely part of the downs.

V

Burderop—The lost waggoner—The ox-carter—
Hodson Bottom—The old gamekeeper—
The gamekeeper's cottage—Tommy Weston

When the wind shot shrewdly on Queen Elizabeth's cheek, height-
ening the colour of it, and adding to the beauty of the royal complexion—which the breath and spirit of the downs are well able to
do—she was descending Brimble Hill; we take the opposite course
and mount up the downs towards Burderop and Hodson. The road
up the hill is steep and winding, and much smoother than it was
in the sixteenth, or even the nineteenth, century, before the steam-
roller made its appearance about the countryside. The material of
the road, as is usual on the downs, is flint. These roads are very
hot in the summer-time. The flints attract and reflect the sun's rays
in an uncommon degree; it is stifling to follow the tracks along
through the hollows on a brilliant windless day in July or August.
The banks of the road, up the hill, are dense with plants and wild
flowers: red and white campion, crane's-bill, cat's-ear, logger heads,
bryony, stachys, and calamint; several large wild apple-trees stand
along the hedge on the brow.

A walk of ten minutes brings you to the top of Ladder Hill. Here,
running up by the side of a large wood of oak and hazel, is a track
which afterwards joins the hard road on the summit, and, passing
by the lodge gate and entrance to the avenue leading to the squire's
house, converges to the south, and shows like a white pillar up the
steep side of Hakpen Hill, a little to the east of Barbury Castle, a

mile and a half away. On the left is a large park and grounds, magnificently wooded, and in the centre of this, reached by an avenue on either side, is Burderop House, where Queen Elizabeth passed the night during her journey from Ramsbury to Down Ampney. The bedstead on which the Queen slept—a fine old English specimen of carved and painted oak—is still preserved, and the room has scarcely been touched since it was occupied by the royal visitant three hundred years ago. Another trophy, hanging in the great hall beneath, is a pair of military top-boots, said to have been worn by Oliver Cromwell, so that here we have the singular mental spectacle of the Protector's boots under Queen Elizabeth's bed. To the east, partly concealed in a deep hollow, and surrounded with woods and trees, is the little village of Hodson, and, below this, a long winding belt of woodland with Coate Reservoir, the haunt of the youthful Richard Jefferies, in the near distance. A railway-line, skirting the wood, runs along the base of the hill towards the high downs; the huge earthworks on Liddington Hill frown over beyond the considerable village of Chiseldon.

There are many stories told of poachers and poaching affrays, which took place round about the woods of Burderop and Hodson in olden times. Then it was quite the usual thing to shoot the poachers, if possible, and bury them in the wood straightway; the game was simple enough, and there was not likely to be much of a hue and cry after the missing trespasser, and the gamekeepers and rustics were not troubled with "nerves" then; they were not afraid to creep about the glades and thickets on the darkest nights. The old gardener still remembers a spirited encounter with poachers in the wood. One night word was brought that there was a party of men in the wood, and the whole staff of game keepers, gardeners, and stablemen set out, armed, some with firearms, some with pitchforks, and others with sticks and stones, while another came running up and fiercely seized the coal-hammer, and so they set out in search of the marauders. By-and-by they came up with them, and let go with their weapons, all together, but did no considerable damage. The poachers shot back at them and promptly retired.

In the chase that followed one unhappy coney-catcher, more tardy than the rest, was sighted clearing over a stone wall. Thereupon one of the keepers shot at him and wounded him in the posterior, but he escaped, leaving a portion of his trousers for identification upon the fence.

The account is related here of the carter returning with a team of six horses, and one of the heavy road waggons used to convey goods and produce before the advent of the railway. Passing through the village, away back on the road, he went into the inn and partook of an extra deep draught of the nut-brown liquor, and went on his way again. By-and-by he fell asleep on the waggon, and the horses, no longer urged with the long whip and shout, came to a stand still, and he fell off his seat on to the grass. About two hours afterwards the old fellow awoke, while the sun was setting over the valley beneath. Starting up with surprise and stupefaction, and rubbing his eyes with his rough, horny fist, he cried out:

"Lord a massy! Is it I, or byent it I? If 'tis I, then I be lost; an' if chent I, then I 'ev found a waggin an' six osses."

The houses in the village of Hodson are very ancient, and nearly all made of chalk. Formerly chalk was the only material used for walls along the down-side, but that has gone out of date now, for several reasons. In the first place, bricks are cheap, and building with them is easy, though hauling up to the hills is expensive, while chalk requires time, and great care in the preparation, and good stuff is not as easily obtained as heretofore in the locality. Here the chalk is soft and inconsistent; all it is fit for is for making tracks and paving yards, though a finer quality is obtained at Bishopstone and near the White Horse. There it is quarried out in masses as big as a horse, and is afterwards broken up, or sawn into squares, and chiselled to requirement. Before it can be used for building, however, it must be dried and tested, which is done by natural means. The chalk is quarried out in great masses and blocks in the summer and autumn, and left in the open; disposed in loose stacks and piles. Posts are then set in the earth, and a roof, generally of thatch, made over the whole, to keep off the wet. When the frost comes disintegration begins. All the soft chalk breaks up and falls away, leaving the hard solid stuff intact; whatever the frost has not broken is counted trustworthy, and carted off to the builders. There are hundreds of houses built of this along the down side, many of which have stood for centuries, and the edges and surface of the chalk are as good now, in many cases, as when they were first constructed.

Sarsen-stones have been used for building purposes, too, but these, also, are gone out of fashion. The sarsen-stone is very hard and difficult to chip, but it was frequently used until a few years ago. The chief objection to this kind of stone is that it "sweats" very much; consequently, houses that are built of it are sure to be cold and damp. Building with enforced concrete is gradually creeping into favour in some parts. Here the concrete is rammed into moulds, and allowed to set; the operation is rather tedious, but when the wall is completed it is as solid as a rock, and almost indestructible.

It is pleasing to meet with the oxen at plough and harrow about the farm, or attached to the cart and waggon, gathering up the hay in the meadow, or the sheaves in the cornfield. The sight of the ox-teams, yoked in pairs, trudging slowly and peacefully along in the furrows, is always a delight, bringing back to mind days of long ago, and old-world customs, centuries before the steam-engine, and when horses were of greater value, comparatively, and were required for more exalted, though not more honourable toils, than that of ploughing the land. The old Biblical picture is recalled to mind as we see the patient beasts toiling side by side, and our thoughts revert to that other spectacle of Jason in search of the Golden Fleece, when he coupled up the dire oxen of Æetes, that breathed forth yellow flames from their nostrils, and how, "marking out with a line straight furrows, he drove them on, and a fathom's length he clove the back of the loamy soil," causing Æetes to cry out with admiration—ινξεν ἀγασφείς—as Pindar beautifully tells us in the myth. Oxen are cheaper than horses for work on the land; they eat rougher food, and are hardier into the bargain, and when they have worked for a few years they may be fatted and sold in the market at a good figure.

Richard Ashton, the ox-carter, dwells in a lonely cottage by the roadside over the downs towards Hakpen; the stables and yards for the oxen are situated in a field a short distance away. The carter is medium in height, stooping a little, with head thrown forward, fair-sized belly, jovial face, laughing eyes, and ruddy cheeks, a picture of health, a very good type of the rural labourer, his slight physical deformity notwithstanding. As a young man he served with the colours, and he is still included in the list of the National Reserve, and caused great amusement at a recent assembling and review of its members locally, when, in the presence of a huge crowd, he marched past with the rest, carrying in his hand a stock of rations, with which he had provisioned himself for the day, ingenuously tied up in a big red dinner-kerchief.

It was evening when I came to the cottage. I found the carter, with his wife and three sturdy children, busily engaged partaking of a hearty and substantial hot meal: meat and soup, with suety dumplings, cabbage, potatoes, and tender, juicy turnips. A monster blue enamelled teapot was set on the hob, and the kettle was steaming away over the fire. The carter's head was leaned well over the table, and his elbows were sprawled out. He was busy with a second helping of the food, and could not tarry yet awhile; the young people quickly finished their meal and prepared to play a game of rings on a board in one corner of the room. A broad smile, nearly approaching a grin, was spread over the carter's features as he picked up the steaming meat and potatoes with his fork and thrust them into his mouth, and turned his head half round, to nod to some remark of mine, or to answer it with a few broken words or sentences. Now the wife and mother took the teapot from the hob, filled it with water from the kettle, and poured him out a large cupful of the beverage, added sugar and milk, and set it down close to his plate, and insisted that I, too, should take a cup, "to kip un company," which I did, sitting next the carter. A moment afterwards he laid down the knife and fork, crossing them on the plate, and pushed them from him, drew up the tea cup and saucer, and leaned back in the chair, wiping his mouth with the back of his hand, and continuing the smile.

"That's a poor tea!" I remarked.

"Is it?" replied he, grinning. "You ent a seed what we put out o' sight afore you come. Jest look be'ind e on that table, at thaay empty dishes yander."

I did as he requested and perceived a great pile of dishes and basins, stacked one within the other, whereat the good wife smiled broadly, and the young people set up a merry laugh.

"Well, you have not done so badly; but I expect you were hungry," I said.

"Bless you," the mother answered, "I don' know how *to* satisfy 'em. Tha comes 'ome like lions; an' these yer bwoys, tha can never sim to 'ev enough, tha ates so well an' 'arty."

The carter is very proud of his oxen, and views the animals with real affection, and tends them with jealous care. He is acquainted with their needs and ailments, is able to discriminate between good, bad, and indifferent beasts, to train them to the toil, and make them useful and docile, understands the proper period of their usefulness, and when they should be superseded, and will not have them ill-used on any account. Their horns are tipped with small brass caps, like balls, to prevent them from goring each other, and no prodding or "fooling" with the beasts, by the lads or under-carters, is ever allowed.

The oxen perform all the various duties to which the ordinary farm horse is liable; such as plough, harrow, drill, hay and corn-cart, turnip-hauling, conveying the manure from the yards, and machine-hoeing. Little Betsy Horton, the quaint old woman who dwelled in the village below in the valley, used to lead the old farm bull in the cart, and attached to the implements, and amused the neighbours with the oddness of her remarks. "What 'ev e bin at to-day, Betsy?" this one inquired, with a smile.

"'Aw bin up yander in the lower ground, a 'oss 'owin' wi' tha bool," she replied.

The ox-carter's day is not a very exacting one. In the summer the teams go out at 7 a.m., and finish at 3.30 p.m., and in the winter the hours are from 7.30 till 3, with an hour for dinner. In the winter, when the oxen lie in, they have to be foddered, which makes extra work, but oxen feed much more quickly than do horses, they are not long in filling their bellies with sweet hay, or nourishing oat straw. When the sowing is in progress the carter helps with that, and receives extra money, and all overtime is paid for. His ordinary wages are 14s. a week, with a large new cottage, and a quarter of an acre of land. "If I was in the townd I should ef to pay six shillin' for mi 'ouse, an no garden, an' work a good many more hours, too; so I be a main bit better off yer wher I be," he says.

There is a tiny dissenting chapel, built of wattle and daub, and which has an interesting history, in the little village of Hodson. This was the first place of the kind to be established in the locality. It is said that a missioner, setting out from Bristol in a canvas tent, constructed on a sort of carriage, which was drawn by large paper kites flying in the air, declared he would build a chapel at that point where he should first come to earth, and that happening to be in the village, he accordingly erected a small chapel there, which has been tenderly cared for by the inhabitants, and is now used as a reading-room.

From the centre of the village the road shoots steeply down into a deep coomb, the slopes of which, on three sides, are thickly draped with towering beech and elm, and plantations of black-looking spruce, and slender brownish-green larches. At the bottom a tiny spring runs underneath the road, issuing from a withy bed, where the slender wands, all of a uniform height, of a beautiful amber in the middle, tipped with crimson, give a charming effect in the mass, lighting up the dark background of the elm and spruce with a rich glow of colour, exceptionally pleasing in the winter, when all else is destitute of foliage. The road leads down between high banks of crumbling chalk, and climbs up almost perpendicularly on the other side. Huge beech-trees grow along the summit of the banks, and are perched immediately on the edge, with half of their gnarled and twisted roots denuded, where the chalk has crumbled and fallen away, leaving the trees deprived of half their grip and sustenance, and dangerous-looking to travellers down the roadway. A mighty gust of wind, such as that we experience on the open downs above, would overturn them, and send them crashing into the hollow beneath; but the singing tempest, raging mightily from the south, shoots like an arrow from the crest of the downs out into the void, and leaves the trees in the hollow almost undisturbed, calm and still in the vacuum created by the leaping elements, or gently swaying their naked tops, as the currents, whirled backwards underneath, eddy and curl over and over about and between them.

The road is strewn with dried leaves of the bracken, which was cut in the woods in the autumn, and stacked there, and has only now been carted away for litter in the cattie stalls. Here and there the fragrant pink campion peeps out from amid the dried grasses and bennets, the herb-robert, with its gemlike blossoms and graceful, bright green or crimson foliage, hangs down from the banks and walls in summer luxuriance, the little celandine, avens, thistle, colt's-foot, mayweed, enchanter's nightshade, and quaint figwort are yet in bloom, though it is January, and a large delicate cluster of pale creamy honeysuckle droops from the bough overhanging the fence, still fragrant, but with a diminished sweetness, which is no more than a hint of her full voluptuousness, like some once lovely maiden, now wasted with sickness, and pining slowly away, lingering on through the dark wintry days, soon to be stricken down and laid low by the cold, pitiless finger of Death. The inquisitive little wren, and equally sociable tomtit, hop about and turn pretty somersaults in the branches, while the tiny brown, woodpecker creeps up the trunk of the old oak-tree with a tap, tap, tap, winding round and round, and searching underneath the limbs, and an occasional red-headed woodpecker the "eke-aw," or "ya-ha"—flies over high up and disappears among the trees of the wood. Away over the silent deep green meadow the hawthorn hedge, with dense red berries, shows a rich colour, most like a long line of crimson lake drawn with the painter's brush, vivid above, but subdued underneath, and intermingling beautifully with the deep brown shades of the hedge-row. The moist scents of the mosses are borne up from the earth, and the souls of the leaves—a dense, spiritual crowd—float listlessly about, or hang steadfast in the air, clinging to their old haunts, till they are gradually sucked out into the open, and scattered broadcast in the profound heavens above.

On one side, at the bottom of the coomb, is a flat open space, containing half a dozen grey old stone-built cottages, standing in the midst of large gardens, completely shut away from the outer world, subjected to fierce heat in the summer, but warmly sheltered and protected from the piercing blasts and cold of winter. The thick spruce plantation is ranged like a dense wall over opposite to the north; from the south a green slope runs gently down, leaving the sunlight free to enter on that side. A short way above, in a small opening of the fir plantation, and almost shut out of view, is the gamekeeper's cottage, immortalized in Richard Jefferies' "The Gamekeeper at Home."

Benny Haylock, the old gamekeeper, and the subject of Jefferies' pages, was a most eccentric person. He would not allow people in the woods under any pretext whatever, but ordered them all unceremoniously away, frightening the timid with his gruff voice and threatening language and behaviour. It would not have done for him to have whole troops of young people coming to gather primrose and violet, anemone and hyacinth, and wandering about the woods at their pleasure, as they do at this time; he would have stormed and raged like a lion. He would not allow even the lady of the House to walk in the woods when the young birds were hatched, but would roughly order her outside, as though she had been an utter stranger, and a suspicious character. One day, when the woodman and his mates were removing some timber from a plantation, the squire came on the scene followed by a small house-dog. "Now, you fellows," said he, "make haste and get out of here before Haylock comes, or you'll be in the wrong."

"Aa, an' so ull you, too, sir, if 'e do ketch ee wi' that ther dog," the woodman replied.

Immediately afterwards Haylock came up. Standing stock-still, and looking at the squire's dog with great displeasure, he addressed the master: "What have you got there along with you? Take the thing out o' the 'ood this minute. I ull not have it in yer, an' you knows it. I not have the birds worritted with the damn thing if you can't come into the 'ood without 'im, stop out altogether yourself." After this he turned and hurried off, crashing noisily amid the dried stems of the bracken, and muttering loudly to himself.

The old fellow wore the top hat everywhere about the woods, and, notwithstanding his rudeness and bluntness, was a sterling example of his profession: "a faithful protection to all kinds of property," as Jefferies styled him. The villagers still remember how he slew all their cats and made a carriage rug from their pelts; they never forgave him for that, though it was done in the interests of the game in the woods. He never partook of but two meals a day—breakfast and supper—and seldom came home, after leaving the cottage, till the evening, weekdays and Sundays the same. As he walked about the woods he ate Indian corn, a quantity of which he always carried in his pocket. When the young gentlemen visitors were out shooting, they had to abide by his instructions, and if they failed to bring down the game, he made scathing comments on their marksmanship, and ground his teeth at them, and told them they could not hit a hayrick, nor a barn-door.

The old keeper was not destitute of wit, and amused them all, sometimes, with quaint tales and exaggerations. One day he came into the gardens, with face aglow, eager to tell them a precious bit of information.

"I've seen this mornin' what I never seen before," he began. "I allus know'd hedgehogs was fond of eggs, but I never know'd 'em to cart 'em off a dozen at a time afore. What do you think I've jest bin an' seen? I warn you wunt believe it, but I stood an' seen it wi' my own eyesight. I seen the hedgehog come along to the pheasant's nest, as ad 'leven eggs in 'im, an' I thought I'd jest see what a *'ood* do; so I stood up, quiet like, an' never made a sound. When the hedgehog come to the nest a smelled all round 'im, as if a was countin' the eggs, then presently a took one in 'is mouth, then rolled over on 'is back into the nest, picked up all the eggs on 'is bristles, an' off a went as 'ard as a was able, and left I thunderstruck. I never seen sich a thing afore, no, that I never did."

Chandler, the woodman, who lives in one of the stone cottages at the bottom of the coomb, knew Richard Jefferies, and James Jefferies, his father, and remembers how the old man used often to come over to the wood to drink whisky, and sit and listen to the nightingales during the summer nights. There was an eccentric old fellow, named Dyke, who owned one of the woods then, and he had a small hut built underneath a large yew-tree; there they assembled and drank small drops of spirit, and hung on the soul-stirring notes of lovely Philomel, as she sat thrilling the woods, with her breast thrust hard against a sharp thorn, as the fable goes. Old Dyke was a gentleman of means, and he had some queer ideas. One passionate desire of his was to produce a blue rose. To accomplish this he planted young briars in the open spaces of the wood, among the hyacinths, thinking that the bees would inoculate the blooms, and thus he would ultimately evolve a blue flower. He was deeply suspicious of his fellow-men and neighbours. Every night, after dark, he came out of doors and discharged his gun several times at intervals, frightening the villagers, and causing them to scuffle off sharply up the roads. This he did to scare away loiterers, and to strike fear into poachers and others. One old farmer I knew always took a double-barrelled gun loaded to bed with him, and placed it at the back of the pillow; at the slightest sound outside during the night he opened the bedroom window and rattled off the contents of both barrels into the air.

The gamekeeper's cottage has not changed very much in outward appearance since the days when Benny Haylock dwelled there, and when the youthful Jefferies stepped therein occasionally to converse with the buxom dame concerning the dressing of the pelts, or to reach the old man's guns down from the rack fixed on the beam in the centre of the ceiling, and minutely examine them, or partake of a few sweet chestnuts roasting in the embers of the great kitchen fire on the dark winter evenings. There it stands, a little way back from the lane, with the Spanish chestnut-trees towering high above it, the dark spruce plantation on each side, and the open coomb winding round at the rear. In front is a large garden and a small bit of lawn; luxuriant roses climb up the wall, over the windows, and underneath the roof; behind are the kennels and outhouses; it is much the same as it was half a century ago. The interior is bright and cheerful, and exquisitely clean still, but there are several alterations visible. The fireplace has been modernized; the rafters and beams of the ceiling have been covered up with matchwood, painted white; and the gunrack, instead of being overhead, is shifted to underneath the wall. Here are four guns: three sporting pieces, and an old military needle rifle, which saw useful service in the Egyptian War, and which was given to the keeper as a present by the squire. The large room is hung round with pictures and photographs; on the side-table, and ranged on a chest of drawers, are several cases of stuffed birds, among them a fine specimen of the red-headed wood pecker, with its large strong bill, and pouchlike throat; a beautiful black and white mottled blackbird; a golden plover—a stranger from the Scotch High-lands, singular as having but three toes; two dainty mountain larks, some of which nest in the locality; and a large hawfinch, with extra stout short bill, also taken in the wood close by.

The gamekeeper is shortish in stature, with a square face, ruddy cheeks, iron-grey hair, and side beard, pleasant and courteous in manner, and abounding with knowledge of wild life. There are many changes in the gamekeeper's profession now from what it used to be, in breeding and caring for the birds, and the task is much lighter than formerly. There is very little poaching done near the woods now, hardly a single case comes to light in the whole year, and that merely the taking of a rabbit or hare, though at the keeper's last place, nine miles distant, he had much trouble, and many midnight watchings, but few encounters. There the method was that of netting; the keepers sometimes took as many as 180 yards of netting in a lot, which was set against the outer edge of the wood, and into which the rabbits and hares were driven by the beaters and their dogs.

The chief things to guard against now in the woods are foxes and other vermin, stoats and weasels, and snakes—which devour the small callow young of birds—magpies, jays, and sparrow-hawks; the kestrel is now preserved, by reason of the large number of mice it destroys. It is remarkable that pheasants and other birds, while on the nest, take scarcely any notice of the kestrel, but rush off immediately they catch sight of the sparrow-hawk, which shoots and darts like an arrow in and out among the bushes and trees.

Foxes play havoc with the pheasants, and especially in the early morning, when the birds first alight from their perches in the trees. Then they are sleepy and "dummel," like human beings, for a short while, unable to realize themselves, and escape from the clutches of the "ruddy reynard."

A short while ago, as the keeper was walking through the wood with a companion, hearing a strange whining sound in the thicket, he stopped short, and thereupon a large fox, with five cubs hanging from her teats, came straight out in front of them, and stood in the way, snarling, and showing her teeth, as if daring them to proceed further, and continued so till all the cubs had got safely away; then she retreated slowly backwards into the thicket and disappeared. When the mother fox wishes to bring her young out of the hole, she first of all emerges and makes a reconnoitre, then stamps with her feet, goes and fetches out the cubs, waits a moment or two, and finally trots off in search of food, leaving them to play with their tails, and with one another. There they run round and round, or roll over on the grass in a heap, and give each other gentle pats, like puppies or kittens, but at the first sound of danger they scamper off into the hole, and remain there in fear and silence.

The gamekeeper is familiar with the cooking and eating of badgers, and especially of badgers' hams, which used to be counted a delicacy, and which he declares to be equal to the best bacon hams in the land. I do not remember whether Jefferies mentions having partaken of the badger or not, but, as the Haylocks ate them, he may possibly have tasted of the dish. Baby badgers are born quite naked, and not all of a litter on the same day. Sometimes the keeper had set as many as three traps at one hole, and then had been outwitted by the badger; he had thrown them all without being taken himself.

Tommy Weston, aged eighty-five, who was plough boy, sheep-boy, carter, and bailiff by turns, dwells in a small cottage in the middle of the village, with his wife and maiden daughter, who is a keeper of pigs, and haulier for the village, going regularly to the railway-station for coal, and delivering parcels on the way. Tommy is tall and erect in stature, finely built, square and boney, with a pleasant face, smiling mischievous eyes, and high, arched eyebrows, a fresh, ruddy complexion, well-seasoned with the down air, and stiff, bristly grey hair, standing straight up from the forehead, which gives him a quaint appearance, and which is yet perfectly in keeping with his general features. His clothes, scrupulously clean, are of corduroy, and he wears a small thin kerchief wound twice about the neck, and tied in a cunning little knot, a fashion dear to the old type of labourer, but which is passing away now. Both husband and wife are hard of hearing.

"'Tis a great denial to have 'em both deaf. It do wear I out so to make 'em understand," the daughter exclaimed. Then she addressed her father, in a shrill voice, shouting in his ear: "Faather, 'e wants you to tell 'e about the owld times."

"What owld times?" he inquired, with a merry twinkle in his eye.

"Why, the *howwld* times, as used to be, when you turned the wind-meell, an' done the grinndin'."

"I don' know nothin' about no owld times; I furgets it," he replied.

"Thelleky! tha's what 'e allus ses," the daughter exclaimed disappointedly,

"Never mind, let me try," I answered. Then, tugging hard at the collar of his coat, and pulling his ear towards my mouth, I began: "You're the finest man in Hodson."

"Whuh?" replied he.

"You're the finest man in Hodson," I repeated. "If you don't take care the recruiting sergeant will have you, yet."

"Ha! ha! ha! He's too late bi seventy year. He ought to a come afore. Them owld times wasn't much good to nob'dy. All as thaay troubled about was manhood, an' scawtin' about."

"Manhood?" said I, puzzled for the moment as to his meaning.

"Tha's it," he repeated; manhood an' strength. Tha didn't trouble about much else. All tha could think on was 'ittin' one another about; an' the rougher tha got trated the better thaay liked it. I've sin 'em grip one another, an' the blood runnin' out in strames atween ther fengers, all down ther bodies, an' thaay was jest landed then. Jimmy Whorl, the carter, had a hand as beg agyen as mine. He was out in the ground one day wi' 'is teamm o' fower 'osses, an' a wanted 'em to 'come hither,' an' cause tha hoodn't do what he telled 'em, he went up to 'em, an' hit 'em ahind the yer wi' his fist, an' knocked 'em down, all fower on 'em, one aater t'other, flat on the ground; an' that's as true as I sets in this cheer. An' he was killed 'isself in the end, fightin' wi' another fella."

"Good heavens! Then what was *he* like?" I exclaimed.

"A fine strappin' chap as ever you seed, he was, I warn," he went on. "That was on Burderop racecourse. When tha brought owld Jimmy whum, his brother went to look at un, an' aater a seed the marks, a said:

"'Tha be good marks, tha be, all fair an' squer, an' honourable gied; an' ef the chap as done't were afront an ma now, be daal'd ef I oodn't ev a packet at un miself too.' A wanted to 'ev a dab at un, simly."

It is furthermore said of Jimmy Whorl, the carter, that one day, when a harrow was wanted for use away over the downs, there being no horse and cart available to convey it up, he went into the farmyard, clapped it on his back, and carried it up to the field, two miles away. The harrow was an iron one, in three sections, and weighed something over 2 cwt.

Hereupon the daughter interposed with: "Will you 'ev some elderberry wine, or be you a tee tot'ler?"

"I should like some, if you please," I said. So she fetched out a small jug of the wine, and warmed it over the fire, as is usual with this kind of drink, and reached down a tin of biscuits from between a set of ancient brass candlesticks standing on the mantelpiece, and granny gently and shyly pushed a big orange into my hand, while Tommy sat smiling, and thrumming on the table with his fingers.

Elderberry wine is a wholesome drink, and stands high in the estimation of the villagers. The berries are gathered when ripe, and placed in cold water; after soaking for several days they are boiled down, and the liquor strained off and sweetened; the wine, taken warm at bedtime, is good to cure a cold. Besides the wine, there is also elderberry jam, or the fruit is used to make tarts and pies, and is sometimes preserved in syrup, as with greengages; some of the old-fashioned sort of people always make an elder berry pie with fruit kept in this way at Christmas. Another use of the elder is that of making a wash for the skin, by steeping the bunches of bloom in boiling water; it is said to be very efficacious in removing freckles, and beautifying the complexion.

VI

Chiseldon—The church and bells—A surprise for
the Bishop—"Clerk's ale"—The Elm-Tree Inn—The
village foundry—Iron moulders—The schoolmaster

FROM HODSON THE ROAD PASSES along the top of the hill for
some distance, then shoots down into a hollow and up again,
running eastward. On the right hand are the open downs, fully cultivated; on the left, the eye roams over a charming picture of woodland scenery. Here the cornfields, intersected with a deep gully, trail
gently away to a continuation of the coomb, which opens out into
the broad valley, and of which the further slope is covered with trees
of oak, ash, elm, and fir. Beyond that, the down-line is visible for
many miles, past Wanborough to the White Horse; and, right in
front, as the road converges, towers Liddington Hill, stately and
imposing as a mountain, and crowned with the ancient hill-fort,
one of the chain that dominated the country round about in olden
times, and protected the system of roads leading this way and that
upon the downs.

> The time sa tranquill is and still,
> That nowhere sail ye find,
> Saife on ane high and barren hill,
> Ane air of peeping wind.

Thus sang the poet, Alexander Hume, writing of the Summer's
Day, over three hundred years ago; and though he was think-

ing of one of those bare, stony hills in his native Scotland, the description might very well be applied to the high mound before us.

The village of Chiseldon is a prosperous place, of over one thousand inhabitants, though a great many of these are town workmen, who take advantage of the facilities offered by the railway-line to live at some distance from their employment; the agricultural element has been sadly reduced in late years. Of the houses and buildings, half are ancient—built of chalk, or rough sarsen-stones—and half are modern, of shabby red brick and tile, ill agreeing with the locality and surroundings. The chalk, or flint-made cottages, with their thatched roofs and quaint gables, fit in exactly with the conditions of the downs, and harmonize so completely with the earth and hills as to appear a natural part of them, while brick-made dwellings are peculiarly unsightly and disagreeable to the beauty-seeking eye of the traveller. The oldest part of the village is situated on the higher ground of the hill, and is grouped around the neck of a deep gully, at the bottom of which, under your very feet, a tiny spring of crystal water bubbles out of the earth and flows down, soon to accumulate in the waters of Coate Reservoir, two miles away. This stream is afterwards the River Cole, which winds away, and enters the Thames at Lechlade.

In times past Chiseldon and the country beyond were the stronghold of robbers and smugglers, and others of an undesirable kind, who committed their depredations, and retired with their spoils into the hidden seclusion of the outlying woods and places, amid the solitude of the downs. There is a tradition among the villagers that the smugglers of the Bristol Channel had a regular trade with the people of this locality, and that they used to convey large amounts of contraband up from the mouth of the Severn, and conceal it about the downs here.

There are traces of the old monks and friars scattered in various parts, far away from the acknowledged sites of the ancient abbeys and convents. In one place the memory of these survives in a name, such as Friar's Mill, on the Cole, near Highworth, or

Quiddington Friars, near Basset Down; in another place local gossip or tradition has handed it on; the people of generation after generation point to a bit of ruin or site where an old church or convent formerly stood. At Chiseldon the memory of the old monkish life and times has been perpetuated in a quaint rhyme, in which the custom of absolving a man from his sins for a fee is clearly alluded to:

> Come all ye honest friends of mine,
> Kill a pig, give me the chine;
> Give me the jaw, give me the jowl,
> Give me the whole, I'll save your soul.

Here the greediness of the monk is in open evidence; nothing less than the whole hog would satisfy him; he would have starved the other's body to save his soul, while he fattened himself upon the sweetbreads and chine, and other choice parts of the unhappy denizen of the sty.

The village church, a large, ancient pile, stands immediately on the brow of the hill overlooking the deep coomb in which the mill formerly stood. The tower is a huge structure, with thick, solid walls, the outer parts of which are of stone, and the interior composed of huge blocks of chalk, obtained from the hillside, and still bearing the marks of the quarry-man's tools, or of whomsoever cut them into the requisite shape for fitting into the walls, many centuries ago. The top parts of the walls have become unstable, and are held together with a strong iron band, which goes round the tower, and is secured with stout bolts, fastened through the masonry. There are five bells on the third floor, the biggest of which is a ton in weight, and the smallest about half a ton. These are hung in a massive framework of oak, half-rotten in places, and crumbling away under the slow finger of Time, and by reason of the rain which for ages has been driven in through the apertures of the windows. From this cause, and on account of the unstable condition of the walls, the bells have not been rung for several years; a little steady chiming at festival times is all that has been permitted by those responsible for the safety of the building.

A few years ago a strike of bell-ringers took place at the village church, and there was no music from the tower for three months. The fact of the matter was, the men missed the old-time annual supper, which had been discontinued, to the detriment of the church's interests and the discipline of the workers. The old bell-ringer was disconsolate at the lack of interest in things about the village; everything is too much trouble now, he says. Only the night before he had been looking at the local newspapers, and wherever his eye alighted there were accounts of the bell-ringer's suppers in all the villages round about; they of Chiseldon alone seemed to have been excluded from the number; no one cared anything about them.

There is a story of the young curate, sauntering through the churchyard, drinking in the beauty of evening, and the music of the bells pealing in the tower. During his walk he came upon the grave-digger, hard at work deep in the earth, and accosted him naïvely: "How beautiful it is, John, to listen to the sweet music of the bells this peaceful evening." The grave-digger stopped work a moment, spat on his hands, and retorted: "I dwun know a bit what you da zaay, zur. I caan' yer nothin' for thaay tarnation bells."

Here, also, the story is related of the traveller who addressed the boy, sitting on the bank by the road side, as to the tolling of the church bell.

"Who's dead yer then, mi bwoy?" quoth he.

"Nob'dy," he replied. "Ther's nob'dy dead yer, as I knows on."

"What's the bell going out for, then?" the stranger asked.

"Oni zumb'dy gwain to be buried," the youth answered.

There were not many words wasted in country courtships in times past, if we are to believe what is said by the villagers. At Clyffe Pypard John over took Mary, one morning, coming out of church, and said: "Ull you 'ev I for a 'usband?"

"Of course I ull," Mary answered; and that was every word uttered at the time, and they married and lived happily afterwards.

There is another story of the farm-hand suing for a wife, but lacking in the art of protestation. He made an open confession of his failing that way, merely remarking: "I don' know much about coortin', but yer's a girt apple var tha.'" And, after all, does not Theocritus tell us of the swain courting the lovely Amaryllis, and bringing her an offering of rosy apples plucked from the highest bough of the tree, and telling her there were some more left for to-morrow?

Once upon a time the Bishop was down to visit Chiseldon Church for a confirmation, and the fact caused great concern to the Vicar and sidesmen, and especially to the old clerk. So he put on his considering cap to invent some means or other of commemorating the event, and of making the Bishop's welcome specially striking. The old fellow was privileged with duties not allowed to the present-day clerk; he stood and played his part in the service, giving out the psalms, and making other announcements. So, when the Bishop and clergy had all come into the church, he stood up, and in a solemn voice began: "Let us sing to the praise and glory of God two vesses of my own compawsin':

> 'Why skip ye zo, ye little 'ills,
>   An' why do ye zo 'op?
> Is it acause 'is Grace is come,
>   'Is Grace, the lord Bi-shop?
> Ace 'tis. Then let us all strik up,
>   An' sing a glorious song of praise,
> An' bless the lord Bi-shop.'

"An tha's the two vesses of mi own compawsin'."

Of what the Bishop thought, or of what the parson said, we have no record; the compliment, if a little inconveniently worded and inopportunely expressed, was sincerely intended, and we cannot choose the time, place, and manner in which our praises are to be sung; we must accept the conditions and be thankful.

There was formerly an interesting custom at Chiseldon which

bore the name of "clerk's ale," but which was discontinued half a century ago. At that time every churchgoer, poor folk and all, paid a pew rent, according to their, means. The money was paid at the Easter Vestry, and after the business was transacted, each man was presented with a pint of ale by the clerk, and in the evening the churchwardens, farmers, and sidesmen met at the clerk's house, and partook of a substantial hot supper, with gin and ale to drink, after which they sat and smoked long clay pipes and passed the hours away.

The Elm-Tree Inn stands in the centre of the village, near the railway, and close to a clump of elms, from which the house derived its name. Before the railway was made there was a broad space, called the Square, before the inn; when a way had to be made for the panting iron horse, with hoofs of thunder, and sinews of steel; the old village meeting-place had to be cut into; the swarm of brawny toilers with pick and shovel attacked it below, and cleaved a passage through the deep chalk up to the open downs above.

Here it was that the feasts and revels were held, with the inevitable back-swording, wrestling, and other games so dear to the older generations of people. Challenges had been issued all round the neighbourhood for wrestlers and single-stick players, stages were erected in the square; there stood the challengers crying out: "Will any young gamester come upon the platform?" The inn had been decorated, without and within, for the occasion; and a mighty bundle of top-hats—fifteen or twenty, trimmed with coloured ribands, and all bound together—was hung out from the signboard.

Formerly the Elm-Tree Inn was a picturesque thatched house, but now it has been rebuilt and modernized; stone, wood, and straw have given place to brick, tile, and concrete, and the interior has been made to match with the outside. The old style of seat and furniture has gone with the walls; pewter pots have given place to glass mugs; landlord and all have been metamorphosed. The nearness of the railway has been responsible for the transformation of things at the inn; where there is continual contact and intercourse with towns-people the atmosphere of the village inn is bound to be changed. Here, now, in the winter evenings, instead of the village gossip of ploughing, threshing, reaping, revelling, and the rest, the talk is chiefly of the town: of football, the cinematograph shows, the theatre, "Sacco" the fasting freak, and a good deal of other sickly mess and rubbish, not half as manly and interesting as the hearty speech and ready wit of the independent crowd of cheerful rustics that assembled in the big room at the Blue Lion, shouting to the landlord for better beer, and singing snatches of song, some of them well worth remembering, such as this of the old carter's, rarely tender, and suggestive of a beautiful story:

> We never speak as we pass by,
> Although a tear bedims her eye;
> I know she thinks of our past life,
> When we were loving man and wife …

or the old poaching song of Thornymoor Fields

> Now Thornymoor Fields are in Nottinghamshire,
> Right whack ti fa lary, right whack ti fa laddie de;
> Now Thornymoor Fields are in Nottinghamshire,
> Right whack ti fa laddie ee day.

> * * * * * * * * *

> The very first night we had bad luck,
> For one of our very best dogs got shot,
> For one of our very best dogs got shot,
> Right whack ti fa laddie ee day.

A good many of these old songs and chanties survived about the villages till late years, but they are fast dying out now, and are replaced by the idiotic airs of the music-hall, or the sound of music is heard no more.

On the opposite side of the road from the inn stands a small foundry, with yards packed full of all kinds of agricultural machinery and implements, of various degrees of usefulness, some falling all to pieces and entirely dilapidated, some stable in parts, and some only slightly defective, awaiting repairs, then to return to the field or farmyard. Here are sets of steam-ploughing tackle, with the huge engines and cultivators, horse-ploughs, reapers and binders, threshing-machines, drills, harrows, horse-rakes, elevators, farm-waggons, and other paraphernalia of the countryside. The wood in many of the implements is rotten and crumbling; here the weight of the ironwork has broken it down, and let the machine fall to the ground; this one, more recently and solidly built, is strong enough, but antiquated in pattern, and has had to be replaced by something more modern, and lighter. Most of the woodwork in agricultural machinery is of oak or ash; if the parts are well covered with paint, and reasonably protected in the winter, they may last for forty or fifty years; but if they are allowed to stand in the wet, only half protected, they will be all to pieces in a third of that time. There is a scarcity of English ash at the present time, and the wood has greatly increased in value thereby; it is quite as expensive as the best oak now.

Little by little, the old machinery—that which cannot be repaired—is broken up, and the parts utilized for something or other—everything comes in once in seven years, the foundry fore-man says—the castings go back into the furnace and are re-melted, the wrought-iron is returned to the smith, who works it up into other shapes, and fits it for new uses, and all that is unfit for local purposes is sold away for ship's ballast, to keep the keel steady against the heaving, rolling waters and buffeting tempest: more than one portion of the plough or reaping or threshing machine that did service on the sunny slopes of the hills and downs amid the beautiful gold of the harvest-crops is lying fathoms deep beneath the dashing waves or the "many-twinkling smile of ocean," as the incomparable Greek poet styled it.

If the machinery is well made in the beginning, it will stand any amount of repair; but if it is cheap and shoddy, then it will not pay for renovating at all. One feature of the yards round about the village foundries is the large quantity of broken foreign-made machinery, especially mowers, binders, and horserakes; some of the premises are full of them. All these, being slightly made, are worn out after a few seasons' use; it is impossible to repair them at a profit, so they are scrapped, and new tackle obtained. Sometimes repairs to the value of £600 are made to a ploughing-engine, and then are profitable. This is when a new boiler, cylinders, and machinery are fitted to the old frame, and the whole made as good as new. The value of a ploughing-engine complete, independent of implements, is from £900 to £1,000.

There is one great disadvantage in steam-ploughing sets—in this country, at least—and the same applies to the new motor-ploughs which have been introduced, and that is, their great weight; they can only be used in fine weather, when the land is dry. After the autumn rains have set in, and the earth has become sodden with the downpour, it is useless to think of employing the steam-ploughs; they would soon be buried half out of sight in the mud and soil. Horse and ox-drawn ploughs, on the other hand, can continue at work all the winter, unless floods and hard frosts intervene: when everything has been said in favour of steam and petrol, there is small likelihood of the horse ever becoming entirely superseded on the land. The weight of a ploughing-engine is 13 or 15 tons—a huge mass of iron and steel to manœuvre around the cornfields—while the ordinary rustic can lift the horse-plough unaided.

The village foundry has existed for nearly two centuries, and, though it is only a small place, it has sufficed for the immediate needs of the neighbourhood. It is chiefly repairs that are executed, and not new machinery made, though there are a few new implements constructed, and especially heavy farm waggons and carriages. Nearly every village of any importance had its foundry till a few years ago, and though the number has diminished, there are still many to be met with here and there: there are no less than seven or eight within a radius of twelve miles of the village. It is true that the amount of work required of them has tragically fallen off of late years, but the owners and staff keep plodding away, with true rural grit, and the determination not to be utterly extinguished. Steam-traction and ploughing sets provided them with much work, and now they are on the decline the steam motor-lorry has come into being, and many of the larger village foundries are occupied with the manufacture of them.

The foundry at Chiseldon finds work in all for thirty-four hands. Of this number about a half are mechanics employed in the workshops, the others are engaged with steam-ploughing and threshing sets, steam-rolling the roads, and acting the part of hauliers. Twenty years ago the owners of the foundry at Swindon, four miles off, had fourteen sets of threshing tackle generally in use, while to-day they have but two, and these not in very frequent demand.

It is a difficult country for hauling, for horse and steam-engine, too, round about the downs. There is great interest in watching the iron steed climbing up the steep, almost perpendicular roads of the hillside, puffing, panting, and snorting, shooting the black smoke and cinders high into the air, with the driver grasping the lever, and his mate at the steering wheel; or to see them running noisily downhill, with steam shut off, and brakes applied, the mechanicians' faces black with the dust and smoke, and the lookout man sitting on the "bob," or tail behind, half asleep with the jolting and jogging.

It sometimes happens that the ploughing will not draw its load straight up the steep hill immediately behind it. In this case it first of all climbs the hill itself, having attached the steel cable to the load, and then turns half round, and winds the cable, and draws it up in that way. Years ago, when the ploughing sets were going from place to place, a man always walked 80 or 100 yards in front, with a red flag, to warn the carters and others, and help hold the horses; in time he took to riding on the fore part of the engine, and now his services are scarcely required at all. What with motor-cars flying this way and that, and the sound of the horns and things, the horses are become used to the traffic; you seldom see them shying and rearing on the highways now at the approach of the traction-engine.

The foundry staff proper includes the working manager— a fine type of the village engineer, tall and square, with ruddy cheeks, bluff and hearty, and clever at his trade, having a practical knowledge of everything connected with his work, in strong contradistinction to the ordinary railway works official, who is crammed full of theory, and lamentably weak in practice, relying on the draughtsmen and mechanics for everything—two smiths, a boilermaker, three fitters and turners, a moulder, and three or four carpenters and waggon-builders. These occupy a small group of buildings connected together, and are able to see each other at work, to communicate with, and consult one another on various points, and to work co-operatively, which is impossible in the big factories of the towns. Here the moulder steps in to see his casting being bored in the lathe, viewing it with real pride, or the turner goes out into the casting-shed, and takes the part in his hand, while the moulder views it fondly, and feels it over and over, bright and smooth with the tools, with an eager inquiry: "How is a? Is a aw right? How do a cut? Nice an' soft, yen a? A wasn't burned. You can kip the metal gentle and mild, or you can burn't up an' make it as brittle as glass. Tha's the caster's look out."

Here also the smiths and turners work side by side, or the fitter and turner goes to the forge, lights it up himself, makes his own tools and uses, and is clever in many ways; there is no jealousy, for that is a natural condition of things at the village works. But in the factory at the town none of this is possible. There a smith is a smith, a fitter is a fitter, a moulder is a moulder, and a labourer a labourer, pure and simple; there is little or no intercourse, and no exchange of work at all among them. In the big factories, too, whatever is made is made in different departments, often situated at some distance from each other; the actual maker of an article or component never sees the user of it to have his approval or criticism; right or wrong the process is continued, and the workmen must accept things as they find them. I have myself made thousands of forgings to the official pattern to discover, one day, from the user of them, that they were of a bad shape, and had either been expensively treated and altered, or else scrapped altogether; but this does not happen at the village foundry.

The mechanics are nearly all young men, smart and up to date, and well skilled in their several crafts. Of their number, some have served time in the sheds at the big railway works, while the others were apprenticed in far-off villages; as they journey from place to place they carry fresh knowledge with them, and enrich the collective wisdom of the local staff. In addition to the more friendly spirit existing among the men, there is an absence of that tension which is the characteristic of big factories; the laws and rules are not so stringent here; there is not the perpetual watching and timing of operations which is so galling to the man of character and spirit, and which never succeeds in the end, unless it be to produce dissatisfaction, and measures of retaliation.

The casting shed is a small stone-built place, long and narrow and ancient-looking; its walls are cracked with the great heat, and appear half ready to topple down. The floor is of sand, black with continual use in the frames, and there is a heap of it just inside the door, waiting to be made up again; it is used many times over for the moulds. The moulds are set in rows down the centre of the shed, and the small furnace, cylindrical in shape, stands near the outer wall. The blast for this is supplied by a small fan, driven from the main shafting. Before oil and steam-engines were thought of, the blast was forced by machines impelled by horses, and also by human power, and the speed was multiplied with gear. In one corner is a tiny furnace, like a washer-woman's boiler, for drying the cores; and near by is a small pitlike place, used as a brass-smelter. There a small fire is lit, and regulated by natural draught, which is sufficient for smelting brass; iron and steel require a much more intense heat to reduce them to a liquid state.

The moulds are made in two sections, within cast-iron frames, made to fit accurately, so as to insure the exact agreement of the counterparts when they are placed together to receive the metal. First the black sand is damped and sifted into the box like frame, then patted down and levelled with the moulder's tools. Next he takes the wooden pattern of the article to be cast, and imprints the sand, filling it up several times, and taking care to have every part firm and even. When this has been repeated in the counterpart frame, the one is turned carefully over and lowered upon the other, and a small aperture left through which to pour the molten iron. When the moulds are all prepared and dry the casting begins: this takes place about once every three weeks at the village. First the furnace is lit up and rammed full of coke, and the blast applied. When the interior is become blazing white-hot the cold pig-iron or scrap is put in above, which mingles with the fuel, all together. As the iron melts it falls to the bottom, and is received into a cavity to which is attached a small shoot, or runner, which is lifted up and stops back the fluid till the moulder is ready; then he brings his iron vessel, lined with fire-bricks, lets down the runner, fills his pot, carries it off, and pours the spluttering metal into his moulds. The next day or so, when these are cold, he removes the top frame, takes out casting, knocks off the waste piece left by the running in of the metal, brushes off the sand, and the part is ready for use, or for the next operation.

The moulder is highly intelligent and very talkative. He lays particular stress on the value to be got from an experience of village foundries, where the work man is required to have a knowledge of many things. "I worked in them big works five year, an' I can tell you, mister, you learns more outside at these small places in one twelvemonth than you would ther in a lifetime. An' why? Cos they wunt let e learn nothin'? Ther's sheens for this, an' sheens for that; everything's cut an' dried, an' ther you be, slavin' like a nigger all yer time, at the same owl' job, an' a girt fool at the end on't; an' if you got to move out anywher' else, you be no good at all'; you don' know nothin'."

It is a well-known fact that the choicest smiths are usually those who have had their forge in the villages. It was said of honest Mark

Fell, at the railway works, that "he could make anything you like, from a shut-link to a steam-engine," and he was only a village blacksmith in the beginning.

The old schoolmaster dwells a short way from the foundry, in a modern cottage, surrounded with piles of books and fusty-looking papers and documents, belonging to an age long past, before the present manner of teaching came in vogue. He is tall and grey, cautious in manner, and not disposed to talk much of his school career. "I am going to have a big bonfire very soon," said he, pointing to the books on the shelves.

I suggested he should give them away to someone or other.

"Give them! You couldn't give them to anyone," he replied. "Who wants books nowadays? I've offered to give them away, time after time, but nobody would have them. They're no good now. Everything is changed in the educational line. They don't do any plodding now. It's all education made easy. They go the short way at it. There was no near cut across the fields in my time, and you were only paid on your successes; so that if you did not do your work thoroughly you lost your allowance; but now they get their salary whether they do good work or not."

The schoolmaster remembers when the ballad-singers went from village to village, singing their rhymes; he had helped to train them when he was a young man. These strolling minstrels frequented all the feasts, fairs, and revels along the downside, and gave an exhibition of their skill. They carried bundles of ballad-sheets with them, and sold them to the rustics at one penny each. The old carter of Woolstone declares that hundreds of these sheets were disposed of at a single fair time. The number of singers varied; there might be four, or no more than two. Very often it was a man and his wife, and they sang alternately, in response to each other. The ballads were some grave, some sentimental, and others comic or satirical. The old carter could only remember two lines of a satirical piece, dealing with the eternal question of authority in the home. After a proposition, relating to home rule, had been set forth by the female singer, the man responded:

I do decline, and you shall find *I* will the breeches wear,

the answer to which was:

Oh, no, not I! for I will die, but I will have my share.

Here we have a form of verse somewhat in the style of the old Alexandrine measure, and though the subject-matter of this fragment is crude enough, there can be no doubt but that there was some good material circulated in this manner. One can readily understand, from this, how it was that the countryside was vocal in the old days, since every cottage contained sheets of the ballads, the airs of which had been taught the people by the singers at the feasts; they could not fail to make a deep impression on the villagers.

VII

The wind-mill—Badbury Plough Inn—"Court Leek"—Ancient cottages—The hay-tier—Old Jonas— "Dabber" Cox—Medbourne—Farmer Brunsden

LEAVING CHISELDON AND FOLLOWING THE road, which runs in the shape of a Z, we immediately emerge upon the downs in sight of the Vale of White Horse, which opens out to the north-east, stretching into the distance as far as the eye can see. On the right hand, as you come from the village, standing in a small field, is the tower of a wind-mill, where much corn was ground till a quarter of a century ago. Now, however, the mill has been dismantled of its fans and turned into a store-house, though a part of the inner machinery remains. There were formerly two wind-mills close together, but one was taken down at an early date, the reason of its removal being—as it is alleged—that there was not enough wind to turn the fans of both. There is another local jest concerning the wind-mill. It is said that an old rustic brought a sack of corn to the mill on his donkey, and, after unloading the ass, tied it up to one of the fans, then stationary, and that the miller set the machinery running, and hoisted the donkey high into the air, where it remained dangling for some time, until the halter broke and let it fall to the ground. The villagers ridicule the narration, and say it is "all bosh," and repudiate the jest, declaring it is made of every wind-mill that ever was erected.

The road continues past the wind-mill till it presently crosses the main highway leading up from the valley to the distant town of Marlborough. The long telegraph wires, strained tight upon the

ALFRED WILLIAMS

poles, stretch far away, gleaming with a copperish tint in the sunshine, while a faint humming sound proceeds from them, where they are in contact with the supports. This sound is many times intensified in rough or wet weather; then the shrill treble of the wind in the wires, and the deep bass of the joints and supports, form together a weird concert of sounds. The country children believe that by laying an ear to the telegraph pole it is possible to intercept the messages.

About half a mile from the junction of the roads towers Liddington Hill, with the *castellum* on top. Another name for this is Beacon Hill, so called because it was from here the beacon fires shone out, in days long past, to warn the people in the vale of impending danger from foes and invaders, and to summon them within the walls of the fort. Formerly, too, it was called Mount Badon, and also Battlebury Hill; and one tradition says it was here that King Arthur fought the Saxons and defeated them in a great battle. The villagers believe there is a subterranean passage leading under the downs from the top of the hill to Burderop, two miles away, which was used as a final means of escape from the entrenchment when the besieged were hard pressed by the enemy.

Immediately after crossing the highroad we enter the small but ancient village of Badbury, of inconsiderable importance at this time, but not destitute of glory in the past, and especially famed by reason of the old inn that stands on the, hillside, and which is known to travellers far and near as Badbury Plough. The village is grouped around the neck of a deep coomb, half full of large elms and firs; the farms and cottages are scattered along the roadside. At the bottom of the hollow a spring, sufficiently large to have driven the mill-wheel till recently, gushes out; the old mill-house is still standing in the bottom. The ground on the slopes of the coomb contains a portion of the original wood and a series of terraces are cut out of the earth there, though for what reason is not evident at this time. The village, by reason of its being in the possession of the Franciscan monks, was formerly exempted from the payment of tolls at Smithfield, as we gather from an ancient document. Of what advantage this remission was to the old Badburians we do not know; there was doubtless a value attaching to the privilege, but it is at an end now; the relation of Badbury to Smithfield, at the present time, is as remote as is that of a thousand other villages about the west country.

Badbury Plough Inn stands some little distance from the village, high upon the roadside, where the main way comes up from the valley to pass over the tops of the downs. The picturesque old building has been taken down in late years, and a new house erected; only the old name and associations remain, but even they are sufficient to invest the new place with an air of romance: many years must come and go before the fame of the Plough Inn will have passed away. The sign-board, hanging over the doorway, is characteristic of the place. Here is depicted a team at plough, and underneath is a rude rhyme, which runs as follows:

> In hope we plough, in hope we sow,
> In hopes we all are led,
> & I am here to sell good beer
> In hopes to get my bread.

How long the old inn had existed here is unknown, but it must have stood for centuries; Farmer Brunsden's father remembered it as long ago as the year 1794, and it was an old building then. The original sign-board, with the verse painted upon it, was hanging above the doorway; there the agriculturists gathered and whiled the hours away, unperturbed by the bloody scenes which were being enacted at that period by the revolutionists over the channel.

As to the games and sports, and "goings on" at the old inn, it is impossible to know all that. "Nobody knows what *hev* bin carred on ther, afore now; summat o' everything, you med depend upon't," the old carter declares, with a sage wag of the head, and in a voice little above a whisper, Back-swording, wrestling, and prize-fighting were of the most ordinary occurrence, and bull-fighting, too, according to one account. This latter sport took place in a small field at the end of the hollow; it is a further proof of the hardihood of the old-time rustics, and their love of fierce plays and games.

There is an ancient custom, known by the name of Court Leek, observed at the Plough Inn twice in every thirteen years. The Court Leek proper is the holding of a feast upon the payment of the quit-rents to the lord of the manor for cottages erected by the roadside. A large portion of waste land by the roadside was utilized for building cottages by poor people formerly. This the squire, who claimed the land, was willing for them to do, charging them a nominal sum as ground rent, which was to be paid once in about seven years. These cottages were worth from £20 to £50 each, and were invariably chalk-made. If, upon the death of an owner, the lord of the manor wished to reclaim the land for any purpose, he might do this on payment of a sum equivalent to the full value of the cottage. When the time drew round to pay the quitrent—which amounted, for the seven years, to 1s. 6d., or 2s. a cottage—notice was given to the occupiers as to the assembling of the Court, and other instructions formulated as to the time and place of the meeting. First of all, a jury of twelve men was elected and secretly sworn in, to whom was delegated the power of assessing the amount of quitrent to be paid by each cottager. After the amount had been fixed, the date of payment was settled; on the evening of that day the whole company met together at the inn, and partook of a feast, provided out of the quitrents, for all the money was to be spent on the entertainment, the squire did not receive any, though either he, or his steward, attended the feast, and revelled till the small hours, sitting among the rustics, who sang or danced to the fiddle and flute, expressing their feelings many times in the words of the old song:

> Come, landlord, fill the flowing bowl
> Until it doth run over;
> For this night we'll merry, merry be,
> For this night we'll merry, merry be,
> For this night we'll merry, merry be,
> And to-morrow we'll get sober.

It often happened that when the account with the landlord of the inn came to be settled, there was a considerable deficiency; in this case a collection was made; the jurymen and farmers contributed a sum, and made good the amount.

The hollow in which the mill formerly stood is called Badbury Bottom. The cavity begins from the centre of the village, and the slope falls steeply down for several hundred feet. Towards the bottom innumerable springs of water trickle noiselessly out all round amid lushest grasses, and run this way and that, finally commingling into one small stream that flowed down and turned the mill-wheel. Around the open space, where the water issues, are clumps of elder and willow, with tall trees of ash and spruce, which are continued down the hollow. A number of pert, trim-looking thrushes and deliciously sensuous and indolent blackbirds frequent the spring head; here they obtain choice sweet mouthfuls, and afterwards perch in the boughs and pour out their rich, liquid notes.

The way down to the bottom is underneath tall elm-trees. Here is one uprooted, and half over thrown, but its sturdy neighbour caught it falling and withstood the shock; now they stand locked fast together, one supporting the other, little the worse for their encounter with the fierce south wind, lord of the downs, of which the wives of the seafarers sing:

> A Southerly wind with rain
> Brings the sailors home from Spain.

In the bottom are several cottages, with large gardens, occupied by farm labourers, cowmen, and others. These cottages are very old, and interesting as showing the type of dwelling constructed for workers on the land several centuries ago. The materials were all obtained close at hand. The foundations are of huge rough sarsen-stones, some of which had lain for countless centuries on the open downs, worn smooth as pebbles, or eaten and hollowed out with the rain and atmospheric change. The walls above are of chalk and sarsen-stones inter mixed, some of the first-named being in blocks two feet square, still bearing the marks of the quarry-men's tools. This was obtained immediately at hand, from the side of the coomb; the crumbling sides of the quarry are still visible not many yards from the building. The old-fashioned bread oven, circular in shape, projects from the outer walls, which are three feet thick and more; a little brick, deep red, and of fine quality, has been introduced here and there over the windows and doors, and the chimney is made of the same material, and is inset with a square stone bearing the date 1689, in which the figure nine is written hind before. The roof is thatch, of many layers; the small bedroom windows are inset into this to the extent of four or five feet, a defect characteristic of that period, occasioning insufficient ventilation and stuffiness, though it appears to have very well answered the purposes of the occupants, for they lived to an astonishing age in the buildings. At one end a mass of ivy climbs up the wall and afterwards leaps upon the roof; in front are large warm gardens, and, before the door, a well with a windlass for drawing up the pails. At the cottage a short way below there is no need of this. There the spring bubbles up beside the doorway; all that is necessary is to scoop a small hole in the ground; it is immediately filled with beautiful crystal water, tempting to the eye and palate.

The rooms within the cottages are large and spacious, sixteen feet or possibly more square, but with rather low ceilings, the only disadvantage, in the light of modern requirements. The fireplaces are wide, roomy, and old-fashioned, and the downstairs windows large, too; the frames of these are of solid oak, and very old. A wooden shelf is fixed along at the bottom of the window: beneath this is a hollow place, used as a receptacle for books and papers, containing also the cottage work-basket, full of needles and thread, reels of cotton, scissors and bodkin, bits of cloth, flannel, calico, and countless buttons, of all shapes and sizes. Some of the floors are of tiles, and others are of large square stones; a broad screen is erected inside the living room to protect the fireplace, and the coal is kept underneath the great broad staircase, leading aloft. The cowman's wife—who was busy removing the potatoes from the pit in the garden—well liked the cottages. The family had recently come from off the downs, where they had dwelled in a brick house. "These housen be twice as warm an' comfortable, an' ther plenty o' room in 'em; too much, if anything," the housewife declared.

The mill house stands farther down the coomb, though only the dwelling part remains at this time. The house is stone built, with massive wooden beams and rafters, slowly crumbling away under the invisible finger of Time. The small stream runs tinkling along under the trees, and between the withy beds, till it comes to where the mill stood, and then plunges out of sight under the ground with a merry, mocking note, and emerges on the other side, among beds of rushes, aild between banks thick with celandine and herb-robert. The huge stones in the cavern-like place, adown which the stream leaps, are overgrown with thick mosses and small ferns; they have probably not been moved for many centuries. There is another cottage close by, built of sarsen-stones with corners of brick. These bricks are much smaller, and of a far finer quality, than those made today; they are known to have stood for a great length of time in the most exposed situations, and are almost unimpaired with the wet and heat. Till recently bricks were made by hand a short way off in the valley. The clay was rammed into moulds, and the top cut away with a sharp tool, then the brick was turned out and burned. A few pounds spent upon these old houses would put them in good repair; it is said there has not been a cottage built in the village for generations.

One of the first buildings on the road above is the old black-smith's shop. The forge, bellows, and anvil have long since been done away with; there is no need of that in the village now, and the smithy has been converted into a labourer's cottage. The yard in which the vehicles stood for repair has been made into a garden, and the old shoeing shed is crammed full of tools: shovels, spades, forks, hoes, reaping- and fagging-hooks and sticks, hedgeing tools, hay-tying apparatus, and other paraphernalia. The occupier of the cottage is odd man on the farm, and can turn his hand to anything about the fields. He is hedger and ditcher, mower and reaper, sheep shearer, rickbuilder, thatcher, quarryman, road-maker, hay- and straw-binder, and many things besides, all of which occupations require skill of a certain kind, though such a one is seldom looked upon as other than a mere menial by those who are incompetent to judge of the matter. For many years his wife went with him to work about the fields, in the haymaking and corn-harvest, and assisted him with the hay- and straw-tying too, leaving home in the early morning, and returning at night, often making long journeys over the downs.

The greater part of this work is done at the piece rate, but the one who is merely attached to a farm can never command such a price for his work as the professional tier. The farm hand will scarcely obtain more than 3s. 6d. a ton, while the other could easily get 5s. by the old method, and 4s. 6d. by the new. By the old method the men twisted their bonds from the hay. To do this they had an iron implement, made on the plan of the augur, with a hook at the end. First they shook the hay loosely into a heap, then one took up a handful and placed it through the crook, and brought the ends round, while the other twisted away. His mate fed the bond from the heap, while he walked backwards. When the bonds were finished they were strained tight, and placed on the ground in pairs and the ends wound round slender wands of hazel or withy thrust into the earth, to keep them secure. The hay was tied in bundles of forty to the ton, while straw ran sixty bundles to the ton; each truss was weighed with balances on the spot. If the bundles proved light, a quantity was stuffed underneath the bonds to make up the deficiency, though a skilful tier can easily guess the weight to within a few ounces.

Great skill is required to make a nice even cut; a good hand with the heavy, pointed hay-knife will fetch it from the rick as sharp and even as a squared block of marble. Straw is more troublesome to bind. That has to be obtained from the ricks in great wide cuts, and afterwards must be well shaken into heaps, and then "hatched up," as though for haulms, before it can be bound, though the price is the same as for hay. Now the hay-tiers use tar cord for binding, and have a machine for pressing the trusses, which makes the operation much more simple and easy, though the old method has to be followed in the case of straw.

As a hobby the old farm hand tills a large garden and keeps bees, studying their habits with great interest and intelligence, and deriving profit from them, too; sweet honey for the house and wax to be sold to the dealers at is 2d. a pound. The bees of the downside obtain much honey from the bloom of wheat, and from thistles—the great beauty and fragrance of which are but little thought of and appreciated—then there are the clover and sanfoin, yielding a rich harvest, and the bright golden charlock, of which the bees are very fond, with the delicious wild thyme of the hillside. The honey of Mount Hymettus was held in especial esteem by the ancients, on account of the great abundance of wild thyme there, which the bees visited.

After taking the honey the good-wife makes a drink called "nath-agalum" from the combs. When the honey has been drained from these they are put into a vessel and a quantity of water is measured in. After being well soaked and washed, the wax is removed and dried, and then the liquor is tested to ascertain its sweetness. To do this a hen's egg is usually placed in the vessel; if the egg sinks, the liquor is too sweet; if it floats, it is correct to taste. After this the liquid is boiled for half an hour, then strained, and afterwards put into casks or jars. In a short time it becomes ripe and strong, rich in flavour, and highly alcoholic. It is very sweet and seductive to the taste; a couple of tumblers full would be enough to make one intoxicated.

Jonas Goddard, the eighty-year-old carter, lives with his son and daughter-in-law in a small cottage facing the houses in the Bottom. I faund the young wife disconsolate over the loss of her firstborn, a daughter, who only lived four days. "'Er was sich a purty little cratur, bless you, an' 'er looked up at I as cunnin', an' laafed in mi face; I knowed 'er was too cunnin' to live. 'Er was born on a Sunday, an' the nurse, 'er said: Born on a Sunday, a sure sign o' prosperity,' but 'er didn't prosper, the purty little dear.

I did grieve an' vex miseif, but 'tis wicked. The Almighty took 'er for a wise purpose, right enough. If you wants to see faather 'es out in the garden."

Passing round the corner of the house I discovered the old carter busy with pick and shovel digging a mighty pit. He was short in stature, sturdily built, and a little corpulent. His features were strong and square, hair grey, short grey beard, pleasant mouth, and merry sparkling eyes. His trousers, much too small around the waist, were drawn together and held with a bootlace; he wore a corduroy jacket, and a waistcoat of the same material, with big brass buttons, each stamped with the head of an animal: a dog, a fox, a horse, a bull, a camel, and a dromedary; a small billycock hat was perched upon his head. He was born at Winterbourne Basset, and came of the old stock. His grandparents had a family of eighteen, he was one of twelve, and his own children numbered half a score.

"You had ten children!" I exclaimed.

"My wife 'ed," he answered quickly.

"And brought them all up?" I continued.

"Hoo, aa," replied he, "an' oni 'ed seven shillin' a wik to do't wi'. I bin pitchin' whate for a whole wik, an' 'ed nothin to ate but bread an' a i-nen, an' never 'ed a day's illness in mi life. But I couldn't get on wi' the barley dampers. What we liked was whum-made loaves wi' the clungy vains," (veins of glutinous matter). "The chuldern oodn't ate it nowadays, tha be pimpered up so, but put 'em an tha land, an' tha'd ate anytheng then. Tha gets this schoolin' an' tha wunt work; you caan't get a civul answer vram 'em."

The carter is possessed of an indomitable spirit, and was a member of the Agricultural Union as long as that existed in these parts. He went to a farmer one day, and asked him for a job.

"Be you a Union man?" the farmer inquired.

"Yes, I be, gaffer, an' a stiff un, too."

"Don' want you, then," the farmer retorted,

"Then you can do wi'out ma; but I shan't channge fer nobody. You can get another fella."

"Yer, wait a bit, I'll gie tha a trial," the farmer said, and engaged him straightway, and proved a good master.

Nearly all the farmers on the downs settled up with the men once a year at that time. Whatever the men required for present use they let them have, and paid the balance in a lump after harvest; the men liked this method very well, because they were sure of a good sum in the autumn. If the man had overdrawn, the farmer allowed him to do some piece-work in the summer and harvest, and squared up in that way; very often it was only a matter of form, to give the man an opportunity of getting clear. The farmers gave the workpeople much food, and often killed fat sheep and sold the mutton to them at 4d. a pound. They also let the men have a sack of wheat at a cheap rate, when they wanted it, and allowed them to pay at their leisure, settling up annually. For fuel, the farmers gave the men the bean stubbles in the fields. The corn was cut off so as to leave a long stubble; this the women pulled up, and the farmers drew it home for the men, and stacked it in ricks. Now the bean stubble is ploughed in so as to keep the ground hollow. All the villagers turned out to help at wheat harvest. Sometimes the reapers had £1 an acre for cutting, and the average savings of a family during harvest was £9 according to the account of old Jonas.

"Dabber" Cox, the chief cowman, corroborated the carter's statements about earnings, but, pressed for a considered opinion, he thought that a man who would stick well to work is a little better off, though not much, now. He sat at the table and devoured a monster tea of bread and meat, looking exceedingly well satisfied. The cowman resembles a Grand Vizier in appearance. He is yellowish in complexion, with long nose, bushy eyebrows, broadish mouth, and thick black hair and beard, which was full of chaff and hay, where he had been carrying the trusses.

"I wonder the dog 'adn't a viod out at e. 'E's main shanky, 'e is," he exclaimed.

The cowman is descended from a distinguished local family. His grandfather, who was head carter, went to work regularly till he was eighty-four, and then was kicked in the head and killed by a young colt which he was "breaking in"in the field. His father was carter, too, and a famous back-sworder. He turned professional, and traversed the whole southern part of the island from Devon to London, and beat all the champions, including the famed men of Somersetshire.

"Nobody couldn't vetch blood out o' 'e. 'E was byet 'ard, 'e was; 'is owl 'ed was as 'ard as iron," the cowman says. This sturdy Wiltshireman, after conquering everyone at home, afterwards went out to Greece and played there, but was killed there in the end.

The head cowman's position is one of responsibility, and the wages are higher than usual for the post; he received £1 a week and his cottage, and, in addition to this, "is for every caaf as drapped alive an the land." The fogger retains a few of the old superstitious beliefs. He declares a farm cannot carry one-hundred cows, it must be either ninety-nine, or one-hundred-and-one; "if you tries to kip jest a 'underd you'll be sure to lose one an em, bi vallin' in the ditch, er caavin' down, er zummat," he says. He furthermore believes that a black calf is a sign of ill luck to the herd; until recently it was the custom to kill it, if one should be born.

Sitting at the table was the cowman's daughter, between twenty and thirty years of age, a helpless cripple, with hands and fingers drawn and contracted, pale and thin with the long suffering and torture of acute rheumatism. On going out to service as a young girl she was put to sleep in a damp bed; there she caught a severe chill, which developed into rheumatics, and blasted her future. Such cases as these are not uncommon; those mistresses who are guilty of such callous disregard of the health of their domestics are deserving of drastic punishment.

From Badbury the road leads down a long slope to where a large coomb, starting from the centre of the hill, opens out into the wide valley. The slopes of the coomb are very steep higher up; near the valley the hollow is funnel-shaped, and the sides are more trailing and gradual. A large spring of water flows down the centre of the coomb, tumbling over and over in its bed, and then rushes head-long through a culvert under the roadway, and blunders noisily out on the other side, laughing in the sunlight, on its way through the fields. While boring in the attempt to obtain water a little distance up the hillside recently, the farmer and his men experienced no less than 150 ft. of solid clay, and had not reached the bottom then. It is singular that that should be there, so high up the hillside; there must have been successive periods of depositing and denudation in the valley in former times.

At the bottom of the hollow are several farms and a group of cottages forming a hamlet, named Medbourne. Less than forty years ago all the valley, visible here, was arable land; now there is not a single patch of corn to be seen. Cowman Cox declares the land was never laid down, "it fell down," and the occupant of the farm in the fields confessed as much. He says that after the three disastrous seasons of 1877-78-79, the land, through continuous rains, had become so full of weeds, and the farmers so disheartened, that they made no further attempts to cultivate it, but laid it down forthwith. The farmer keeps a dairy of eighty cows, and a large flock of cheviots. His wages bill is £500 a year, and often more. He thinks milk to be the best investment at present, though he is of the opinion that the milk industry has seen the best of its days; the cost of producing it, and especially of the winter supply, is rapidly rising. By keeping his flock on the downs by day, and bringing them below into the pens by night, he makes the hills feed the valley—that is to say, the sheep, by manuring the lowlands, enrich them at the expense of the downs; by following this up, and constantly shifting the pens, it is easy to manure a big tract of ground for nothing.

Henry Brunsden, of Coate, the broken-down farmer, nearly ninety years of age, who nursed the infant Richard Jefferies, and gave him the freedom of his occupation, to shoot, fish, and otherwise amuse himself in his boyhood days, was ruined by a big milk swindle. A London firm contracted with him for 260 barn gallons of milk a day, and when he had become deeply indebted to all the farmers round about, whose supplies he took, he was suddenly made aware that the firm was a bogus one, and that he was a ruined man. His long hair and thin beard are snow white; his face seems to be all smiles, his head shakes slightly as the result of his great age, yet he is a veritable chatterbox. His sons laughingly tell him to "stop it," and "shut up," and tease him with this and that; he yields to their commands with an affectionate smile, and a gentle inclination of the head, but soon commences again in great glee, and faster than before. His memory is remarkable; he can quote poems and recite rhymes innumerable, and compose them himself, too; he commemorated his eighty-seventh birthday in one of these, while sitting in his arm-chair by the fireside.

> O'er Life's road, rough and uneven,
> I have dragged to eighty-seven.
> What have these years left for me?
> Nothing but infirmity.
> Sitting in my chair content,
> Thinking of the years I've spent,
> Of the future, and the past,
> Wondering how long life will last,
> Thanks I give for old and new,
> And that's the most that I can do.

VIII

Liddington Hill—The village—Characteristics—
"Pebble soup"—The old village constable—
The thatcher and carter

THE HILL, AT THE BASE of which the road runs along, is the largest and most imposing down at the western end of the Vale of
White Horse. Its length, from end to end, is about three-quarters of
a mile; from the crown to the base is an almost equivalent distance.
On the top of the hill is a level space, gradually narrowing into
another ridge, and running back wards to the south, past Upper
Upham, towards Aldbourne and Ramsbury. At the western extremity tower the walls of the ancient encampment, impregnable to
the besieger, enclosing an area of eight or ten acres; at the eastern
end is a beechen clump, or folley, planted there for a landmark,
to denote to the dwellers in the wide valley the existence of a
refuge by day, as did the beacon-fires by night, in the old times
of war and sudden danger. The branches of the trees, by reason of
the almost continual setting of the wind from the south-west, are
blown north-eastwards, and have grown in that direction; while the
outer walls of the *castellum* have slipped away in several places, and
so lost their former symmetry: great would be the distress of the
original constructors and occupants of it, if they were suddenly to
be called back to life and required to defend it against a determined
assault of the enemy. Situated near the clump is a dew-pond; a
little way to the rear an old grass market road crosses, leading to
Marlborough; halfway down, in front, the ridgeway—here a hard

road—passes along over Wanborough Plain, soon to resume its scarce-trodden green in climbing up the steep side of Charlbury Hill, a mile or so to the east.

There are several views, producing different impressions and states of feeling, to be obtained from the hill-top. In front the eye ranges over a magnificent panorama of fertile valley and woodland, stretching away for forty miles or more into the blue horizon, rousing the imagination to its highest flights; behind, it alights on a series of gentle curving hills and slopes, winding dells and coombs, soothing to the most troubled mind; on one side is visible the beechen clump of Barbury Hill, with the railway-train creeping slowly across the intervening plain; to the east, high up, are to be seen the ramparts at White Horse Hill, which I can never view without a sense of something half revealed, a feeling of eternity. The light, dry atmosphere, and invigorating breeze fill you with surprising strength and vigour, and produce great mental clearness; there flesh and blood are overcome, hunger and thirst, passion and fear, vanish under the purifying influence of the down current. In dull weather, and during the dark days of winter, the long brown-grey ridges and deep blue backs of the downs are *morne* and solitary, producing an air of sadness, and even of dejection, in some people; the valley, too, is vague and obscure; everything in the distance is blotted out with mist and cloud, or dense fogs hang for days in the air, to develop at length into a downpour of drenching rain, which is always heaviest along the hillsides, and round about the lone walls of the *castellum*.

The village of Liddington is situated about half a mile from the top of the hill, grouped upon a terrace adown the slope, and round about the head of a coomb. From the hill itself the village is almost invisible, concealed, as it is, below the beetling uplands, and shrouded with elms and beeches; only the grey square tower of the old church can be seen rising through the tree-tops on that side. The cottages are very old, and nearly all chalk-made, and they seem to have been built, some here and some there, facing this way and that, in rows or pairs, or isolated, without regard to plan or design. Wherever a building was wanted, there it was made; one is perched high above the roadside, another deep down out of sight in the coomb, and several more are standing at the angle of the roads, or a little way out in the fields.

There were formerly two mills in the village. One of these stood at the bottom of the coomb, near the spring-head; and the other a short way down in the fields. After turning the wheel of the upper mill, the stream flowed down till it came to the narrow road, where it was dammed back; now it foams out between huge stones on the other side, ten feet below the level of the highway. Water-threshing was also carried on at the upper mill, before the all-conquering steam-engine came on the scene. The machine was of the same kind as that driven by horses; it was connected with the wheel by a spindle, and the speed obtained with gear. The land around Liddington, immediately beneath the hill, is accredited with having grown no less than eighteen sacks and two bushels of prime wheat to the acre, and vast quantities of roots to the same, before it was laid down, and yet the yield of hay is said to be no more than one ton to the acre now.

A good many villages have characteristics peculiar to themselves. Thus, the inhabitants of one place are noted for hard-headedness, of another for wittiness, bluntness, sturdy independence, soberness, noise, quiet, or political fervour, and the fighting spirit. By some means Liddington has obtained the reputation of being a "newsy place," so that the quality of inquisitiveness would seem to apply to the inhabitants there. It was said you could not pass through the village on foot without being accosted by someone or other requiring to know where you were bound for, and what your business might be. A friend of mine, recently, on being acquainted with the matter, refused to believe it, and made a wager that he would pass through the village unchallenged; but he lost the bet, for he had scarcely entered the street before someone—a total stranger—smilingly addressed him with a cheery: "Hello! where be you off to this way, then?" The inhabitants are spoken of collectively as "The Liddington Pig-diggers." This came about, in the beginning, through a remark let fall by a rustic about digging for a pig upon the hill-top, which was wrongly received by the hearer, and clownishly construed into meaning that he had actually been digging for a pig, in the same manner as the folks of another village were accredited with having raked after the moon. The true interpretation of the remark is something far different. It was an ancient privilege of the parishioners to go upon the downs flint-digging. This they did in spare time, and when other work was slack. The flints, when unearthed, were sold for road-making and repairing, and the money was very often used to buy a pig for the cottager's sty. Accordingly, it became the fashion, when one was about to go flint-digging, to say that he was going to dig for another pig; and so the story became current that pigs were dug out of the flint-beds upon the hill, and the villagers were branded with the title of "Pig-diggers."

It is well known that dialect survives longest in the villages, though it still remains in most of the provincial towns, too, where the population is consistent, and where there are not many factories. But besides dialect, with its many quaintnesses and local variations, such, for instance, as: "Yella," "Yellacks," "Yellocks," "Yelleky," "Yilliky," "Thelliky," and simple "Lacks," and "Locks," ("Here, look," and "There, look,") you often hear Elizabethan expressions made, too, such as, "Gad," "Begad," "God's truth," or "This is God's truth," or "Code struth," and sometimes a Latin or Greek expression, as *bos* for calf, *rumpus*, a sudden noise, from the Latin verb *rumpere*, and *smame*, to smear, from Greek *sman*, meaning the same. Here at Liddington an old man told me of five brothers who "had a envy" against a certain farmer, and went into his field one night by moonlight and mowed down five acres of beans in full bloom, in return for some wrong he had done one of them. Here we have a perfect reproduction of the Greek phrase φΦονον εχειν τινι, which means, literally, "to have an envy against someone," but it is remarkable that it should have become translated into the English, and preserved among rustics in a small out-of-the-way village perched upon the down-side.

The population of Liddington, in common with their neighbours, regularly indulged in the old sports, games and autumnal revels. The great event of the year was the feast, held at the inn, which continued for a week, and the opening of which was always marked by the cutting of an acorn pie, in continuation of an ancient custom, the signification of which is not known now. During the week the street was lined with stalls and booths for dancing and mirth; here Fiddler Jack, the Orpheus of the downs, discoursed sweet music, while the village nymphs and swains executed the motions of the dance at a penny a tune, and the children played at "snuff-boxes," and "spandabs."

Besides acorn pie, the villagers used occasionally to make a dish of "pibble sup," (pebble soup). At first thought it would seem to be a difficult matter to do this, but the cottagers say it is "yezzi anuf, when you knows the waay." First of all you obtain water, and boil it in the pot, adding a bit of bacon, several potatoes, a little salt, some celery, a cabbage, turnips, and ketchup, and afterwards drop in a small pebble, and well boil the whole, and you have the soup complete.

The poor people of the down-side still eat many herbs which would not appear palatable to dwellers in the town, but which, as a matter of fact, are both agreeable to the taste, and highly whole- some, too. In this list are stinging-nettles—used also for tea—hop- tops, charlock, boiled rhubarb leaves, boiled lettuce, dandelion leaves and roots, sorrel, wild landcress, and succory. Potatoes were very cheap during the first half of the nineteenth century, when wages were low about the downs; they could easily be obtained at 2s. 6d. a sack. There was a special kind of potatoes common to North Wiltshire, called locally "Yarth evvers" (earth heavers) by reason of their great productiveness; there is no need to explain away the denominative.

North Wiltshire was always famed for its bacon; it was a chief part of the staple food, of farmers and labourers, too. The farmers, however, only ate the hams, gammons and chine, and the best of the pig-meat; they gave the inferior parts away to the labourers, together with the imperfect cheeses, and occasional presents of mutton. Both masters and men ate a good deal of the bacon raw, and especially when in the fields; but so great was the power of their digestive organs they seldom felt any inconvenience arising from it.

On the hills, and in the valley, too, down to recent times, the farmers, instead of paying Sunday wages for milking, used to give the men their breakfast and supper, of bread, meat and ale, and the amount of fat bacon consumed at such times is almost incredible. One morning, at a small farm, where there were only three to sit down to breakfast, the farmer's wife had brought out a whole belly-piece, of six pounds, boiled, and set it on a large dish, and when the meal was finished there were about two pounds left. Hereupon the carter addressed his two mates:

"Ev you chaps finished?"

"Aa," they replied.

"Don' e want na moore?"

"No," they answered.

"Byen agwain to lave that mossel," the other proceeded, and took it from the dish and ate the whole piece, without bread.

Immediately afterwards the farmer's wife looked in and roundly scolded them for not calling out for more meat.

"But we 'ed anuf, thenk e, missis," one said.

"I never thinks you 'ed anuf when you cleared the dish," replied she.

There is a characteristic story of the boy minding a herd of pigs, and being accosted by the traveller.

"Whose pigs be they, mi bwoy?" inquired he.

"That owl' fella's ther, locks," the youth answered soberly, pointing to the father of the herd.

"Very good, mi bwoy, very good," the other replied. Then he proceeded: "Wher do this road goto, mi bwoy?"

"Dwun go nowher. A's yer every night an' marnin' when I comes along," the boy answered.

"Capital! capital!" the stranger exclaimed; then, "Wha's thy father's name, young un?"

"I dwun know, but if thee't stop yer an' mind thase pegs a bit, I'll go whum an' ax mother. Dursay 'er can tell tha," the youth replied.

The road that passes through the village of Liddington up over the hills being a chief highway to London, it was frequented with much traffic, and especially in the early days, before the railways were made. Then the huge, heavy waggons, laden with burdens of produce for the far-off Metropolis—ordinarily drawn by eight horses, but requiring no less than thirteen to fetch them up the long steep hill—plied regularly up and down; the jingle of bells and crack of the carter's whip, with the rumble of the waggon wheels, were heard every day along the rough flint roads. The chief produce carried this way was flour, with other food-stuffs, such as beef, mutton, veal, bacon, butter, eggs, and cheese. Halfway up the hill, in an even space, stood large stables; here the horses were changed, and the carters rested, sometimes sleeping in their vehicles, and sometimes at the inn. After leaving the village they proceeded by way of Hungerford, Newbury, and Reading; it usually took them two days to reach London from Liddington, a distance of seventy-three miles. Considerable quantities of food were stolen from the waggon *en route*, by thieves and idlers, who regularly subsisted on what they could purloin from the vehicles, and the waggoners themselves used often to feed on the contents of the load, skilfully cutting off pieces of beef and bacon soon after the start; it is a common saying, about the country side, that "a slysh (slice) is not missed off a cut loaf."

Young New, the aged carpenter and wheelwright, at one time also village constable and mail contractor, had often lent assistance to the waggoners to haul their loads to the top of the steep hill. He made his own mail-van, and selected his horses for the journey with the post, which lay between Swindon and Hungerford. The roads were very rough at that time, and were often blocked with snow in the winter; then the mail-man always carried a shovel, with which to dig his way through the drifts. Before the railway was made coal was conveyed by barges, along the canal. One year the canal was frozen over for fifteen weeks, and there was a coal famine along the down-side. The ordinary price of coal—locally—in the year 1830, was 50s. a ton.

Local letters cost 4d. to deliver, and the postman traversed the down-side daily, for twelve or fifteen miles, mounted on a donkey; for this he received 10s. weekly. Newspapers cost 6d. each. The farmers co-operated in the purchase of these; one newspaper had to suffice for half a dozen farmhouses.

The old carpenter held the post of village constable for twenty years, before the institution of the County Police. This office was one of responsibility in those times, and was not unattended with danger; the old man bears many scars as the result of encounters with roughs in the execution of his duty. The chief offenders against the law were gipsies, tramps, and travelling navvies; there was seldom any trouble with the villagers. There was no regular salary attached to the post of constable; the only sum he received was 5s. every year when he went to the court to be sworn in. His personal equipment comprised a loaded baton, and hand-cuffs for the prisoners. Several times, on making arrests, when the prisoner would not walk to the town, four miles away, he had clapped the hand-cuffs on him securely, tied his feet and legs together, and hauled him along on his back to the cells. At a neighbouring village the constable was often required to lodge prisoners for the night, on their way to prison. To hold them secure he had two mighty staples driven into the strong woodwork, one each side of the wide fire-place, and the culprits were chained up to these all night, while the constable took his rest. If there were three prisoners, the great, heavy pig-killing bench was brought into requisition, and the third was unceremoniously chained down to that; there was small fear of escaping from such a custody.

A short distance from the ex-constable dwells the old thatcher, of over ninety years, who enjoys as good general health now as ever he did. He is of moderate height, well-built, with aristocratic features, strong, clear, brown eyes, dark hair and beard, only just tinged with grey; he is very erect, and he walks firmly. "I ates an' drenks as well as ever I did," he says. He was sitting by the fireside, lamenting a wet afternoon, and wearing a thick pair of nailed boots, leather gaiters, and an old frayed, blue felt hat on his head. If it had been fine he would have been at work, for he cannot be idle; all that morning he had been busy wheeling manure from the cow-yard to his allotment.

As a boy he played "trippant" from school to go with his father; then he began to thatch by himself. Altogether, he had thatched over 3,000 ricks, besides innumerable cottages and farm buildings. The average number of ricks he thatched per annum was 50, though sometimes they came to not far short of 100. For thatching a rick he received 2s. and his food for the time; with good luck he could cover an ordinary sized rick in from four to five hours. For cottages and farm-buildings the price was 3s. 6d. a square, a square being of 10 feet—100 feet in all—and his services were required in no less than ten parishes. When there was no thatching to be done he turned his hand to the making of sheep-cages, and built cottages of wattle and daub, or rubble (chalk-stone), and sold them to poor labourers, or let them at 1s. a week. By doing this, and by following his work as a thatcher, he became fairly well-to-do, and is now the possessor of many "housen," and other property in the place. A large number of the cottages, and farms, too, along the hill-side, were built on the "life-hold" system. The builder agreed to pay a sum of money down, securing the ground for his lifetime, and when he died the house reverted to the landlord, or his next of kin might pay down another sum, and secure it for his own lifetime, and so on.

The old thatcher's interest in life is as keen as ever it was, and his memory is unimpaired; all the scenes and events of his past career roll before his eyes in an unbroken panorama. He remembers the "mobbin'" and "sheen breakin'"—the agricultural riots of 1830—and how his father lifted him up on the garden gate to see the "cavalry" go by, to quell the disturbances. His mother used to take her children to leasing in the cornfields. She wore a very large red cloak, "as ood kip out no end o' wet"; when it rained she gathered her little ones together under the cloak, as the hen gathers her chicks; there they stayed till the storm was over.

He had often seen the revelling and back-swording, but had only been upon the stage once himself, then he got a broken nose with his opponent's stick, and that quenched his ardour for the game. The youths of Liddington went footballing on Sundays, and the young thatcher accompanied them, much against the will of his father, who was a local preacher. One Sunday, on the way back from a distant village, where he had been playing, he called at the little chapel, where his father was preaching, and the parent respectfully asked the congregation to "make room for the bwoy," adding, "dursay e's tired, for a bin a futballin' aal day." For the present generation of people he has but a qualified admiration; he thinks the besetting evil of to-day is laziness and pride; but he is sorry for some of his doings, and "blaggardness" in the past, and adds: "We was a lot o' girt fools; I caan't a-ber to thenk on't."

There is another nonagenarian living a short way from the thatcher. This is Maslin, the old carter, who has spent all his life on the downs around Liddington and Marlborough. "This owld 'and o' mine 'ave sowed twelve acres o' whate in a day many a time, an' sometimes as much as sixteen acres. P'raps you oodn't thenk that," he says, with, a proud smile. He also remembers the riots of 1830, and saw them "smaishin' up the sheens" in the farmyard, when he was a boy. The rioters' chief hatred was of the threshing-machines; these they attacked with especial violence, and afterwards assailed the farmhouse, and demanded money and food from the farmer. When the horse-threshing machines first came out the corn was not thrown into a drum, as at present, but was fed between rollers, which conveyed it into the thresher, as in the case of the chaff-cutter. Four horses, attached to as many levers, supplied the power for this threshing-machine. In the centre of the ring, round which they walked, was a kind of cage, in which a boy stood, to drive the animals. At first only the biggest farmers had one of these; then, after a time, they found their way into most farmyards where there was much cornland. So, also, when the drill was invented, farmers used to hire one from the foundry or warehouse, until such time as they could afford to buy one for them selves.

The old carter, with long, grey hair and beard, fine features, and kind, smiling eyes, is delighted to talk of the hard but happy times of yore, when the bright cornfields, full of reapers, stretched for many miles, and the crowds of women and children after wards came to lease in the stubble, while the stroke of the flail sounded "thwack, thwack, thwack" in the barn all the winter, and the teams came forth to plough in the matches held yearly upon the broad downs; he had many times carried off the prize for this as a young man—e.g., £4 for the head-carter and £2 for the under-carter. There were two styles of ploughing in vogue—the "flat work" and "brick work"; the former kind being when the earth is turned over flat, and the latter when it is turned up edgeways. The allotting of the prizes depended upon the taste of the judges for this or that kind of furrow; but brick ploughing is usually considered the best for harrowing and cleaning. The carter thinks the old wooden ploughs were much better than the new iron ones; they left the ground rougher, but you could clean out the couch better; the new style is better to the eye but worse for the crop.

Whenever the teams went out on the road the carter received what is called "road-money," and some times "straw-money," too. In the case of corn to the market or mill, he received 1s. for twenty sacks from the farmer, and 4d. for every twenty sacks from the miller—1s. 4d. a score in all—which is the amount still paid in the locality. "Straw-money" is the money derived from the sale of straw used to cover the corn and other produce in the waggon. This the carters usually sold to innkeepers; each waggon carried about a shilling's worth, and sometimes more.

It is a singular fact that a great many of the down labourers, and especially carters, have a shrill, piping tone of voice quite peculiar to them, and which is not to be met with anywhere in the valley. This can only be accounted for by the climate of the downs, and the continual breezes there; such conditions must of necessity tend to affect the voice in time.

A favourite dainty of the carter's, years ago, was a "twud in the 'ole." This was not the same thing as that which bears the name to-day—viz., a piece of beef-steak wrapped with white flour paste, and baked, or boiled, but a large kidney potato, enclosed in a jacket of barley-meal paste, and baked that way. This "made anybody a good breakfast," the old man declares; and though it was frugal fare indeed, the healthy, hearty, sturdy folks seem to have derived wonderful strength and muscle from it.

The little cottage at the foot of the hill is typical of the carter. The great, long-handled whip, adorned with numerous brass ferrules, hangs on the wall behind the door, while here and there, about the room, are numerous decorative brasses, well polished, with a set of bells, buckles, and straps for the horses, a hempen halter, and the broad flag dinner-basket, lying on the floor underneath the wall.

Crack, crack, goes the whip, I whistle and I sing,
I sit upon the waggon, I'm as happy as a king;
My horse is always willing, and for me I'm never sad,
There's none can lead a jollier life than Jim the carter's lad.

There are those to-day, and especially the town bred, who turn up their noses at the sentiments expressed in the words of the old rustic songs, and pretend the breezy cheerfulness and jollity of carters is a myth, but they are mistaken. The fact is, the towns do not understand the country, and the countryman's simple feelings and natural joy in the freedom of the life out of doors; it is as natural for carter boys to whistle and sing as it is for them to eat their breakfast or dinner; what is more, when you are mounted in the waggon, off on the road, or down the fields, you cannot resist a feeling of elation and optimism; there is a real inspiration to joy in the time and place, the company of the horses, and the motion of the farm waggon.

SONG: "WAIT FOR THE WAGGON"

Will you come with me, Phyllis dear, to yon blue mountains free?
Where the blossoms smell the sweetest, come, rove along with me;
And every Sunday morning, when I am by your side,
We'll jump into the waggon, and all take a ride.

CHORUS:

> Wait for the waggon, wait for the waggon,
> Wait for the waggon, and we'll all take a ride.

Where the river runs like silver, and the thrushes sing so sweet,
I have a cabin, Phyllis, and something good to eat;
Come, listen to my story, it will relieve my heart,
So jump into the waggon, and off we will start.

Do you believe, my Phyllis dear, old Mike, with all his wealth,
Can make you half as happy as I with youth and health?
We'll have a little farm and cot, a horse, a pig, a cow,
And you shall mind the dairy, while I will guide the plough.

Your lips are red as poppies, your hair is thick and neat,
All braided up with dahlias, and hollyhocks so sweet;
And every Sunday morning, when I am by your side,
We'll jump into the waggon, and all take a ride.

Together on Life's journey we'll travel till we stop,
And if we have no trouble we'll reach the happy top;
Then come with me, sweet Phyllis, my dear, my lovely bride,
We'll jump into the waggon, and all take a ride.

> Wait for the waggon, wait for the waggon,
> Wait for the waggon, and we'll all take a ride.

IX

Wanborough Plain—Wanborough—Roman
remains—Home industries—Soap-making—
"Hudson's pudding"—"Boney"—The old bootmaker

Between Liddington Hill and Charlbury Hill the lower
chalk down projects outward a mile or so to the north and
forms a plateau, semi-circular in shape, about two and a half miles
round the verge, intersected with several coombs, abounding in
rich cornland, and studded with farmhouses and buildings. This
plateau—about 600 feet above sea-level—is known as Wanborough
Plain, and is famed as being the site of two desperate battles fought
in the early days of our history, one in A.D. 590, when the Britons
and Saxons, combined under Ceolric, defeated Ceawlin, the long-
victorious King of Wessex; and the other in A.D. 717, when the
Mercians under Ceolred attacked the men of Wessex, and were
defeated by Ine. As at Ellendune and Barbury Castle, there is nothing to indicate the encounters, except several barrows, situated near
the road on the way to Aldbourne: the eye alights on broad fields
of waving green or golden corn, or vast squares of purple clover
and sanfoin.

There are several roads running north, east, south, and west,
across the plain. There is the main road from Liddington, up which
the heavy waggons came, climbing the steep hill, and stretching
away towards Hungerford for London; next is the Ridgeway—here
a hard road, crossing straight through the plain to Charlbury Hill
on the other side—there is a narrower track running through the

cornfields down to the valley by Kite Hill; and another highway to the east, which is a Roman road—the old Ermin Street—leading from the Shepherd's Rest Inn and down Callis Hill, and continuing far away, as far as the eye can see, past Cold Harbour, towards Cirencester and Gloucester. The oldest and most famed of these roads is the Ridgeway. This is an ancient British track, from ten to fifteen yards wide, bordered with banks or ridges, leading up from Avebury, and running along the tops of the downs, first connecting the chain of camps or "castles," from Barbury to Uffington, and then stretching away towards Streatley and Reading. In early days it was a military road, along which the fierce warriors passed and repassed, the victors and vanquished, the proud conquerors, chanting and singing their battle-songs, or the demoralized mob, fleeing pellmell before their pursuers: in more recent times it was used by the smugglers to convey their contraband out away from the towns and villages, and conceal it in the woods about the downs, and also by the Welsh drovers, who brought their herds along Ermin Street, and then passed by the Ridgeway—thereby escaping the charge of the toll-gates—and wandered leisurely towards their destination, grazing their cattle on the pasture of the hillside; Below, in the valley, and running parallel with the Ridgeway, is another old track called "Pilgrims Path," but this has been cut off, and enclosed in the meadowlands in so many places, that it is impossible to follow it for any distance.

The village of Wanborough is one of the most ancient in the whole island. Long before Julius Cæsar set foot on English shores there was a settlement here, on the hill-top looking to the west over Swindon, which was probably a fortified camp ages before the one was constructed on Liddington Hill opposite. Here, according to a well-maintained tradition, stood an old heathen temple, used by the Sun-worshippers; and here, on the identical site, stands the grey old church to-day, the tower and steeple of which rise high above the valley, and are visible for many miles in the country round about. The ground beneath the hill lies flat and marshy; at the time of the prehistoric village it was forest and swamp, abounding in game and wild-fowl; and the site of the camp agrees well with Cæsar's description—a place surrounded with marsh and swamp, in a strongly fortified position.

The village is divided into two parts—Upper and Lower Wanborough. The upper part is the more ancient, dating far back, long before the advent of the Romans, people after people having successively had their township there; according to local tradition it would seem to resemble Homer's Ilium, that was built over seven times, or more. It is said there were many churches and chapels here before the existing building; one report goes so far as to put the number at 32, which is evidently an exaggeration.

Lower Wanborough lies at the bottom, between Kite Hill and Callis Hill, and is packed with ruins full of historical interest; it is said that a considerable Roman town extended for nearly two miles, from the foot of the hills down to the Nythe—the Nidum of old times. There are traces every where of huge buildings and mansions, in the massive stone foundations, traces of columns and bridges, and ruined moats remaining. For generations the farmers have been digging out this stone for building and road-making, and unearthing all kinds of interesting and valuable remains—such as fragments of pottery, stone and lead coffins, war implements, and thousands of coins, and bits of jewellery. As long ago as 1689 a vessel was discovered at Nidum, containing 2,000 Roman coins, and there have been hundreds found since.

The reason why so much money and valuables have been found buried among the Roman ruins everywhere is that when the Roman residents in Britain were warned to retire from the island, they had confident hopes of returning when the trouble was past, but they little anticipated what was really in store for them. Their own troubles at Rome, and in the East, increased to such an extent as to shatter all hopes of ever returning to Britain; and the terrible Saxons, who, almost alone of the German tribes, knew nothing of the Roman arts and civilization, razed all that was Roman to the ground, and left scarcely anything to remind them of their predecessors in the island.

Soon after the Roman merchants and residents left, the Saxons fell upon the land like a fury; the towns and villas were destroyed, and the stones and material scattered broadcast, and finally used for making other houses and works; and the temple of Nidum shared the same fate with them. Little by little, the débris was carried off; what human hands did not remove became embedded in the dust of centuries, and overgrown with flowers and grasses. In time the wilderness assumed a more pleasing aspect, and finally took the appearance of beautiful fields, though betraying, by their unevenness, some traces of their former state. The vastness of the period between the departure of the Romans and the arrival of the Conqueror from Normandy, and down to our own day, is scarcely conceived by most people; they are apt to speak of a thousand years as an insignificant space, whereas, in reality, it is an appalling length of time.

At the time of the Doomsday survey there was a mill paying forty pence, which points to considerable progress in agriculture; the good folks of Wanborough had become established on the land, and were busily employed in the cultivation of crops. The mill stood upon the banks of the little river Lidd, which wound down from Liddington, and sang merrily underneath the willows and hawthorn, before it tumbled noisily upon the old wooden waterwheel. Local tradition says this stream was formerly spanned by a bridge made entirely of copper, but there is no trace of it at this day. There is a satirical, yet pathetic rhyme, engraved upon a stone in the churchyard on the hillside, to commemorate a worthy miller of this place.

> God works his wonders now and then;
> Here lies a miller, an honest man;
> This world's glory he did not mind,
> Nor was his heart to pride inclined;
> Vile enemies him oft oppressed;
> God set him free as he thought best.

Perhaps, after all, an honest miller is not such a rarity, in spite of the proverb; though even this one had his detractors, and was not above suspicion, according to the rhyme. But "virtue soars above the dirty earth, and scorns the vulgar crowd," as the poet tells us; no doubt the miller was happy at his task, and fond of his wheel, and the foaming, spouting stream that constantly leapt over it.

From olden times, down to the early part of the nineteenth century, Wanborough was the seat of cottage industries: spinning and weaving, straw-plaiting and soap and candle-making. The farmers' wives spun the flax—part of which was grown in the neighbourhood—afterwards they took it to the weavers in the cottages, who manufactured it into linens, and made sheets, checks, and other dress stuffs. They also wove blankets, and carpets. The wool, grown upon the downs, near at hand, was first sent to Oxfordshire to be dyed, then it was woven, and afterwards sent back to be milled, to obtain the "nap" or "fluff." But the local weavers succumbed to the Irish hawkers, who carried their wares in bales and packs, and undersold the Wanborough men; they were not so efficiently equipped as were their competitors beyond St. George's Channel. By an old law no weaver was allowed to keep a "tucking" or "fulling" mill, or use dying, or to have above two looms in a house, on pain of forfeiting 20s. a week, and he was moreover forced to serve an apprenticeship to a weaver or clothier for seven years, or be fined to the extent of £20.

The manufacture of soap and candles in the villages is a further proof that the countryside was entirely self-supporting, and independent of the towns. In the case of Wanborough alone, the people grew their corn, ground their own flour, made their own farm implements and waggons, and harness for the teams—with leather from their own tan yards—made their own footwear, spun their own flax, wove their own woollens, made their own clothes, and manufactured their own soaps, candles, and rush-lights.

There was no gas, or electricity, or even lucifer matches then; only the old tinder-box, with flint and steel. The tinder-box was replenished with linen rags, which had first been held to the fire, and scorched brown. Then there were the sulphur matches, which the rustics made themselves, at dinner-time, or in the evening, cutting up, and shaving the wood with their pocket-knives and dipping the ends into the brimstone, and allowing them to dry. When a fire was required, the cottager took the flint and steel, and struck a spark, which fell upon the tinder and ignited it, not to a flame, but causing it to smoulder—or "swilter," as the rustics say—then a sulphur match was applied and kindled, which was the instrument for communicating the fire from the tinder-box. When linen rags were scarce the cottagers were driven to many expedients, and, if everything else failed, there was the goodman's shirt—all rustics wore white linen shirts in those times—the tail of which was unceremoniously ripped off, and baked, to provide fuel for the flint and steel.

There were several kinds of soap in use among the villagers formerly, the chief of which was the grey Bristol soap at 1d. a pound, and black soap at ½d. a pound, that is, before the imposition of the duties. White soap was imported from the Continent, chiefly from Spain, and bore a duty of 2d. a pound. In time the home production was taxed, too, to the, extent of 1½d. a pound, and the most rigid precautions were taken to prevent the soap-makers from escaping the duties, while severe penalties were inflicted on those who broke the law. The villagers' soap was made with the lees drawn from ashes of potash and lime, boiled up with tallow and oil. There were two processes—the half-boil and the final boil. The first of these half prepared the soap, the second finally purified it, and made it ready for cutting up for use. The rustics often used soap as an aperient medicine, swallowing it in the shape of pills, or dissolving it in syrup, or warm milk, thereby putting home manufactures to yet another use, and so escaping the payment of doctors' and apothecaries' fees. Although soap-boiling is, at best, a humble occupation, the local maker indulged in thoughts and aspirations as high as those of other men. In the churchyard is a stone, which tells us that:

Near this place is deposited the terrestrial part of
JOHN SMITH,
Soap-boiler and tallow-chandler of this Parish. 1794.

Almost every village of any size had its malthouse and brewery, and produced the old-fashioned brown farmhouse ale, and supplied the local inns, or those farms and cottages, the occupants of which, through lack of knowledge, equipment, or convenience, did not brew their own. There were three qualities of the liquor: strong beer, fresh beer, and ale; and whatever modern temperance advocates may allege, the old folks of the down-side are unconquerable in the belief that it was drinking plenty of wholesome ale that made them strong and hardy.

Some of the farmers made cider, and gave that to the men, instead of ale. At one farm alone they made 3,000 gallons a year, and consumed the greater part of it in the summer and harvest. During the cider-making the men lived in, and had everything found, besides extra wages. At such times it was usual for the farmer's wife to make monster puddings of cruttons, currants and sliced apples. This was an especial favourite with the men, who ate huge quantities of it. "Lar, maaster," the old rustic exclaimed one day, "I do like yoor mince puddin'. I awps yool 'eve some moor when we comes agyen."

The old-fashioned roly-poly pudding is honoured with a special name at Wanborough; there, by reason of a quaint incident, it is called "Hudson's pudding." Old John Hudson, the farmer, was a bachelor, and was very fond of the roly-poly kind of pudding. One day, while at table, when the pudding had been brought in, he sat viewing it with great pleasure, and a broad smile on his countenance, and fell to moralizing on his lot, and that of the steaming dish before him, and was overheard by the domestic.

"Ha!" said he—taking a knife, and measuring off the pudding into slices—"if I had had a wife and children, ther'd a bin a slice for mam, a slice for Tom, a slice for Bob, a slice for Dick, a slice for Sue, a slice for Sal, a slice for Nance, an' none at all for I, and now"—putting his arms around the dish and drawing it from off the table on to his knees—"'tis all John Hudson's." Thereupon the domestic told the tale out of doors, and the roly-poly was after wards called "Hudson's pudding."

The Greek Socrates used to carry a wooden spoon with which to eat his lentils. Seeing a boy, one day, taking up these with his fingers, he threw away his spoon with the remark: "This child beats me for simplicity." So, too, at the harvest-home, when the food was brought in, one hungry rustic, eager to start the meal, began grabbing up the cabbage from the dish with his hands. Then the carter interposed with: "Owld on a bit, owl' man. Ther'll be some knives an' farks tareckly;" to which the other promptly replied: "Tith an' vengers was made afoore knives an' farks, mun."

There were many quaint sports and games held in the village and neighbourhood of Wanborough in bygone times, but they are all at an end now. The oldest of these festivals was one called the Lot Mead. This took place at mowing-time, and was the occasion for much merriment and feast-making. There the leader of the games appeared wearing garlands of flowers, and the mowers were enter-tained with one pound of beef, and a head of garlic apiece. This is reminiscent of pagan times, for the mowers in ancient Italy, accord-ing to Horace, used to drink a decoction of thyme and garlic.

Another annual event was the Cow Fair. This was a great gath-ering and sale of beasts, at which all the farmers of the locality attended to inspect the show, and to make purchases. There was much cattle from Hereford and Wales, which filled the villagers with astonishment; they were especially struck with those "with the whitey faces." After the sale, the remainder passed up Callis Hill and away over the downs to London. When the herds of cattle passed through, they were sheltered in pens or yards, at the inns. A guide preceded each herd by one day, and arranged for food and water along the road; there was no telegraph then with which to despatch messages beforehand. Oftentimes the number of cattle passing through exceeded 800 in a week.

When the heavy waggons, conveying food and fodder, went

through, as at Liddington, the farmers around the village killed their fat sheep, calves, and pigs, and despatched them off with the rest. Dealers travelled with some of the waggons, buying and collecting food-stuffs along the journey.

There were great flocks of sheep kept upon the downs above the village formerly, and many depredations were made on the folds by the hungry poor. The old rustics still point to a spot where stood a great hollow pollard ash-tree, in which the carcases of the stolen sheep were concealed. The menfolk of several families used to visit the field, kill and carry off a sheep, dress it, and hang it up in the hollow tree; the mothers went at night and cut off a portion as required. The first thing to be done when a sheep was missed was to search the cottages of suspected persons; by carefully following this plan, a sheep was never found at one of them.

In addition to the Cow Fair was the Autumn Fair and Market, held under an ancient Charter granted by King Stephen, in the year 1252, when the booths for contests and amusements extended for a mile along the roadsides; and afterwards the Feast, or "Revels," at which the inevitable back-swording and wrestling took first place. Then the old village band turned out, with their quaint instruments, the chief of which was one called "the serpent," being in fact, a brazen serpent in a coil, into whose mouth the player blew; and, besides this, the "horse's leg," so-called from its resemblance to the limb of that animal. The rest of the band was made up of fiddles, piccolos, and clarionets—"clarnets," as the rustics call them. On Sundays the serpent went to church, and was played from the old gallery, to the great admiration of the smock-frocked farm labourers.

"Dobbin Sunday" is the name given to the day for the distribution of charity bread to the poor of the village. The bread was made into small rolls and loaves, and the distribution took place at church, on the Sabbath. After the folks from the neighbouring town took to attending the ceremony and obtaining the bread in order to waste it, the day of the week was changed, but "Dobbin Sunday" is still remembered by the villagers.

Jonathan Keen, the old farm hand, nearly ninety years of age, remembers the old sports and games, and regularly frequented them when they were held on the village green. He is big made, tall and boney, a fine physical type of the rustic, but he is trembling and feeble now. "I feels mi age terrabul. 'Tis a hard job to get about much," he tells you. When he was nearly eighty the mare in the stable kicked him severely, and broke two of his ribs; but even then he walked home unaided, the distance of a mile. As a boy, before he was fourteen, he could carry a sack of wheat with the men, while his wages were no more than 2s. 6d. weekly. His school chum, the ninety-one years old thatcher, of Liddington, pays him a visit occasionally, and Jonathan never omits to remind him of the fact that he stole his marbles in the lane over eighty years ago, when they were minding the cows. "We was oni bits o' urchins then," he adds.

The old man was a distinguished gamester in his younger days; there is nothing like the old times and amusements, according to his view. "The owld games ought to a bin kipt on wi," he says.

"Us could hae a bit o' fun then, an' 'twasn't allus rough; 'twas oni now an' agyen as us 'ad a bit of a row, an' then 'twas nothin'. We bwoys ood run fer miles to see a bit o' back-zoordin' an' wrustlin'." His old head is covered with scars—several of five inches in length—which he received at play with the single-sticks, but these are his marks of honour; he feels no disgrace in the possession of them. His legs, too, are covered with marks of the wrestlers boots; but he is not ashamed of them, either. The wrestlers were forbidden to have iron tips on their boots, so a great many used to soak them for a month in horse urine; this made the leather very hard, and they were enabled to kick their opponents black and blue.

One of Jonathan's old mates had both his thumbs bent right back in the wrestling, which happened somewhat curiously, from our point of view. There was a trick in wrestling called "reining up." This was to get your two thumbs into your opponent's mouth—one each side—and force him backwards with it. How difficult that must have been may be surmised from the dislocation of the thumbs; but the other's mouth must have been very hard to occasion it.

The Wanborough back-sworders were very clever with the sticks. It was a common exercise to practise with a lighted candle on the table, and, so skilful were the players, that they could time after time extinguish the flame without bending the wick. A favourite trick of the players was to strike each other on the funnybone, and then take immediate advantage of the blow to break a head. After the sword-play at the "Revels" the company was entertained by the prize-winners who paid for a repast of bread, cheese, and ale at the inn.

But the darling sport of old Jonathan was cock-fighting, which was far more frequently indulged in than the sword-play. The champion cock of the whole neighbourhood was one "Boney," who had slain dozens of competitors, and, though minus an eye, was still unconquerable in the field of game-fighters. One day a game-breeder brought Jonathan a small rough cock.

"Ull e buy a good little tom?"

"I don' mind! 'Ow much?"

"Aaf a crownd to you. An' 'e's a game un," the dealer replied.

"I'll 'ev un," said Jonathan, and he took the bird home.

Immediately a challenge was issued by "Boney's" owner, and accepted. When the time came round the birds were brought out, the small cock crowing lustily under Jonathan's arm.

"'E's a good un, I back. A crows like billiool," the umpire remarked.

Soon after the start the small rough cock gave a mighty bound, and struck poor Boney's other eye out, blinding him completely, and ending his career in the ring. Boney understood and felt his defeat very much, and ran about squalling with rage and pain. "I took my little cock, aater that, an' slenked along whum as ef I'd bin an' killed a fella, an' didn' Boney's missis let it into I!" quoth Jonathan.

"Ya ant a zeed thaay little kines it, 'ev e?" remarked he, rising from his arm-chair, and reaching down a small box from the mantelpiece. The "little kines" proved to be a collection of Roman money, coins impressed with the figures of Constantinus and other of the Emperors, which the old labourer had found from time to time about the fields, and digging in his cottage garden. There is a tradition to the effect that the Roman road that passes through the village was made by local labourers, who carried the stones in baskets, and received one penny a day in wages. Whether this knowledge was really handed down from one generation to another or not may be open to question, but old Jonathan heard it from his father, who had received it from his parents before him.

At the boxing and fighting matches which took place in out-of-the-way spots, the mothers of the young men frequently attended with whips and whipped their sons up to the line, calling them cowards if they gave way at all. Old Betty Seymour, who dwelled in a small cottage by the canal-side, regularly attended the matches, and often gave active support to the combatants. The London, Somerset, and local teams of back-sworders met annually at Coate, in a contest for the championship, and thousands of people attended to see the games.

How vexed the old bootmaker was to think he had wasted precious time watching the sword-play, when a young fellow. "What, I to stand here and watch this ungodly work! To see men knockin' one another about an' the blood a runnin' down in strames," said he to himself one day at the Revels. He would do so no more. After leaving the games he got over in a field, and, kneeling down on the grass, asked God to keep him from the back swording, and never attended another contest afterwards.

A short while ago the vicar invited him to church to hear a sermon, and was afterwards indiscreet enough to call on the old man to beg a compliment.

"What did you think of the sermon?" said he.

"What did I thenk o' the sarmint? Why, I didn't thenk nothin' an't. Ya dun't understand the Gospel!"

"Yes I do," the vicar replied.

"Why don' e praach it, then," the bootmaker answered. "I never yerd sich a skippin' awver in mi life. 'Tis a fine beg buildin' ya got, but 'tis some middlin' poor stuff praached inside on in."

The old bootmaker, though past ninety, is hale and hearty, and uncommonly vigorous. He is quick and keen in conversation, has a clear, strong voice, and warms to his subject amazingly; he would put many a youthful orator to shame, and overwhelm him with his unanswerable logic and wisdom. Strongly and sternly Puritanical in view, he interprets your thoughts, and sums you up in a moment; you feel his quick, penetrating gaze piercing you through and through, and are quelled in his presence.

Though at such a great age, he still works at his trade, and earns a few shillings, repairing the villagers' boots. When, many years ago, his master died—who left a fortune of £2,300, acquired at the village shop—he took on the business, and made boots for all: farmers, labourers, game-keepers, and the rest, warranted all his goods for twelve months, and gave a year's credit, which he had no cause to regret, as long as his dealings were with rustics; only the jockeys and town folk defrauded him of his money. The country labourers used to settle up every year at the end of harvest. He had been to the village of Bishopstone, three miles off, and collected £70 in three nights, and £22 at the tiny hamlet of Idstone. A shepherd had paid him as much as £7 10s. at a time for boots for himself and family.

Once a farm labourer owed him 33s., and came to him sorely vexed, one day, to tell him that he was so "hard drove" he could not pay, and he did not know when he could do so, either. "Well, you must let it stop till you *can* pay't, you know, and don't worry," the bootmaker replied. A short while after this the labourer removed from the locality, and the money was considered lost. Thirty-three years afterwards a registered letter came addressed to

GEORGE FOWLER,
Shoemaker,
Wanborough
(If alive),

and containing the 33s. in payment of the debt, and 1s over as a kind of interest on the sum. The old labourer had not forgotten it. Another who owed him a similar sum sent the money along in the same way, saying the debt "haunted him when he was at home, or in company, or in church, or following the plough, or about the stables; he couldn't rest till he had got it off his mind." There are practically no boots made in the villages now; instead, the folks go to the nearest town and purchase cheap pairs, which are all to pieces in a few months. Jonathan Keen was still wearing a pair of everyday boots made by the old shoemaker eight years before; he would have worn out half a dozen pairs bought at the town in that time.

Though the old inns have been metamorphosed and the old games and amusements done away with, and there is a dearth of those

> Who riddles tell, and merry tale,
> O'er nut-brown cakes and mugs of ale,

as the old rhyme has it, there is at least one inn in the village where a right good song may still be heard occasionally. Here the landlord leads the way, and entertains the company, dressing up in smock frock and chimney-pot hat, to sing "The Life of a Farmer," and in some sort, to keep alive he traditions of the countryside.

Extract from "The Life of a Farmer"

> My dad was a farmer, staunch and true,
> And I lead the life that he used to do,
> For I brew my beer, and I drink it, too.
> Then, hoorah! for the life of a farmer!
> I love to jump on the old grey mare,
> And gallop away to Weyhill Fair,
> Or to hunt the fox, and course the hare,
> Then, hoorah! for the life of a farmer!

Chorus:

> The black sheep starts with a baa, baa, baa,
> And the old black crow goes caa, caa, caa,
> There's a week, week, week, and a bow, wow, wow,

And moo, moo, moo, from the brindle cow,
And the cocks and the hens go cluck, cluck, cluck,
And a quack, quack, quack, from the old white duck,
Hee-haw, hee-haw, the donkeys bray,
And cock-a-doodle-doo at the break of day,
Then, hoorah! for the life of a farmer.

Etc.

X

Callis Hill—The flint-diggers—The sheep-fold—
Aldbourne—The willow-weavers—Chair-making—
Baydon—The wheelwright

THE OLD ROMAN ROAD OF Ermin Street enters Wiltshire near
Cricklade, in the bed of the Thames Valley, and, after climbing
up Blunsdon slope by Coldharbour, runs as straight as an arrow
for six or seven miles, then leaps upon the downs at Wanborough,
and continues away towards Newbury and London. The steep,
chalk-flint road of Callis Hill (*Callis*, Latin= a track) shows like a
white pillar from the valley, formidable to the eye of the waggoner,
but this is partly the effect of distance; the track is not quite as
precipitous as it looks to be when you come to mount it, though
it is difficult enough to ascend with a heavy load. Formerly the hill
was much steeper than it is now. Then it took six horses to draw a
load of hay or straw to the top of it, and, in wet weather—when the
chalk was slippery—the horses could not stand at all. Once, when
the carter was climbing up with a load of hay, and had reached
the steepest part, the shafts of the waggon broke off, and let it run
back. In a moment the hind-wheel struck the bank, and the whole
lot turned over, and slid nearly to the bottom, with the wheels
of the waggon spinning round, to the great consternation of the
carter and his boys. After this, and several other accidents, steps
were taken to lighten the ascent; the road was raised and made up
at the bottom, and the top planed down, though even now it is
very steep and difficult to mount.

A short way over the brow the Ridgeway crosses along, and afterwards ascends Charlbury Hill, running to the White Horse. Here, in an angle of the road, shaded with a large chestnut tree, stands the far-famed inn, The Shepherds' Rest, the halting-place of shepherds and drovers in past times, and a welcome refuge for travellers along the highway, and rustics employed about the broad plain. Years ago, when the fairs and markets were held all over the country, as many as 80,000, or 100,000 sheep passed this way annually; now there are scarcely any, beyond the few kept on the farms in the immediate neigh bourhood.

The Roman road continues, running underneath the steep downs on the left, with Wanborough Plain to the right, till it turns off to the east towards Baydon, while another road brings you through a charming dale to the village of Aldbourne—locally called A-burn—several miles away. At the end of the plain, and dotted about, in an amphitheatre of hills, are many ruins of Ancient British and Roman villages, while on the tops of the high downs, outlined against the sky, bare, lonely and windswept, are the "barrows," or burial-places of the old chieftains and men of note, keeping guard over the lowlands beneath.

All the roads about the downs are made of flints. These are obtained in two ways, with very little difficulty, and always near at hand; there is very little charge for hauling, and no railway carriage, as with most other stones and materials. A great many of the flints are picked up on the ploughed land after the harrowing has been done, and then the farmers sell them to the road authorities. This work is done by women, who are paid at the rate of is a square yard, twenty bushels being counted a square yard. The down-land quickly dries after the heaviest rains, and the work, though laborious enough, is not altogether uncongenial; the women can earn 8s. or 9s. a week, when the weather is fine.

Flint-digging also is carried on by men everywhere about the downs, and is done at the piece rate: 2s. 6d. a square yard being paid for all flints duly dug out and riddled. The flint-beds usually lie immediately under the turf on the high parts; you have merely to turn back the top spit, loosen the stones with the pick, and shovel them out. Generally, each man has his own station and tools, and works singly. His apparatus consists of a pickaxe, a stout iron drag, a steel fork with eight grains, a shovel, a riddle, or "ruddle,"(sieve) and a wheelbarrow. Along the winter and spring he has a movable shelter made of a couple of close hurdles covered with a rough canvas sheet; whichever way the wind is setting he adjusts this against a stout prop, and works behind it. Like most other rustic labourers, the flint-diggers believe in the horseshoe as a sign of luck; you often see one nailed in the centre of the hurdle at the top, as they fix them over the doors of the cottages. Flints which are gathered up from the ploughed land are better for road-making and repairing than those newly dug out, being much harder and more durable, by reason of their long exposure to the sun and atmosphere.

In the field a short way from the road winding through the dale to Aldbourne is a large sheep-fold, barricaded round with thick walls of warm straw and otherwise protected against the cold winds and rain, made cosy for the ewes and lambs. The fold is about forty yards square, and contains several hundred pens, or "coops," arranged in rows and lines, the whole set out like a little town within; all the coops are securely thatched over. Besides the pens, there are two large open folds; in one of these are the ewes waiting to bring forth, in the other are those which have had their lambs successfully. The shepherd, by observation, and the experience of his trade, by means quite unknown to strangers, can tell which ewes will bring forth first. These are put in the coops, and, after lambing, stay there for two or three days, then pass out into the fold, and others take their place. There are about 800 ewes altogether. These, with good luck, should yield 1,000 lambs, but a great deal depends on the weather. The lambing season begins about the middle of January, and is not over till April. During five or six weeks of this time the shepherd and his lads sleep in their wooden house beside the fold, so as to keep watch over the sheep, day and night. To neglect the ewes would be disastrous; a good many of the lambs, and ewes, too, would die. The shepherd's credit, and his livelihood would be gone; no one would employ him if he failed in his duty to the fold. Moreover, it is to his advantage to have everything go off well, since he gets a share of the spoils: besides his wages at this time he receives 1s for every lamb "over the number," so that if his 800 ewes should yield 1,000 lambs, born alive, he would be the richer by 200 shillings. If one farmer is deficient in the number of lambs, he commonly buys some from his neighbour to make up the amount; for these he pays 2s. each.

The shepherd's two sons are in charge of the fold for an hour or two to-day, while he is gone with the farmer to ferret rabbits on the downs a little distance off. The elder of these is aged eighteen, the younger one fourteen; he has just left school, and is come to help with the sheep, to carry hay and corn, and to run errands for his father. The elder brother was sitting in the doorway of the house, shaving a ground-ash stick with his pocket-knife, while the other—a small, bright, healthy, happy child, with heavy boots, and great, leather gaiters—was fondling the ewes and lambs, which were well-pleased with his attentions. The senior brother is a fine, sturdy, handsome lad, with fresh complexion, dreamy eyes, and soft, musical voice. He speaks the dialect of the mid-downs, using "pert" for part, "zide" for side, and "taak"for talk, but it all sounds pretty and sweet, harmonizing well with the idyllic surroundings of the yellow-brown hills and the sheep-fold.

"Do you like the lambing-time?" said I.

"Yes," he replied, gently and emphatically, while his eyes lit up with wonderful pleasure. "This is the happiest time of all the year."

"Tell me why," I said again.

"Because of the lambs, and especially when we has good luck with them, and no trouble with the ewes," he answered.

Then he took me into the fold, and round the coops, talking all the while of the characteristics of the ewes, the love and devotion of one mother, and the indifference and even dislike of another, for her babe, taking up first one lambkin and then another in his arms, and nursing them on his breast, while the proud ewes bleated fondly or timidly, looking up with large, intelligent eyes, or followed behind, coming to thrust their warm noses into our hands, or to lick our fingers, as a dog would do. Some ewes will not recognize their lambs for three or four days, nor yet allow them to suck. These have to be "tiddled," as the shepherds say—e.g., fed with a bottle, or the ewe must be forcibly held, while the lamb sucks the sweet milk for itself.

The lambs vary much in size when they are born, and for the first few days look to be all ears, legs, and tail; their legs especially seem to be out of all proportion to the rest of their body. Their skins look much too large for them, and their coats are hard, like bark to the touch, and they are almost black in colour. Their ears, for the most part, project out at right angles, though sometimes they lop and droop down, and, together with their black noses and pretty, bead-like eyes, give them a most quaint appearance. Here and there was a little creature blind of one eye; this, the shepherd-boy said, was caused by the draught through the corner of the coop. Several of the ewes were limping, which I thought might be due to foot-rot, but the youth explained it was a little earth, wedged, and hardened in the cleft of the foot.

Hereupon we came to a sheep in travail, and when she was delivered of the lamb, he laid it on the clean, dry straw, lifted the ewe upon her feet and made her smell the babe, which she immediately began to lick clean: the ewes recognize their lambs by smell. The mother is not long in recovering from the pains of giving birth to the lamb. In about half an hour she is usually well again, and goes on eating her food with the rest; though sometimes she falls ill and dies, or has to be fed on corn—chiefly split peas—to restore her to a fit condition in which to suckle her offspring.

The village of Aldbourne is situated in a large hollow, where the ridges of the high downs slope and meet as do the spokes of a wheel towards the hub, and in the centre of which six roads come into conjunction, leading, one to Liddington, one to Wanborough, one to Bishopstone, one to Baydon, one to Hungerford, and one to Ogbourne. Numerous springs gush out of the downs all round in the winter, flooding the cornfields, and overflowing the roads, and even bursting out underneath the houses, and from the very centre of the street itself. The waters of these are finally collected in a course by the roadside, and go tumbling down to meet in the centre of the place, and afterwards run away to join the River Kennet near Hungerford. From being built in the hollow, and from the prevalence of the springs—though the village is some 400 feet above sea-level—the inhabitants call it a "rheumaticky place," though, as soon as the winter passes, the springs subside, and there is no water at all to be had from the surface in the summer and autumn months.

The village is one of the most interesting in the land, both by reason of its antiquity, and especially of its industries, which were many, and the principal of which have only recently died out in the face of other methods of manufacture. The streets are broad and spacious, with plenty of freedom and light. A large wash-pool is in the heart of the place, and near to this stands the principal inn, The Crown. Opposite the pool, under the wall, is a long wooden seat, where each day, when it is fine, you may be sure of seeing half a dozen of the aged grey-haired villagers, sitting in the sunlight, talking over every day matters, or reminiscences of old times. A fine, ancient church, built in the Norman style, with a magnificent tower 80 feet high, stands back against the downs and overlooks the village with majestic grandeur; in front of this is a large square, and in the centre the ruins of a fine church cross. The rectory—said to have been the hunting-box of John of Gaunt—stands near the pile, half concealed among tall beech-trees. The amazing tower was built a year later than Salisbury Cathedral, and we can imagine what an object of pride it must have been to the villagers for years after its completion, but that rapture is excited no more now, or only in the occasional visitor, at least. Eight bells, of an exceedingly rich, sweet tone, hang in the tower, and are the product of the village; for the people of Aldbourne cast their own bells, and not only so, but made them for others, too; the greater part of the church bells for miles around were cast at Aldbourne. When Oliver Cromwell was thundering through the land he attempted to batter down the tower, but that was too stout for his puny artillery; the slight damage he did to the exterior has been eradicated, and the pile looks prouder and more defiant than ever.

Aldbourne is the centre of a large agricultural district, and is inhabited by an easy-going and independent population, who, according to a local critic, "work when they like, play when they like, go where they like, do what they like; are happy and careless, civil and honest, and beholding to no man." Cottages are cheap and plentiful, if a little antiquated in appearance; the average rental of these is £3 or £4 a year. Many of the cottages are very old, some of the fifteenth century, and some later, built in the Early Elizabethan style; while others are of flints, chalk, and sarsen-stones. In the latter half of the eighteenth century a big portion of the village was destroyed by fire. Before this it was called "Little London"; after the conflagration it was nicknamed "All-burnt." The villagers still relate how the carter, being at dinner, and warned to leave the house, declared he would not budge till he had finished his meal; but the flames increased so rapidly that he had to rush from the house, and leave his dinner unfinished in the end.

It is related of Aldbourne that a wag one day brought a dab-chick from Ramsbury and put it in the pond, thereby rousing the natives to the highest pitch of curiosity to know what kind of bird the stranger might be. After a consultation it was decided to fetch the oldest inhabitant; as he was an invalid he had, perforce, to be produced in a wheel barrow. On trying to come up with the water-fowl that naturally swam over to the other side. "Wheel ma round," the old man shouted; then, as the bird swam back: "Wheel ma round agyen"; and so on, till, failing to get close to the bird, he gave his opinion afar off. "'Tis a dab-chick," he declared, with oracular gravity. Thereupon the natives were satisfied, but when outsiders came to know the story they laughed heartily, and ever since the good folks of Aldbourne have been styled "dab-chicks" about the down-side.

The land around Aldbourne is either arable, or else grazing ground for sheep; there is scarcely any pasture at all, and very few cows are kept. There is an abundance of fine wheat, barley, oats, rye, and beans grown in the locality, all which are easily disposed of, some at home, and some transported abroad for seed; while there is an increasing demand for straw of all kinds as fodder and litter for cattle. Even wheat straw is cut up into chaff in great quantities for cows and yearlings; there is a greater demand for straw now than at any previous time, and all this gives a fresh impetus to corn-growing.

In consequence of there being no cows and dairy work about the downs, wages are a little lower than in the fertile districts of the valley, but the work is easier, and the hours much shorter, and there is no Sunday labour, except in the winter, when the horses lie in, and in the case of the shepherd, who must always attend to his flock. In the summer the teams go out from 7 a.m. till 3.30 p.m., and in the winter from 8 a.m. till 3 p.m; after feeding the horses the carters are free to go home and enjoy a long evening, in strong contrast to the factory workmen, who, year in and year out, toil from 6 a.m. till 5.30 p.m., and often till 8 p.m., shut away from the air and sunlight, half suffocated with the smoke and stench, and driven almost to distraction with the iron rules and system, and the crafty wiles of overseers.

The carter's weekly wage is 13s. or 14s., which looks small at first, but there are other benefits to be taken into consideration, which, in all, amount to a value of £1 a week, from year's end to year's end. Chatting with the carter, whom I met on the road walking with his team, hands in pockets, and pipe in mouth, well dressed, and well fed, sociable and cheerful, he told me, with many smiles, that besides his 13s. a week, he had a cottage and forty perch of land, rent free, £3 at Michaelmas, with one ton of coal, one hundred beech or hazel faggots, 10s. for every foal born alive, 2d. an acre for all drilling, 2d. an acre for mowing—clover, sanfoin, etc.—and a like sum for reaping and binding, and the same rate obtains throughout the locality. The day labourers fall a good way short of this, and only receive 11s. and 12s. in the dead of winter, but when the spring comes the hoeing begins and continues through the summer till harvest, which is done piece work, and brings the average wages up to a better figure. One day-man told me that before the advent of so much machinery he used to draw from £12 to £15 in the harvest, but there is nothing like so much obtained now. Another old fellow, who is ditcher and drainer in the valley, and who walked about the garden paths with naked feet in a bitterly cold wind speaking to me, makes 7s. and 8s. a day at his work.

Formerly Aldbourne was much bigger and more thickly populated than it is now. A century ago the inhabitants numbered 2,000; but they are shrunk to 1,100 to-day, and the migration still proceeds apace, though the men go not so much to the towns as to the colonies, which is a mark of courage in them, and is not to be deplored too much. But the chief cause of the village's prosperity was its cottage industries of spinning and weaving, which made the villagers peculiarly independent and self-supporting; it is said there was not a cottage in the place but had one or two looms worked by the women and girls, whose average weekly earnings were from 9s. to 10s. 6d. In early times, down to the close of the eighteenth century, silk-spinning and weaving was the chief industry; after that time fustian and linen-weaving was in vogue, and silk gimp-making—the ornamental bordering in upholstery—which finally gave place to willow-weaving and plaiting. Besides these purely cottage industries, there was a bell foundry, and a general foundry, a soap and candle factory, two wind-mills, with powerful machinery impelled with six large fans, malt-houses, rope-walks, and a chair and table manufactory, which is still active, and where everything is hand-made, with the exception of the table-tops and seats of the chairs.

The silk-weaving was the oldest industry. In the time of William the Conqueror an inundation of the Netherlands took place, and drove many of the Flemish weavers into other countries. Some of these came to England, where the King established them, first at Carlisle, and then in the Western Counties, so that the Aldbourne

weaving may date from that period. The last of the home employ-
ments was the Willow-weaving and plaiting, which has not been
discontinued above sixteen years, and which might be revived, if
the cottagers would do it; but they are disinclined to undertake
the work again, so this important trade has fallen to decay, though
there are manufacturers ready and anxious to take the woven material when it shall be forthcoming.

Willow-weaving was done with the loom, and the process was
almost identical with that of woollen and other stuffs. First of
all, the young withy poles and trees—and sometimes lime-trees
also—were cut, and the bark removed. Then the wood was sawn
up into pieces a yard long, and the small logs split into quarters.
After this it was passed on to expert cutters, who, with the use of
specially contrived hand-tools, cut the wood into very thin strips,
and separated the fibre, tearing it apart, into something smaller
than wheat straws. These fibres were tied in bundles and afterwards
passed on to the weavers, who wove them into sheets a yard square.
One thread was called the "sharp," and the other the "shoot," in the
loom. The price paid for weaving was 1s. 6d. for a dozen squares,
and the sum earned in wages every week averaged £50. When the
squares were done, they were received into the proprietor's depot,
and despatched off to London for hat-making; and some of them
went abroad, too, to be utilized for the same purpose. The material was very tough and pliable, and would last a long time, in any
weather.

Willow-plaiting moved on the same lines as the weaving, but
this was done without looms. Here the willow was cut into thin
strips with hand-planes, and the women and girls plaited them,
using five strips at a time. This fabric the folks called "tuscin,"
which may be the local rendering of "Tuscan." About fifteen years
ago willow material was displaced by compressed paper, but this
would not stand the wet, and the London manufacturers came and
tried to revive the industry, but to no purpose. A company was
formed in the village, and the looms were got into order again, but
the cottagers would not take to the work any more, so the looms

were carried off to the towns, and the experiment tried there, but it was unsuccessful.

The manufacture of chairs on the easy-going, old-fashioned lines still proceeds in the village. All the work is done by hand, and is of the most skilful and efficient kind; there is a great demand for Aldbourne chairs all round Wiltshire and Berkshire, and the output is often at the rate of 100 a week. Every kind of chair is made, together with a few tables, though it is chiefly chairs, large and small; polishing and all is done on the premises. The wood is obtained in the locality of Marlborough, and, except the elm-boards for the seats, it is cut up with hand-saws. The frames of the chairs are chiefly of ash, and the legs of birch and beech. Some of the chairs in olden times were made of yew; these lasted for a century, or a century and a half, in constant use, but none are made of that kind of wood to-day.

The skill of the village chairmakers, and especially of the turners, is most remarkable; though I have been for many years acquainted with all kinds of elaborate turning in metals, I have never seen any thing made so simply, quickly, and beautifully, as are the ornamental legs and spokes of the chairs and tables, and everything made, too, without gauges, absolutely to the eye, with unerring precision. The lathes are very primitive and simply constructed, but remarkably effective, machines. There are merely two sharp steel centres, fixed in "dogs," for holding the rough wood, and a wooden rest for the tools before, with a treadle underneath. About ten feet from the ground is a long thin strip of fir-wood, or larch, fixed at one end, and bearing on a cross support in the middle. From the free end of this plank, immediately above the lathe, a small cord is suspended; when the wood is fixed in the dogs, the cord is passed once round it, and fixed to the treadle beneath. As the operator pushes down the treadle with his foot, the rope is drawn down quickly, and the wood in the dogs revolves with great rapidity; as the treadle comes up the spring of the plank above draws it back, and the wood spins round again in the other direction. The cutting is only done as the wood turns towards the operator, but it all moves so quickly and regularly, and the turner is so highly skilled, that he can work at a great speed. From the time of taking up a rough piece of wood for a chair-leg from the ground, and handing it back, perfectly turned, as smooth as marble, with not the slightest tool-mark about it—except for the ornamental cuts—is no more than three minutes.

The work proceeds by easy stages, the master and owner toiling with his men; there are no stringent laws framed for employes: "If there were, they would be useless," the master says. "It is best to jog along comfortably together. If they want a pipe of tobacco, I tell them to slip outside and have it; and if it is wet they go into the next room where there is no danger of a fire; it would never do to attempt to proceed on the lines of the big factories here in Aldbourne."

As well as being skilful, intelligent, individual, and independent, the folks of the ancient weaving village are noted for longevity; life is usually lived to the full in the majority of places about the downside. Granny Bird is one of the oldest inhabitants today.

She is over ninety years of age, and is as nimble as a top; she skips all round the village in a few moments. When the beautiful, bonny, rosy-cheeked boys and girls come out of school in the afternoon, they always run up to Granny in the street, and shake hands with her, with pretty modesty and bashfulness. "They allus does that whenever they ketches sight o' I," Granny says. She points to the high tower, which she climbed as a young girl, and to the large square before the church, round which they ran for gown lengths nearly a century ago, and to all the cottages in view, where the busy shuttles plied to and fro, in happier days than these, and she remembers all sorts of feasting, sporting, and revelling, but this is at an end now; only the old, grey tower remains unchanged, with the evergreen downs, that lie all round like the billows of a mighty ocean; all the rest is passing away.

Living near to Granny is the aged roadmender and back-sworder, who continued his daily work till he was nearly eighty-five, and, on the other side, the old bricklayer and well-digger, who has carried out many difficult tasks, and bored no end of wells about the downs, and assisted at opening the ancient barrows on the hill-tops. In addition to this, he has had much to do with dew-ponds, and has frequently measured the dew-fall, which, according to his statement, often amounts to three inches in a night, during a thick mist. The water in the ponds attracts the mist, that may be seen rapidly drawn into the pools; the mist will fill the ponds much more quickly than would an ordinary shower of rain.

From Aldbourne the road climbs steeply up the high downs to the east and continues away, rising higher and higher, till it reaches the pretty village of Baydon, nestling amid tall elms and beeches, and surrounded with fresh green meadows. The road, leading along the hill, commands a delightful view of the Aldbourne vale. In the distance lie the downs, ranged along with graceful and exquisite ease, green and golden, or faint blue, rising and falling in a series of lovely lines, softly blending and intermingling, while below is a panorama of fertile cornfields, studded with farms and ricks, and numerous clumps of beeches dotted about, and the long white road winding through the middle of the hollow towards Liddington Castle, visible on the sky-line, four or five miles away. Immediately underneath nestles the compact village of Aldbourne, surmounted with the magnificent church tower, with the white smoke of the afternoon fires rising from a hundred cottage chimneys, preparing for the return of the toilers; on the one side stands the engine and thresher, and a dozen men and women busy at the ricks, while the mournful, humming sound is carried out by the down breeze; on the other are the teams returning from the field, and unloosed from the ploughs, the shares of which, polished with the hard, dry earth and chalk, gleam like silver in the bright sunshine.

The village of Baydon enjoys the distinction of being the high-est inhabited village in the southern counties, and possibly in the whole land. It is perched upon an eminence at an altitude of nearly 900 feet above sea-level, high above the ordinary down-land, and yet the subsoil is a stiff clay, which is remarkable at such a height, and where all for miles around is a succession of chalk lands. This clay grew large crops of corn in times past, but the fields have been laid down for pasture now, though there are no dairies, since the railway is afar off; instead, the farmers rear young cattle, and graze the fields. The village stands on the old Roman road of Ermin Street, and is possessed of a pretty Norman church: its population is about 200. Formerly it had many more inhabitants, but when the cornland came to be laid down, the people drifted away; the cottages fell into ruins, and were taken down; it is a repetition of the old story. Here it was that the steam-plough and scarifier were first invented, and the first tackle made, by one John Allen Williams, but someone or other improved on the device, and carried off the rewards of the invention. From that time the work of the little foundry dwindled in importance; now it has ceased entirely, and the premises have been demolished.

There was one sturdy old family in Baydon, known and celebrated for miles around, by reason of their prowess in wrestling and back-swording. This was the Beckinghams, who were blacksmiths and farmers, too, skilled in the art of ironwork, and also in that of tilling the earth; able to beat out the spluttering, hissing mass on the anvil, and cognizant of "Nature's gentle doings" as well, besides being able to cope with every competitor in the games about the down-side. The combination of black-smithing and other trades with that of farming was very common formerly; nearly every proprietor of the forge had a few acres of land, and kept horses and cattle.

The last of the kind living at Baydon is old John Alder, who was carpenter, wheelwright, and farmer, thereby uniting yet another trade with that of husbandry, and being doubly qualified to construct carts and waggons, since he was not only a good judge of materials, but was also versed in the actual use and running of the vehicles, and could put his own handiwork to the test. He received his tuition as a boy in the village, and considered himself for tunate to get 16s. a week as a journeyman, fifty years ago. A good farm waggon costs about £32, and a heavy cart £12 or £15. The wheels of waggons and carts are generally made of three kinds of wood: oak for the spokes, elm for the hub, and ash (or elm), for the felleys. Of these, ash is the most costly now, chiefly by reason of its use for motor car frames, and in aeroplanes; it is very light, pliant, and durable. This the poet Spenser knew, and intimated as much in his catalogue of trees:

> The yew, obedient to the bender's will,
> The birch for shalts, the sallow for the mill,
> The myrrh, sweet-bleeding of the bitter wound,
> The warlike beech, *the ash for nothing ill*,
> The fruitful olive, and the plantain round,
> The carver holm, the maple seldom inward sound.

The old wheelwright has retired from farming now, and lives at the little shop with his grown-up daughters, who carry on the business of the village Post Office, and sell all kinds of curious odds and ends, such as are in demand in country places: as marbles for the children, and whipcord for the farm-lads, needles and thread, hooks and eyes, and buttons for the good-wives, shoes for the feet, hats for the head, clothes for the body, sweetmeats, jams, pickles, foodstuffs, pictures, newspapers, clothes-pegs, postage stamps, and a host of other sundries, of varying degrees of usefulness. The little room within—the window of which looks out upon the old Roman road by which the Emperors used to pass—contains many curios; bits of antique chinaware, books, stuffed animals and birds in glass cases, the most interesting of which is a "dove-cuckoo," i.e., a dove crossed with a cuckoo, which was shot in the high beech-trees standing by the roadside.

Though the village of Baydon is small, life there is not dull, or not from the point of view of the inhabitants, at least; they have their cares and businesses, and are serenely occupied with them. If the winter is stark and keen, the summer-time is beautiful; there is no loneliness where the heart is satisfied and at peace with itself; melancholy and dejection are usually dependent more upon the individual, than upon the surroundings of a place.

XI

Russley Downs—The down feeling—Little Hinton—
The coomb—The church and mill—The old
blacksmith—Earl's Court Farm and Ghosts—Dressing
up the corpse—Bourton "Rout"—Danish traditions

THE DOWNS BETWEEN BAYDON AND Charlbury are intersected
with a beautiful dale, full of rich corn-fields, and dotted with
farm buildings, clumps of firs, and beeches. Here and there is a
dew-pond, perched in a small niche high upon a slope, or built up
against the bank artificially; on the one hand a flock of sheep, snow
white, are descending the hill-side with a swift whirling motion,
like that of a cloud changing in mid-air; on the other, the narrow
white road lies like a thread along the valley, soon to rear up perpendicularly, and disappear over the brow into the next hollow. To
the east the dale opens out into a broad valley, the confines of which
dwindle away, and are lost in the faint blue distance; farther off, in
the other direction, on the ridge of a down, is a long hedge of beech,
the form of which is exactly like that of cavalry on the march, the
resemblance is so striking that when the eye first lights upon it it
seems possessed of real motion; the whole mass seems visibly to
advance some distance along the hill-top against the sky-line.

In the bottom of the dale, where the narrow road winds steeply
down, stands a large farmhouse and several cottages, and about
half a mile further on is the hamlet of Russley, famed for its racing
stables and grounds, and from which, according to local report,
a subterranean passage formerly ran to Ashdown House, a mile
and a half away, though the tunnel, if it ever existed, is blocked

up now, and rendered impassable by reason of the fallen debris. Many of these underground passages are supposed to exist about the downs, but few actual traces of them remain. Besides these concealed ways, there are other covered ways above ground, running like deep ditches over the hill-tops and through the hollows. These were probably made by the early Britons, to afford them means of passing from village to village in the shelter. In the valley trees and vegetation would conceal their movements, and afford protection; where these did not exist on the downs, resort was had to artificial means to supply the deficiency.

The openness and strategic disposition of the downs between Russley and Lambourn make them an ideal ground for military manceuvres; many brilliant spectacles have been witnessed here in modern times, and many mimic battles fiercely waged along the slopes and plains, amid the wheat stubble and turnip fields. Here we small boys used to come, tramping ten miles from home in the happy harvest holidays, and be inextricably mixed up and confused with 70,000 or 80,000 troops, driven this way and that, now in the firing line, exposed to the terrific fusillade of the infantrymen's rifles, now under the heels of the cavalry, nearly trodden to death, running mile after mile, thirsty and sweating in the hot sunshine; at one time scolded out of our wits by the testy corporal, at another chaffed and encouraged by the fat, jolly cavalry sergeant, loitering among the sweet-smelling turnips, and singing a snatch of song by himself:

The girl I love, and the horse I ride.

The thin red line of the infantrymen, stretching as far as ever the eye could see, the glint of the sun on helmets, and the flashing of sabres, with the boom, boom, of the cannon, and the continual crack, crack, crack, of the rifles, formed a scenre never to be forgotten; though we somehow managed to lose our tiny stock of pence, lying down on the beautiful short turf studded with harebell and scabious, and had to perform the long journey home on empty stomachs, singing as we passed down the narrow lanes of the valley.

The feeling of the downs is quite different from that experienced in the vale amid the deep green meadows, the trees, and hedgerows. There it is a sense of vast, cumbersome wealth, of unspeakable riches, a luxury of possession, and imprisonment with it; you feel to be hemmed in and circumscribed with so much treasure of tree, plant, and flower; the view is shorter, the outlook limited, the spirit chafes and frets, and tries to soar, but is prevented by its surroundings, confined, as it is, within a fortress of beauty and loveliness. But here, on the downs, you are not compassed about with trees and boughs, and locked fast in rich meadows, out of sight of the great expanse of the heavens and the magic-moving horizon. Instead, there are bareness, simplicity, and spaciousness, coupled with a feeling of great strength, and uncontrolled freedom, an infinity of range, and an immortality of purpose. The soul goes out with the vision, shooting fleeter than light itself to every point of the heavens, penetrating everywhere, seeing, divining, and understanding all things, to shrink into bondage and comparative insignificance when you withdraw and descend the slopes into the heart of the intricate and bewildering valley.

Little Hinton lies at the foot of Charlbury Hill—called also Shelbarrow and Sharborough by the natives—bordering on the rich fertile fields of the vale on the one hand, and skirted by the corn-growing downs on the other, half hidden in a grassy hollow, and one part out of sight amid a profusion of tall elm-trees, which thrive well on the hillside. From the top of the hill itself the village is almost invisible; but from the valley, six or seven miles away, it can plainly be seen, nestling peacefully underneath the huge hill, which, from its exquisite shape and graceful disposition, gives an impression of delicious ease and rest where it lies slumbering in the sunlight. Immediately below the hill, washed out of the chalk, and opening into the valley, is a large hollow, called "Cowtail Coomb," at the bottom of which twenty springs gush out and flow away down into the bright fields beyond. The bottom of the coomb is tilled, and several broad terraces run round on the shallow side.

A mile or so to the west, near the Roman road, is the entrance to another remarkable coomb, which winds round in a zigzag fashion, and joins the valley in the centre of the village. The striking features of this coomb are its abrupt beginning, its great depth, and its sharpness of outline; human hands could not have carried out an excavation with greater precision, and there has been no wearing away of the ridges, at whatever date the gully was formed. At the bottom of the hollow, and along the tops of the slopes, are terraces and excavations, unmistakably the work of human beings; here, in some far-off, remote age, before the dawn of history, dwelled a little community, and tilled their small lands, happy in their seclusion, and unscorched with the fires and lust of ambition. Some of the pit dwellings of the prehistoric village were inhabited, as late as a century ago, by a family named Clargo, the last of whom, Mary Clargo, an old woman, counted a witch by the villagers, lived there alone, with the pit thatched over, to protect her from the rain and cold. Here and there, slanting down the side is a track made by the horses, that come to drink in the pool at the bottom, with many other small paths formed by the hares, which plunge straight down among the long grass and spring up on the other side, without troubling to deviate to make the ascent easier.

Years ago the place was said to be haunted by witches and goblins, who caught the horses turned out by moonlight, and galloped them furiously up and down the coomb, and so wore out the tracks. This the carters and rustics believed from often finding their horses foaming with sweat in the early morning; not knowing how to account for it other wise, they thought upon evil spirits who took the form of witches by night and vanished into thin air with the dawn. To stand at the entrance to the coomb and look towards the centre, where the high ridge is crowned with dark spruce and fir, gives one the impression of looking down a mountain gorge; the formation is one little to be met with about the smoothly carved and evenly shaped downs.

The village is divided into two parts, about a quarter of a mile distant from each other, one of which is called West Hinton, and the other Church Hinton, because the church is situated there; though when the old folks are speaking of the other part from that in which they live, they merely say "t'other 'Inton"; that denominative answers their purpose very well. To further localize the divisions—if that could be necessary in such a tiny place—the villagers have named one corner "The City," and another "Wopham"; and where the road climbs up to connect the two Hintons is called Body Horse Hill, because the outline of the road resembles that of a horse.

The pretty church stands adown the slope at the foot of the hill, in the midst of a group of picturesque chalk-built cottages and farmhouses, out of sight of the highway, except the red-tiled roof of the tower, which rises up and peeps over the tops of the trees and the cottage chimneys. The little building is very ancient, Saxon in style, quaint without and within, with round arches, beautifully carved oak woodwork, centuries old, and old-fashioned box-pews, the whole pervaded with a sense of calm peacefulness, answering to the description of Lamartine's Retreat, where,

> … jamais ne s'élève
> Bruit qui fasse penser;
> Jusqu' ce qu'il s'achève
> On peut mener son rêve
> Et le recommencer.

Without the porch, and shading the entrance to the tiny burial ground, is a splendid elm, the branches of which droop low down over the heads of those entering in, as though to bless them, while all around, in the season, bloom beautiful primrose, snowdrop, and daffodil; a magnificent yew-tree, with large, perfect trunk, and graceful drooping branches, almost resembling a cedar in shape, stands on the other side. The small square tower is covered with ivy from base to summit; the whole makes a charming picture, pleasing to the beauty loving eye of the stranger. Inside the church is a very quaint stone font, carved with the figures of birds, fishes, a hog, and a serpent, which the Saxons loved to depict on their fonts and vessels, but the Normans considered all such as Pagan emblems, and destroyed or defaced them whenever they found them. Within the tiny porch are fixed sundry notices, of vestries, the amounts of the weekly offertories, sums payable to the rector on certain occasions, and a card containing the sexton's fees, which are interesting, as showing a person's indebtedness to him at the time of marriage and death.

FEES TO SEXTON

		s.	d.
Funerals:			
	For 6-foot grave	7	6
	For 8-foot grave	10	0
	Toll bell, one hour	1	0
	Toll bell, two hours	2	6
	On erection of memorial stone	10	0
Weddings:			
	Publication of banns	1	6
	At the service	1	6

Digging a grave is not always an easy matter, especially in localities where stone is encountered; very often the digger has to force his way through five or six feet of closely packed and almost solid stone, and must work hard to complete his grave after a couple of days' laborious toil.

The old mill stood afar off, nearly two miles from the village, in the centre of a tract of meadowland known as Hinton Marsh, or "Mash," in local parlance. The road down to it is through a delightful lane bordered with fields of great fertility, producing an abundance of rich sweet grass, and the hedgerows teem with birds: blackbirds and thrushes, linnets, goldfinches, bullfinches, redpolls and others, while the magnificent downs, rising up to Charlbury Tump in the south, standing bold and clear, or soft and subdued, mingling with the hazy blue heavens, form a picture which, for pure sweet beauty, might be equalled, but never surpassed. Numerous small springs run rippling along under the boughs, and through the tiny copses, presently to leap through the hatches and fall below with a musical plash, afterwards winding round and round in the midst of the fields, clear as crystal, and glistening like silver in the sunlight, overflowing their banks here and there, to form small lakes in the hollows, finally to meet in several larger streams and be received into the River Cole, and flow thence away to the sea. Here, besides the smaller birds, dwell the wild-fowl: ducks and moorhens, the heron, or "mollern," snipe, and kingfishers; the large gold-brown hares limp or bound across the fields, the ruddy fox lurks in the dingle, or plays with its cubs in the corner of the meadow, and the sagacious-looking water-rats paddle to and fro in the streams, and tunnel in the banks, letting the water trickle through, living lives of supreme quiet and indolence.

The stream was diverted, and carried along between raised banks for half a mile or more to form the mill-pond, and to obtain sufficient fall for the water to turn the ponderous wheel, and escape again to its natural bed. The mill-head, where the wheel stood, is twelve or fifteen feet above the meadows; but the building has long since fallen to ruins; there is little trace of it remaining, except a pile of large stones, and a bed of masonry, covered over with thick, delicious moss, where the water oozes out low down. Rows of bullace boughs and apple-trees mark the spot where the mill-house garden and orchard formerly stood, and tell the sad tale of departed days; there is no sound of the mill any more, or of the teams conveying the rich grain and pearly flour; all that is gone never to return. The last one to operate the mill, by a curious coincidence, bore the name of Spindle, but he was the victim of a cruel act in the end, which brought about the ruin of the mill thirty years before they ceased to grind higher up on the down-side. About half a century ago, the land adjoining changed hands, and the new owner, contending that the lower road which led to the mill was private property, set stout posts in the way, and prevented the carts and waggons from approaching it, and so the grinding stopped, and the building fell to pieces.

There are two small blacksmiths' shops in the village, one of which, half tumbling down, is held by a farmer, who merely does a job now and then when he feels disposed, and repairs his own implements; and the other in daily use, by the old blacksmith, John Johnson, or "Young John," as the villagers playfully name him. His shed—which he built himself—is of iron, and stands immediately alongside the school playground, through which he crosses, in dirty weather, to gain the forge, stepping on wooden boxes to assist him over the low fence. At playtime the children come out to watch him at work, to hear the roaring bellows and tinkling anvil, and to see the bright yellow sparks whizzing out, and shooting through the small doorway. The old smith is very fond of the children, and they love him in return; "Young John" is a familiar figure, and a favourite with all the villagers. The farmer gave him the ground, free of rents, for his forge, glad to have a regular smith in the place; "Young John" executes all the small repairs to the machinery and implements, and shoes the horses, settling up with his patrons every three months.

The little forge is a curious place, containing all kinds of rough tools, with other odds and ends, and everything is in a muddle, as is usual with the village smithy. Once, at Ashbury, young "Strawberry" and his mates, in the absence of the smith, took it upon themselves to clean up the shop, and received a good spanking for their pains when he returned, who promptly kicked the tackle right and left, all over the place again. The bellows for the forge are in a tiny box-like place behind where the smith stands; there are several iron "boshes" for the water, and the dust-like coal is kept in a large two-handled pot, which once did service over the kitchen fire. The chimney is a very simple contrivance, being merely a milk-churn, with the bottom knocked out, hung in the iron roof, the broad bottom forming a kind of bonnet, to carry off the smoke and sulphur. This suits the old blacksmith very well, because, as he says, he "can look up the chimmuck at night, an' see the stars a-shinin' outside."

The smith is tall and boney, but none too robust since he had the severe attack of bronchitis last fall, which played havoc with him; he is hard on seventy now. In manner he is extremely gentle and agreeable, a lovable man, with a playful, yet serious mind, full of quaint sayings and sparks of wit, able to converse on matters of the deepest import, and to make rhymes while he beats out the fizzing metal on the anvil. His voice is soft and mellow, and he sings the tenor part in the choir at the tiny church; he has been a chorister all his life, from early childhood. He is ripe for a chat at all times, whenever you care to look in upon him, and is desirous of taking every one up to the coomb to see the ancient dwellings, to tell you the names of all the hills, and point out the spot where the old grey mare "Merriman" slipped over the steep side of the coomb, and tumbled down one hundred feet with a load of manure behind her, shattering the cart to fragments, but escaping unhurt herself. He has no mate to help him at the forge, except when he has an extra heavy job in hand; then he gets an old neighbour to come and give him a blow, but be "soon gets out o' bread" (breath). His hammers are all named: there are "Slogger," the sledge; "Dragon," the intermediate one; and "Useful," the hand hammer. When he wants either of them he cries aloud: "Now, Useful!" "Come yer, Dragon!" "Stop ther, Slogger, till I wants tha agyen!" Where "Useful" is not big enough, and "Slogger" too mighty, he "goes at it, an' 'its into 't wi' Dragon, an' yarns mi bit o' rooty" (bread).

He remembers when the terraces in the coombs were cultivated and grew famous crops of wheat. The ploughing of the sides of the coombs was done by oxen which are more surefooted than horses, and the corn grown there was of an extra good quality, because of the great heat, and shelter from the wind. The old fellow has pondered on the formation of the coombs, and is convinced they were made by water action, but, being unskilled in geological lore, his opinion is that they were washed out at the time of the Flood. In connection with the pit-dwellings there is a local tradition to the effect that "our owl' foore-faathers lived ther in times gone by, an' scrawp ther tayls off a climmin' up the stip slopes." Besides being blacksmith and choirman, "Young John" scares the birds from the wheat in the fields, and is empowered by the farmers to shoot rabbits and destructive birds. Many fieldfares visit the coomb in the winter months, in search of food; these the old man takes with the gun, and boils, them into broth; the smithy is often full of feathers plucked from birds obtained in this way.

A short distance from the blacksmith's shop lives the old thatcher, Steven Gray—whose brother, of the same trade, after half a century of work on ricks and roofs, fell from the top of one in the autumn, and was killed outright—and also Bill Adams, the carter, whose old dad drove a team of eight horses with one of the big waggons plying between Gloucester and London, before the railway-line to the west was made, or even thought of. When the track was laid hundreds of people swarmed off the downs, and ran for miles to see the first train pass along. The engine was the "comicallest theng" the carter "had ever seed"; a good many of the villagers took to their heels, saying the engine had "brawk the gyet down, an' runned away."

Adders have been found from time to time on the downs beyond Charlbury Tump, but they are rare hereabout, as also are snakes on the high ground, though they frequent the hollows, and especially the banks of the springs, where they obtain plenty of food. Both adders and snakes, when suddenly disturbed, occasionally, swallow their young, and disgorge them afterwards. I have heard of a grass snake having been taken and cooked, in the same way as one would serve an eel, for an experiment; the flesh was said to resemble that of the eel some what, and to be palatable enough.

In the fields below the village, not far from where the mill stood formerly, situated in a beautiful but lonely spot, on an eminence, is the farm of Mount Pleasant, and near by is an old mansion and farm called Earl's Court, which has had a romantic past, and which might provide abundant material for the imaginative writer to produce a masterpiece. The rambling old house, surrounded with deep pools, dates from the fifteenth century, and was once the abode of a Sir Anthony Hinton, whose antecedents gave their name to the village, which has happened in more cases than one

along the down-side. The rooms of the house are beautifully pan-
elled in the original oak; the old carved mantelpieces and cup-
boards remain intact; the massive wooden locks are still on the
doors, with the great curved iron keys within them, the wheel and
rack have not long dis appeared from the dark room at the back
on the ground floor; an air of mystery, like a spell, pervades the
place. In one of the upstair rooms is a shrine, used by the priests
in olden days, and near this is an apartment called "Taffy's room,"
which was bolted and sealed up for several centuries, and has not
been opened many years. The house was declared to be haunted,
years ago—the belief is not wholly dead yet—an attempt was
made to lay the ghost in this room, but the plan failed; instead,
those who undertook the pacificatory rites perished themselves,
and their spirits remained shut in the compartment.

The occupation of the place by spirits began at the time of the
Reformation, when the monks were turned adrift, and finally banished from Earl's Court. According to the account handed down,
before the monks were driven out they begged the fulfilment of one
prayer, which was granted—viz., that the house should be haunted
by ghosts for ever afterwards, and so it has been, as every successive
occupant has certainly believed. The first sign of the haunting was
that of the owls coming daily to perch upon the gable ends, blink-
ing at the farm folks, who were not long in finding a solution of
the phenomenon; they perceived it was the ghosts of the monks,
embodied in the owls, come back to enter the old haunts, and
continue their revels. From this time forth the visitations began in
deadly earnest; there was rattling of chains at midnight, shrieks and
cries, slamming of doors, gusts of wind down the passages, a sound
as of the rolling of cheeses about the bedroom floors, white hooded
faces peering through the windows, and all kinds of weird and
ghostly happenings. After this had been in progress for some time,
efforts were made to bring about peace with prayers and offerings;
some gave large donations to the church, some besprinkled the
walls and rooms with holy water, and others went on pilgrimages
to the shrines of the saints, but everything was in vain; still the

owls sat at noon on the gable ends, hooting and shrieking, and the house was disturbed with the unearthly visitants.

At last it was decided to lay the ghost, once and for all time. Accordingly, the "weirds," who had their home in the caves on the hill, were summoned, and their aid invoked; after a consultation in secret with the "powers," they made the announcement: Seven was the mystic number. So the "Seven" came—from where, no one knew—draped and hooded, in ghostly secrecy, and driven in coaches attended by serving-men as mute and inscrutable as the Seven themselves. First of all they sought out a room in the middle of the house, which henceforth was to be locked and sealed, and entered by no person. Here they chalked out a circle on the floor, and, standing within it, mumbled over a bookful of prayers backwards, one against the other, while the spirit flew whizzing round and round the circle, howling like a wild beast. After they had fixed it in human form with their incantations, the chief of the Seven addressed it saying: "In the name of the Us, I command thee to tell why thou art troubled." Hereupon, the spirit, that of one of the monks, entered upon a long and incoherent narration of griefs and sorrows that had befallen them consequent on their having been banished from the shrine at Earl's Court; when it had finished the Seven declared it to be laid for "a thousand years to-morrow." But there was a cunning cheat in the "to-morrow" part, which broke the spell, and prevented them from laying the spirit; instead, there was a mighty clap, like thunder in 'the house, and the Seven had vanished, leaving their own ghosts behind, black as rooks, confined in the room, moping and whimpering, and floating about, spinning and whirling, and scratching at the walls, but unable to escape from the doom appointed them.

After that the spirits of the monks assumed various forms. Sometimes they appeared in the guise of a fair lady, roaming about among the flowers in the moonlight; at another time they shone a flickering light, like the goblin Lanthorn Jack, to ensnare the unwary into the deep, dark pools standing alongside the house; now they hovered with faces infixed upon the window-panes at daybreak; now cutting hay upon the high stack in the farmyard; and again they were a hen and chicken clucking under the servant's feet as she descended the dark staircase in the winter mornings. One day the servant girl, in a fit of bravado, broke into the chamber with her broom and duster; there was the magic fire blazing up the chimney, and the seven dark figures nodding around. She shrieked with terror and fainted; when the farmer's wife came on the scene there was nothing visible but the white wood-ashes on the hearth, and the prostrate servant girl.

Following this, the pump was bewitched, the keys would not turn in the locks, the doors would not shut, the calves were still-born, and the quivering milk would leap out of the pail on to the dairy floor. So, too, a funeral bier, with nodding plumes, and seven dark figures seated upon it, kept coming and going, advancing and receding, over and over all night in the lane, and the foggers, coming to milking in the early hours, frequently saw an old hag, gripping a stout staff, floating across the large pool on a black calf, whom they several times accosted with: "Mother, you be late gwain whoam," to which she responded, with a wave of the stick: "I've heard un crack; I've heard un crack;" and suddenly vanished into thin air.

Such are the stories told of Earl's Court, and much gossip besides, which may not be true, but certain it is that "Taffy's room" exists, and equally certain is it that it was bolted up for centuries; what is more, traces of the ghosts are said to exist to-day, for it is not many months since a guest at Earl's Court, a complete stranger to the place, and one absolutely unacquainted with its history, surprised the farmer and his wife one morning by resolutely affirming that in the early hours he awoke to find a strange white face, enclosed in an antique hood, looking in upon him through the window.

A short way below Earl's Court, spanning the River Cole, is Acorn Bridge, the scene of many famous contests between prizefighters and others, before the railway was made, and brought civilization to the spot. The last great fight there, remembered by the rustics, was between two champions nicknamed "The Mouse," and "The

Earwig." This time the fighting lasted for five hours, and one of the combatants fought with a broken arm for half the period.

There was a small inn standing a short way off, on the roadside, kept by one named Ricks, whose son, being half-witted, and not to be managed, was despatched off to the workhouse at the neighbouring village of Stratton St. Margaret. Being here intractable also, and refusing to eat, the master of the place, thinking to frighten him into submission, shut him in the dead-house all night with the corpses. But the idiot was not to be overcome so easily, and was far from being terrified with the presence of the dead. During the night he lifted one of these from its coffin, stripped off his own clothes, and dressed the corpse in them, and stood it against the wall, just inside the door; then he put the dead man's shroud on himself, and lay down in the coffin, and remained silent. By-and-by the workhouse master came, bearing food for the prisoner. Unlocking the door, he approached the corpse, standing up, and held out the food, at the same time saying: "Will you have it now?" As there was no answer forthcoming he asked again: "Will you have it now?" Then, before he could realize anything, up jumped the idiot, clad in the white shroud, from the coffin, and cried: "If he won't have it, I wull." The workhouse chief dropped the food and ran off, but so great was his fright, and the shock so severe, that he died from it soon afterwards.

A little more than a mile east of Earl's Court, perched upon a small hill, and surrounded with tall elms, beeches, and apple orchards, the rosy-white bloom of which scents the air with fragrance in the early summer, is the pretty village of Bourton, whose inhabitants, undisturbed by the noises and fever of whirling life, dwell in peace and quiet, and follow their pursuits on the farm, leading a simple, guileless existence. Here every house and building is of stone, well made, with large gardens, and plenty of room and light; it is altogether a model village. This was brought about by a beneficent landlord, who came a stranger, and sympathized with the poor; he had all the ruinous cottages removed and filled their places with substantial modern dwellings. Nearly every cottage has gardens and parterre in front; these the occupants tend with great pride and care, vying with each other in the production of beautiful blooms.

In the centre of the village, on the hill, is a large open space—formerly the village green—where stands the shattered trunk of a once mighty elm tree, shading an ancient monolith, round which the children play; and hard by is the blacksmith's shop, where, from morn till night, toils the brawny man with the hammer and tools, puffing up the yellow flames from the forge, and making the place ring with the blows of the hammer on the sounding anvil. Here it was the ancient games were kept at Feast-time, formerly called "The Rout," as is indicated in the local rhyme:

> Shrivenham Revels, and Bourton Rout,
> The Watchfield pot boils, and the fire is out.

The games, however, were not of the boisterous and vigorous order, such as took place along the hill-side—back-swording, wrestling, and the rest; instead, the chief diversion was bowling for cakes, climbing the greasy pole for a leg of mutton, and, most loved of all, step-dancing, sometimes in the open, and sometimes in the big barn near by, fitted out for the occasion. To compete for the leg of mutton, a waggon-wheel was first laid on the ground, and a Dutch Barnpole, well-greased, with the leg of mutton on top, infixed into it; the men had to climb up and reach the mutton from the top. The winner was usually one who stood by and waited till several others had nearly gained the top, and so cleaned the pole, then he, smothering his front with dust, "climmed up an' ed un," to use the rustic's own words.

The step-dancing was a very pleasing pastime, exceedingly popular with all. In these young and old, male and female, took part, and the young girls and women wore pretty caps of lace and silk, and those who were possessed of the daintiest received prizes, awarded by judges on the spot. In the step-dancing the ground was marked out with parallel lines, and the dancers were allocated to certain spaces; as the fiddles played they proceeded along the lines, working out figures with great skill and pretty motions to the tune of:

> Charlie over the water,
>> Charlie over the lea,
> Charlie loves to kiss the girls
>> As sweet as sugar-candy.

Old Elijah Wheatley, nearly ninety, with shaggy, grey hair, and smiling face, still hums the airs played on the fiddles at the dancing when he was a young man. He says: "There was never any rough games at Bourton, but everything was for happiness and jolliness, you know. The little children used to come, and the mothers and fathers, and the poor old folks, and smile at the dancers, and everyone was happy and glad."

The old man relates a striking tradition in connection with the monolith, standing near the elm-tree. He says it was neither a church cross, nor a market cross, but was originally set up by the Saxons to commemorate the driving out of the Danes, in the time of Ethelred. There is another relic of this in the Hocker Bench, at Bishopstone, near by, where the villagers kept a festival to celebrate the same thing, and it is known that this locality was well-loved by the Danes. What is more striking still—and there is that which is pathetic about it—is that the Danish settlers' parting words to the Saxon villagers should have been perpetuated all these years, and brought down to the present time. Thus, old Elijah declares that the Danes grieved deeply at having to leave the lovely land; they said England was their country, and they should come back again, which the villagers always expected, and which Elijah even now believes. "They allus said they'd come back, and they wants to come back, and they *hull* come back, too, some day, right anuff," he tells you. As to this, there would be some difference of opinion, but the tradition itself is a unique and extraordinary thing.

XII

The stream and water-meadow—Flight of
plovers—Bishopstone—The coomb—Dab-chicks—
"Hocking"—"Time bushes"—Watercress beds—The
village tailor—The basket-maker—Idstone

At the bottom of Cowtail Coomb, underneath Charlbury Hill, a
spring bursts out and flows down between beds of bright amber-
coloured willow, tipped with crimson, and plunges under the
narrow road leading along the hillside, then leaps through into the
meadows, soon to join a larger stream that turns the mill-wheel at
Bishopstone. Immediately after the confluence the brook, running
between steep banks, and shaded with boughs of ash and maple,
shoots sidelong, and dives through a narrow bridge beneath the
highroad, and roars out on the other side, and then goes foaming
away round a bend, under tall willows, out of sight of the traveller,
known only to the wild things of Nature, the farm-folks, and the
cattle in the fields. The bridge is of two walls, with large flat stones
overlaid; at the end, where the stream emerges, above the water, is
a recess, large enough to contain two persons, and concealed from
the road with thick boughs of maple, which droop down to the
level of the stream. Large moss-covered stones oppose the passage
of the water, roaring through the bridge; the spray is dashed widely
around. It is delightful to climb down from the road above when
the fierce summer sun is scorching hill and valley, and refresh one-
self in the cool dewy shelter. The stones of the walls are green with
ivy and herb robert, and there is usually an inquisitive redbreast or
wren hopping about in the maple bushes.

There is a water-meadow, fed by the spring a short distance back, on the upper side of the bridge. Some parts of the meadow are high above the stream-bed; it almost seems as though the water had flowed uphill to reach them, but that has been carried down from a greater height at the other end of the field. Near Liddington Mill is a water-meadow twenty feet above the stream-bed. This was brought about by damming up the stream and diverting the water; by this means land that was naturally dry and barren was made to produce an abundant crop of grass. It is astonishing to what a depth the springs carve down for some distance after leaving the hillside. This is caused by the powerful rush of the water leaping down the slopes when the springs are full; as it reaches the level fields the force subsides, and there is scarcely any wearing of the bed and banks.

In winter, during the sharp frosts, when everything else is rigid and iron-like, the water-meads will not have frozen over, especially where they are elevated and uneven; the flow of the water will prevent the ice from forming there. A great many birds flock to the water-meadows then, and among them crowds of plovers, which alight in the shallows, and wade about in search of food. Before alighting in the water they fly round and round, and to and fro, many times, as though shy of the pools, then presently swoop down and lodge all together. Their manoeuvres in mid-air are extremely swift and interesting to follow. The beating of their wings is rapid and regular; at one time they mount up in the form of a black pillar, now wheel quickly round, turning half over, their breasts gleaming like silver in the sunlight, then, as they right about, and fly in a level line, they almost vanish from sight, and only show a faint thin line, till they execute another turning movement and come flying back once more towards you.

The village of Bishopstone lies along the hillside, about a mile from Charlbury Tump, and is almost concealed on three sides, with dense elm-trees, which tower above the farmhouses and cottages. These elms flourish well around all the down-side villages, which may be because of their being situated in the coombs, since the soil is deeper there; you can locate all the villages of the hillside by observing the density of the trees, standing afar off in the valley.

The village, by reason of its location, compactness, and fine natural scenery, is the prettiest of all the down-side, taken as one view. It is grouped around the mouth of a magnificent coomb, and the houses stand in terraces, or singly, perched one above the other, beginning at the bottom of a series of dells, which branch off from the centre of the place. Pretty walks and paths wind round and round, and up and down, between evergreen box hedges—often twenty feet in height—leading to the cottages; the slopes of the dells are covered with gardens and orchards. Flowing through the coomb, for nearly a mile, is a powerful spring, which forms a large pool in the centre of the place, supplying the folks with abundant water, and turning the mill-wheel by the roadside. After leaving the mill the sparkling water is conveyed hither and thither, through numerous hollows, each containing several watercress beds, and finally emerges into the meadows below.

Nearly all the cottages are built of chalk, and have thatched roofs. The majority of them are ancient, and many are of a great size, rambling in structure, with big rooms, and beams like huge trees, supporting the floors above. Roses and creepers climb up over the porches and windows, adding a grace to the almost snow-white walls; large trained pear-trees spread their arms along from end to end between the windows and roof, and down to the ground, bearing beautiful clusters of brilliant bloom, and choice rich fruits. Some of these trees are nearly 300 years old, and are still healthy and prolific.

The coomb is the greatest and most remarkable of all throughout the down-side. It has its beginning immediately under the northeast side of Charlbury Tump, and is about half a mile in length. The head is scooped out in triangular form, and is terraced round on all three sides, the whole resembling a vast amphitheatre, with banks of huge seats for the spectators. Half-way down a narrow gorge, sharp and steep, enters from the east: the bottom of the coomb is level, like a track, and bears the trace of water, while the gorge, from its abruptness, appears to have been carved out by ice. A square dew-pond gleams like a lucid gem in the centre of the hollow; rough patches of long grass are dotted about the slopes; while here and there a great hawthorn bush, centuries old, is outlined against the blue sky: the view is one of rugged grandeur with features of exquisite beauty. As you walk around the banks of the coomb—called "The Linches"—towards the village, you are confronted with an optical illusion; the ground and cottages underneath seem to be proceeding rapidly ahead of you, while the avenue over opposite appears to be approaching and receding behind. The sound of the horse's gallop along the village street echoes loudly up the coomb; you may plainly hear it three-quarters of a mile away.

In the centre of the village is a large square pool formed by the waters of the spring, which are dammed back by the road passing along the hillside; and, higher up, beyond a series of watercress beds, surrounded with cottages and gardens, is a square troughlike place—fed by a rippling spring of crystal clearness—called William's Well, where the cottagers obtain their drinking-water, and which has never yet been known to fail. Two hatches regulate the water in the pool. One of these admits the current, passing beneath the road, to the mill-wheel exactly opposite; the other carries off the overplus, which runs under the road and falls below for a distance of twenty feet with a loud plashing noise, and hurries away, white with foam, among the beds of brown and green cresses.

The pool is inhabited by a score of moorhens and several pairs of dab-chicks, which swim about quite unconcernedly with the ducks, coming quite close to the edge of the pond, and even stalking about the cottagers' paths around the doors. These live chiefly on the insects about the pool and beds—such as freshwater shrimps—and the miller feeds them twice a day with bran and meal. The dab-chicks are smaller than the moorhens, roundish in shape, and brown in colour. Their motions and doings on the pool are very interesting; it is amusing to watch their curious antics in the water, swimming to and fro, and plunging down out of sight among the green, gauzelike weeds. The ducks and moorhens merely stand on their heads and grope about on the bottom, but the dab-chicks, being much smaller, with a pretty effort, dive right under and remain there about one third of a minute before coming to the surface again.

The mill stands on the opposite side of the highway, and is built up from the hollow beneath. The great iron wheel is situated outside the building, with its top slightly below the level of the pond; the third floor and entrance are even with the road. Here, in times past, the corn was brought from off the hills, and converted into flour, to supply the village and the countryside round about. The machinery is still used for gristing, but not for fine flour; almost every day the huge wheel revolves under the weight of the foaming water, and rumbles beneath the high wall. The school, the blacksmith's shop, and the mill are all close together; the children are happy in their situation, and in the opportunities they have for viewing the several industries; they throng around the smithy door, and peer over at the mighty wheel each time they pass along, delighted to see the gleaming waters leaping down, and to view the merry fizzing sparks shooting out underneath the stroke of the blacksmith's hammer.

The village church stands about a stone's-throw from the mill. This is a fine large building in the Norman style of architecture, with a high massive tower, which has been girded about with several stout iron bands, made by the village smith in the churchyard itself. It is said that the old peal of bells—lately destroyed by a fire—were cast in the churchyard; this was to save carriage, according to the sexton's account. There are eight bells in the tower in place of those that were destroyed; guilds of ringers come from a great distance to "ring the changes" on these, while the parish team exercise their skill, ringing out the "Grandsire Trebles," the "Double Norwich Peal," and the "Peal of Bob Major." The big bell of the tower is rung every night during the winter from eight till nine, as a guide for any who may be lost on the downs. This the villagers call the "kyfew" (curfew). The custom was instituted by one who was himself lost on the downs, who heard the bell ringing in the darkness, and was guided by it; accordingly he left a sum of money to pay the ringer for all time.

In the belfrey, preserved in a case, is an ancient clock, made by an old-time village blacksmith, which recorded the flight of the hours for no less than 238 years. The frame and wheels of this are very stout and strong, and every year, at spring cleaning, the sexton took it out into the churchyard and set fire to it, to burn off the oil and grease; afterwards it was replaced in its position and went all the better for the cleaning.

A century ago, when the villages of the down-side were infested with robbers, the thieves used to bring their plunder to Bishopstone, and conceal it in the tombs, with the bones and dust of the dead. Here, too, in times past, the poor folks used to assemble in the porches to receive their alms, wearing a red badge on the arm, containing the letters B.P.—Bishopstone Paupers—while the villagers' sheep were brought regularly to graze in the churchyard on the Sabbath, the tinkling of the bells agreeing well with the music of the anthem inside.

In the centre of the village, near the blacksmith's shop, is a spot called Hocker Bench, a title which is almost meaningless to the inhabitants to-day, but the place was a noted rendezvous in the past, and the site of the annual revels of Hocktide. The festival of Hocktide, which fell about Easter-time, was the survival of an ancient Saxon custom called Hocking, a kind of joy-day held to commemorate the death of the Danish tyrant Hardicanute, and the final extinction of the Danish power, in the year 1042. Here the oldest men of the village, calling themselves Aldermen of Hocker Bench, and wearing badges and insignia, resorted to keep good order, and to be spectators of the dancing, and pastimes of the younger. There was formerly a play of Hocktide, which the good men of Coventry petitioned they might act before Queen Elizabeth, and received her consent to do so. When it was produced—at Kenilworth—the Queen "laughed right well," and gave the players two bucks, and five marks in money.

The villagers blame the police regulations for the extinction of the old festivities; by prohibiting all concourse in the streets and open spaces, and driving the feasters and revellers into far-off fields and obscure corners, they brought about the death of the old fairs and amusements. In many cases the village clergy took a leading part in smashing up the old games, without increasing their congregations, however; it is common knowledge that the churches in country places are barer and emptier than ever before.

Some of the old feudal customs still continued at Bishopstone till a century and a half ago, although the manorial system has long since gone out of date. Then every plough, or team, belonging to the tenants of the manor estates, at three days' warning, made, in the old husbandman's phrase, "three journeys," viz: ploughed three days for the lord of the Manor, at 2d. a day, and bread and cheese gratis. At wheat-harvest, likewise, every tenant was bound, at three days' warning, to maintain a reaper. These had their breakfast at home, and were afterwards entertained at the lord of the Manor's expense. At dinner-time every man had one pound of beef, one pound of mutton, a handful of salt, four pounds of bread, and a liberal supply of home-brewed ale. This was served to them in the field; at evening they all came to the Manor House and again each had four pounds of bread, one pound of cheese, a large cup of ale, and a candle.

The old-fashioned farmers around Bishopstone and Idstone, down to few years ago, used to give their workpeople three meals a day—dinner, tea, and supper—regularly throughout the hay and corn-harvest. The dinner was a hot meal, consisting of boiled legs of mutton, and pieces of beef, several kinds of vegetables, and a huge roly-poly suety pudding. This was cooked each day over the faggot fire in the brew-house, then it was carefully stowed in the clean bright milk-pails and carried out into the fields with the yokes. "This used to put some life into us, an' mek us strong an' 'earty; we didn't mind buckin' in an' doin' a bit extra aater that," the old carter declared.

The farmers used also to sell the tail-wheat to the men, at a low rate; this was sent to the mill near by and ground into flour, and afterwards baked in the cottage oven. The bread made from this was very brown and sweet, but cheap and nutritious. When bread was wanted in a hurry, and the housewife had no time in which to heat the oven, she used to mix the flour thinly and make cakes in the frying-pan over the flames. The old style of making emergency bread—and which is still in vogue in foreign countries—was to make a wood fire, and place a fair-sized smooth stone therein, and when the stone was well heated, to remove it from the ashes, clean it, and wrap the flour paste around it. We have all heard of King Alfred tending the cakes cooking on the hearth, and how he allowed them to burn, and was scolded by the good-wife. Respecting the kind of cakes, there has probably been some misconception; there can be no doubt but that they were the famous "barley bangers," baked in the old three-legged pot, which were such favourites in great King Alfred's land, and, later, throughout all the western counties.

The tops of the downs above the village are widely cultivated and grow abundant crops of wheat and oats; here the teams are at work all the year round: ploughing, harrowing, and drilling. The bright plough-shares are visible a long way off in sunny weather; each time the plough turns at the headland the polished share gleams like a diamond in the sunlight two miles away.

A short distance from the Ridgeway are the remains of a Roman station, and, high upon the downs towards Russley, are two aged hawthorn trees, known respectively as the "one o'clock bush," and the "two o'clock bush." These are so called because the ploughmen and harvesters tell the time with them: when the sun is exactly above the first it is one o'clock, and when it is above the other it is two o'clock. The labourers on the downs still make for themselves sundials for use in the fields. To do this they merely thrust a wand into the ground and note the shadows at the different hours, cutting out marks in the short turf with their pocket-knives.

The village could formerly boast of many industries. At one time nearly all the cottages had spinning-wheels and looms, and wove woollen stuffs and willow fibre. Large quantities of hemp were grown in the neighbourhood, and the fibre prepared at

Bishopstone, and afterwards sent away for manufacture into ropes and sacking. There were also premises for making whiting from the down chalk, a bone mill, a soap and candle works, and glove-and gaiter-making. Besides this there is the watercress industry, and the village has its smithy, its tailor, and basket-maker. One of the curios exhibited in the village is an old fire-engine that did service for 300 years, and has only recently been superseded. Formerly fires were very much more common about the downs than they are now; ricks and farm buildings were often ablaze: there was more incendiarism prevalent sixty years ago than there is in our day. During the time of the agricultural riots the old engine was in constant demand to put out farm fires; it is a wonder the rioters did not single out that, too, and smash it up with the new-fangled threshers and other plant.

The watercress beds lie along the bottom of the coomb, from where the spring bubbles out of the hillside, down to the mill-pond, and all about the hollows in the centre of the village, sheltered with the high, warm hedges, and overhung with the elm-tree boughs. The beds are divided with banks of turf or stone, set across; a small opening is left for the water to run through, passing from bed to bed, or, if the current is too swift, that is conducted along a channel at one side, and only allowed to filter through the loose stones and so keep the cress supplied. The beds are renovated each year, in the early autumn, when all the cress has been cut. First the bed is cleaned out, and well raked over, in order to remove all the old roots and weeds; then fresh rootless stems are set in the loose sand or gravel, about six inches apart, and in about half a foot of water. If the springs are high, and the bottom "brashy" (stony), a small stone is laid on the stem to keep it in place; roots very soon shoot from the stalk and find a holding in the bottom. The plants grow all through the winter, and are ready with a yield in February, under favourable conditions; though if the springs have been low and the weather severe, it will be later; the cress cannot stand hard frost, and unless it is covered with water, it will soon be withered up, especially in the bleak winds of January.

There is no fertilizer used with the cress in the beds; a sprinkling of lime to destroy the insects is all that is needed: the springs abound with freshwater shrimps, and these would soon devour a bed of cress if they were not seen to. It is not advisable to replant from the same bunches each year, otherwise the cress would very soon deteriorate in quality, as in the case of vegetables and corn crops; the plants need changing to insure a vigorous growth. Some of the owners of the beds search along the small brooks and ditches in the fields, and by the road-side, and obtain fresh plants there; these thrive best of all, and yield a heavy crop when they are transplanted into the clear spring waters. Blight attacks the cress in the beds, and gets stronger every year, interfering with the industry. This is brought about by a small blue fly, like a lady-bird, which lays the germs in the banks beside the water. The occupiers of the beds tar the banks in order to destroy the germs, but every year the pest increases.

The watercress industry, if conducted thoroughly, is a profitable one; a certain income is assured to those who are willing to pay sufficient attention to the beds. It is difficult to obtain labour in planting out the beds and cutting the cress, on account of having to stand in the water; a great many men who do this are afflicted with rheumatism. The men wear top-boots at the work, and are paid at the rate of 3s. a day. The value of the cress is not as high as it was formerly; twenty years ago it fetched 15s. a flat (hamper), whereas to-day it is sold at 8s. for the same quantity. The Bishopstone product is far-famed, and was in great request in the markets of London, Birmingham, and Manchester; but many of the beds are dilapidated now, there is not nearly as much cress grown as there used to be.

The old tailor and breeches-maker, whose father and grandfather were masters of the craft, still carries on his trade and does good business with farmers and others for many miles around, in spite of the competition of big concerns, which tend to crush out the small village workshops. But the old fellow has methods of his own, together with a rare skill in the use of scissors and needle; his customers are numbered all over the world: in Africa, Germany, India, America, and elsewhere. His father and grandfather were makers of the old leather breeches, and one of them may possibly have made those belonging to unhappy Job Cork, whose pair was baked in the oven, and caused the wearer such inconvenience, since Bishopstone is not far from the White Horse, where the old Shepherd tended his flocks three-quarters of a century ago. But the old leather kinds have passed away now, and have given place to cheap corduroys and shoddy, in the case of the labouring classes, at least.

The tailor's shop stands near the True Heart Inn, and but a few paces from Hocker Bench. The house is ancient and rambling in structure, with a roof of thick, warm thatch. Here three journey-men are constantly employed, usually seated on the floor, cutting out, stitching together, and finishing the suits. The tailor's "goose," "gander," and "gosling," are cooking in the oven near by, as they jestingly say: these are the three flat-irons, used for pressing the seams of the cloth.

The old tailor, though drawing near to eighty, is as quick-witted and energetic as ever he was. He is tall in stature, with fresh complexion, sharp keen eyes, and a bit of grey beard underneath the chin. His speech is short and quick, with a kind of Scotch accent, and he is very deaf. Every year he issues a special almanac, prefaced with a quotation from his old Breeches Bible: "And they sewed figge-tree leaves together, and made themselves breeches," adding that "improvements have been made since the first pairs." His grandfather was the village constable at the time of the Chartist Riots; the ancient sword and staff used during the disturbances are still preserved behind the counter at the shop, with many other curios: tinder-boxes, flails, venerable books, handcuffs, Roman horseshoes, and a cow-bell, six pounds in weight, which used to hang around the necks of the cows grazing on the common lands, before they were enclosed. In the lot is a huge old leather-bound Prayer-Book, such as the rustics used to carry under their arms to church every Sabbath morning. This particular one belonged to a labourer, and has a tale attached to it. One day the parson came into the labourer's house; there was only the boy at home.

"Ha!" said the cleric, looking round the room; "I'm glad to see you've got the good Book in the house, my boy."

"Ya-as, zur," the youth answered.

"And when does your father use it?" continued the parson.

"Every Zunday marnin', zur," was the reply.

"And how does he use it? Does he stand up and read it to you like this?" inquired the vicar, taking the book in his hands.

"No-o-o! A oni sharpens 'is razzur on in," replied the youth, with a contemptuous toss of the head.

The basket-maker, who is almost blind, dwells alone in a large old cottage standing by the road side as you come up the hill. His small yard and garden are packed with bundles of withy, fresh from the beds; other bundles, some of a bright amber colour, and some stripped of the bark, ready for weaving into white wicker-work, are brought indoors, and placed under the window, or stacked in the large pantry. He has his seat on the floor in the large room, and works away unmolested, for he is his own master, and pleases himself as to the number of hours he toils, and the quantity of baskets he makes. There are three kinds of withy in general use for basket-making, these are: "Black Jack"—of a dark colour—"Spaniard"—dark green—and "Black Sally," the commonest kind of all, which is very brittle and inferior. All withies vary in quality according to the situation and soil in which they grow; a clay ground produces the best willows. The basket-maker's tools are: a shop-knife, a pick ing-knife, shears, a bodkin, a shave, an upright, a plane, a cleaver, a heavy iron with a ring at one end for straightening out the knots, a screw-block, and a lap-board. He makes baskets of many kinds, great and small, good serviceable stuff, warranted to wear well, and, though very short-sighted, he is quick and clever at his trade. By working hard he would make three round bushel baskets a day, which would earn him about 5s. 6d., but flat cress-baskets are those most usually required. The beams of the old house are as large as trees, and the chalk walls are much worn with the wet, and almost ready to tumble down in places. The average weekly rent of cottages in Bishopstone is 1s. 6d. or 2s., with large gardens, but actual wages are low: shepherds and carters only obtain 13s. or 14s. and day men 11s. to 12s. a week.

About a mile to the east of Bishopstone, under the hill, is the hamlet of Idstone. Long lines of tall elms, clustered with ivy, stand along the hillside, and shade the roadway and farm buildings; the whole surroundings are softly beautiful, and typical of the hill scenery. From the village a hard road runs steeply up to the broad downs, and joins the Ridgeway about half a mile from the crest. Half-way up the hill, near the road, is a pretty dingle wood of hazel, guelder-rose, spindle-tree, and wild cherry. The ground, in the open spaces, is blue with violets in spring; the hedges are so thickly overgrown and interwoven with bryony that you cannot see into them. A green path, used by the shepherds, leads through the midst of the dingle, and brings you out on to the open corn-grounds above. The stems of the spindle-tree continue a deep green after years of growth, and they are very tough and strong. The brilliant scarlet berries of the guelder-rose still hang on the boughs, throughout March, and the peggles, too, though the birds, and especially the fieldfares, have fed on them all the winter. In Berkshire the rustics call hawthorn berries not peggles, but "haggas."

The hamlet of Idstone, though formerly of some importance, has fallen away now, and dropped out of notice. It contains a few rich farms, and cottages for the labourers; there are no other residents. The romantic-looking old Inn, which bore the name of "Trip the Daisy," has been closed this many a day; there is nowhere for the labourers to go in the evening, to while away an hour, unless they choose to walk to Ashbury or Bishopstone. The little children, after school, play about in the farmyard, or in the sheds, at hide-and-seek in the carts and waggons, or scamper about among the trusses of hay and straw on the ground, or peep through the fence and watch their fathers milking the cows, or foddering the young cattle.

In days gone by the tiny hamlet was noted for spinning and weaving, and especially for the manufacture of woollen rugs and mops, which all the farmers' wives used at that time, instead of house-cloths. Granny Dobson was the last to do weaving in the place, nearly three-quarters of a century ago. The aged carter at the farm, who is eighty-five, remembers the industry, and has a touching story to tell of the poor old woman, who, too old to weave any more, was starved to death with a wretched allowance of 2s. a week, granted by the parish. One bitter winter's day, after a severe fall of snow, while he was in the stable attending to his horses, something seemed to tell him that the old woman was without food. Being obsessed with the thought for a long time, he went home and acquainted his wife, and she set out for the cottage. When she arrived, there was the old dame, sure enough, foodless and fireless, and half perished, but too resigned to beg; she had had neither food nor fire for three or four days. Thereupon the carter's wife, with none too much for themselves, fetched a loaf and butter, warm drink, and fuel for the fire, while granny knelt down in tears and thanked God for putting it into the carter's mind to come and visit her at such a timely hour.

The old carter, though so full of years, has about twenty hives of bees, which he himself sees to, and disposes of the pure honey at 6d. per pound. He loves the tiny denizens of the hives, and pays careful attention to their habits and haunts, and is fully persuaded that the bees understand what he says to them as they enter and leave the hives, and crawl over his hands and arms. The custom of "telling the bees" is common all along the down-side, and one old lady was certain that the bees sang the Psalms at night in their houses, but this the carter is inclined to disbelieve, and he half doubts the other, saying: "Dursay 'tis oni a lot o' owl' tales as folks have hatched up."

XIII

Features of the downs—Ashbury—The old Manor
House—The hurdle-maker—Ashdown House and
Wood—Kingstone Coomb—The Upper Mill—
The wheel and machinery—Grinding operations

THOUGH ALL THE VILLAGES OF the down-side have many things
in common, the same physical characteristics, and general
scenery, the same type of cottages and farmhouses, there is still a
delightful variation all along the line in their altitude, disposition,
and aspect, and in the individual features and detailed beauty of each
separate place. The slopes of the downs, if they have general forms,
are continually changing and interchanging in localities, assuming
new and strange shapes, charming and surprising with their grace
and exquisiteness, at one time standing out bold and abrupt as a
mountain ledge, at another sweeping, curving, and winding round
in a serpentine, or blending and interfusing, full of sweetness, of a
delicate green, or rich brown, golden, purple, or faint blue, or indigo,
or robed in pearly mist; for ever reflecting the mood of the heavens,
and sympathetic with the heart and feelings of man. The coombs,
which are such a remarkable feature of the down-side, are seldom
alike in formation, and by their diversity and mystery compel us to
explore them all, and linger amid their gentle beauty, grandeur, or
solitariness.

The cottages, too, though of the same general type, have endless
variety of form and picturesqueness, especially those old ones which
are built of chalk-stone. These, often with their fifteenth-century
pattern of architecture, their huge beams, overhanging courts and

windows, quaint gables, and walls held and riveted together with strong irons, leaning here, and bulging there, marked and figured with endless hieroglyphics, together with the crooks and bends, and angles of the streets, are always productive of new interest. Here the grey old church tower looms high upon the hillside, as at Wroughton, Liddington, and Wanborough, or peeps out from among beautiful trees, as at Hinton Parva, and Bishopstone, or keeps majestic guard over the closely nestling houses and streets, as at Aldbourne; the compactness of one, the diffuseness of another, the height of this and the depth of that, the light and shade, and local colour of grass and corn crops, and the quiet natural beauty common to all, give to each its distinctive feature, and make them consimilar, too: the view is of a complete panorama, with fresh charms and delights scattered everywhere throughout the picture.

The village of Ashbury, midway between Charlbury Hill and the White Horse, is perched upon the hillside, higher than Bishopstone and Hinton, at an altitude corresponding with that of Wanborough and Liddington, but lower than Baydon, out of sight over the downs, five miles away to the south. The village is very ancient, dating, historically, from the early Saxon times, when it was a bone of contention between the men of Wessex and those of Mercia; in the end it was wrested from the West Saxons by Offa, King of the North countrymen. The whole of this district, from the River Thames to the chalk range of Ashdown, was a kind of debatable land between the Kings of Wessex and Mercia till the latter were finally subdued by Egbert. Later on, the village became an important ecclesiastical centre, being connected with the two great medieval Abbeys of Abingdon and Glastonbury.

The name Ashbury signifies "the hill of the ash," for which tree the locality was famed, though the wood is become scarce at this time. The land beneath the hill lies low and swampy, and the spring that rises at Idstone has a difficulty in finding a passage out, before it saunters away down the valley. At first view it looks to be actually flowing up-hill—a common kind of illusion near the down slope—but this is because of the several gradients, which are deceiving and puzzling to the eye of the novice.

The majority of the cottages are chalk-made, and very ancient; many of them are strengthened with iron bars passed through from side to side, with a flat S piece bolted on the exterior, to hold them together. Here and there you meet with a cottage built entirely of sarsen-stones, or of flints with brick corners, or of small, hand-made bricks, many centuries old, exceedingly quaint in structure. The walls of the chalk-built cottages are very thick and warm, and the interiors large and comfortable, and the roof is invariably of thatch; slates and tiles are rarely found in conjunction with chalk materials. The windows of many of these cottages are strikingly picturesque, showing a deep clear blue in contrast with the gleaming walls; and no one possesses the art of making a window appear beautiful in a greater degree than do the village housewives. The clear, polished panes of glass, the dainty lace or muslin curtains within, and the brilliant red or ivy-leaved geranium, lily, or cineraria growing in the china or earthenware pot, often standing in a tea-saucer, take the eye of all who pass down the streets, and every cottager's wife is adjudged by the appearance of her windows from the roadway. Dwellers in the town have not the art of window arrangement, to make them look attractive and beautiful; though there are the dust and smoke to contend with. Here and there the rustics keep their few books or musical instrument in the window, and I have seen the cottage store of best china and glassware arranged there, too, which looked very pretty and sweet.

The old church stands immediately above the village, on the hillside, and is reached by a steep, narrow roadway bordered by several cottages of unusual quaintness, singular in having their corners bevelled off, which is unusual even in the oldest houses of the down-side. The church is a large, flattish building, of mixed styles and dates, with a little Saxon, Norman, and Early English architecture, full of strange nooks and crannies, all "higgledy-piggledy," as the sexton calls it, with exquisite bits of workmanship here and there, and many curios, dear to students and others, who revel in romantic lore and antiquities. Running round the church, on the side facing the hill, is a stone gutter, six feet deep, to carry off the water during heavy rainfalls; and the large burial-place is surrounded with tall elm-trees on the east, south, and west. The tombs are in a very dilapidated state; the walls of some are fallen away, discovering the interiors, and the stones are covered with a luxuriant growth of purplish-brown ivy, some of which has entered the gaping sepulchres and half filled them with the foliage. The graves and open spaces, in the spring, are golden with crocus and celandine; in the summer-time the delicate harebell, trefoil, scabious, and mallows mingle with the short green and brown turf. The several families of the village have a separate corner allotted them in the churchyard; and there is a sweet confusion in the disposition of the graves, which is pleasanter to find than the conventional rows and lines in most burial-grounds.

Near the entrance to the village, alongside the road, is a small coomb with very steep banks, thick with tall, stately elms, the bottom of which contains several watercress beds fed by a copious spring, and, immediately on the other side, half hidden behind the foliage, is a magnificent old manor house of the twelfth century, round which the imaginative writer might weave a deathless story, for there is no lack of suggestiveness to provide him with suitable materials. The huge, grey buttressed walls, covered with rose, pear, and ivy, the old porch with original door, heavily studded with iron, and the ecclesiastical looking windows, beautifully carved, still retaining the stout iron bars, together with the tall, taper chimneys, form a solemn and stately picture, and its close proximity to the dark, pitlike coomb invests it with a suitable gruesomeness. The interior of the building is splendidly furnished with fine oak panelling, carved beams, and cornices, and the dining-room, before its partition, was a superb apartment. There are traces of shrines and cells in the upper parts, and a large corridor passes through the middle of the house, by which a right of way was bad for horsemen and others by a path leading down through the valley. At the rear of the house are the remains of several gigantic trees of ash and walnut, many centuries old; a large mill-bay and fish-pond extended round below the garden and grounds.

There were formerly two mills at Ashbury, besides the two still working at Kingstone, near by, but they have long since been done away with, though the mill cottages remain to mark the spot where the wheels were situated. One of the mills was burned down, many years ago, through the instrumentality—it is said—of a rival miller at Kingstone, who was promptly apprehended and transported for the offence, but as the industry was already on the decline, the mill was not re-erected.

The village of Ashbury, in common with others of the down-side, had its cottage industries till half a century ago. These were spinning and weaving wool, straw-plaiting, and bonnet-making, which was a regular trade of the neighbourhood. Both wheat and rye-straw was used for the plaiting, with a preference for the rye product, since this retains its brightness of colour much longer than the other, and is more durable also. The straw for the plaiting was obtained direct from the farmers' barns, and the heads of the wheat and rye were cut off before the threshing, so that the straws were unbroken, and in excellent condition. When the straw had been plaited into strips, it was passed through a small hand-roller machine and pressed out, and the strips were afterwards sewn together. The local name for a spinning-wheel is a "lath"; many of the cottages contained these till a few years ago; they have not long been broken up and destroyed by those of a younger and unsympathetic generation.

Uriah Partridge, the old hurdle-maker, the last of his kind in the village, and the only representative of the trade for many miles around, dwells with his son and daughter in a big roomy cottage, and still makes a few hurdles, farm-gates, ladders, cow-cribs, and sheep-cages for use in the locality. Formerly, when there were more flocks kept upon the downs, there was a constant demand for close and flake hurdles, and cages to contain hay for the sheep, but since these have dwindled the trade has fallen off; the hurdles and things are now more commonly made at shops and workyards in the county towns.

Old Uriah is a gentle, cheerful soul, getting hard on for eighty, of medium height and healthy appearance, with kind smiling eyes, musical speech, and pleasant behaviour. His mother was a straw-plaiter and bonnet-maker, and his father was of the same trade as himself. He began work as a boy in Ashdown Woods, two miles away over the hill, and received 1s. 6d. a week in wages, which his good old mother described as being 1d. a day for walking up the hill, 1d. a day to come down it, and 1d. a day for the work he did. In the winter-time, in frosty weather, the hill is very slippery; one old carter declared he had to "craal up an 'is 'ands an' knees like a vrag."

The old man's tools are not very numerous, but several of them are curiously made, and interesting, being specially adapted for splitting up the wood, and fitting the parts together. The splitting is performed with a tool which he calls the "frammerd" (fromwards). This has a blade similar to that of a billhook, and is fitted on a shaft like that of an axe, with the sharp edge on the outer side, pointing away from the user. To split the wood the edge is placed in the centre of the piece at the end, and driven in with a small mallet; by working the tool to and fro the cleaving is continued to the end of the pole. The other implements are a mortising knife—in shape like a weather-vane—augurs for "barrin"—boring—bill-hooks, axes, saws, and shaves. To hold the wood for shaving, the work man has a simply contrived vice, operated with the foot, and fixed on the end of a bench; sitting astride this he infixes the part, presses the treadle with his foot, and rapidly shaves off the bark and rough knots with the sharp tool.

Hazel-wood is used for making close hurdles, and ash or withy poles for flakes, cow-cribs, and sheep cages. Hazel is cut once in eight years for faggoting, or earlier if it is required for hurdle-making. The old man usually buys his wood growing on the tree, and cuts it himself, which is the cheaper method, or else he buys it at the sales of underwood cut in the copses round about. The charge for making hurdles is 6s. a dozen, or 14s. the dozen, if he finds the wood. Cages take longer to make; for these he receives 13s.

a dozen; they cost exactly double if purchased off the big makers in the towns.

Old Uriah's hands are amazingly hard and "nummel" (feeling-less), by reason of the continual holding of the wood and tools, and the tops of several fingers have fallen quite off, as the result of handling the green frozen wood in the winter, and getting them frost-bitten; but he is able to grip the tools and material in spite of this, and is very clever and quick in shaping the stuff and fitting it together. His neighbour, Ruth Westell, has been fogger at the farm for the last thirty years, milking and foddering the cows, and attending to them winter and summer, Sunday and week-day, with her gown tucked up, like Canidia in the poem, and having a cloth cap on her head. Her hair and woollen bodice are usually full of chaff and hay from the trusses, and her clothes are redolent of the sweet milk. She is very happy in her occupation, and as sharp as a needle in conversation. Though poor, she is not forced to do the work, but she loves the cattle, and the work of the dairy. Her cot-tage is packed with curious pictures and things; the sides of bacon hang under the kitchen wall, and the fat hams are suspended up the chimney-back, drying in the heat nd smoke of the fire beneath.

Two miles from the village, over the hill, lying along a gentle slope beneath a precipitous down, upon which King Alfred is said to have fought his great battle with the Danes, is a magnificent wood of oak, ash, and beech, a mile long, in the centre of which, in an opening, stands Ashdown House, the seat of an ancient family, the founder of which served under, and was commended by, the great Gustavus Adoiphus of Sweden, and was one of the most remarkable characters of the seventeenth century. It is said that, flying from the plague that was raging in London in 1665, and riding aimlessly over the downs, he came upon the site of Ashdown House, then occupied by a solitary farm, bought it, and built a place of refuge, thinking the plague would surely never come there. There is also a local tradition to the effect that he had a coloured servant in attendance upon him, who reproached his master with the remark: "Then massa's God is in the country, and not in the town," which saying struck him so forcibly that he returned to London, and remained there assisting the poor and afflicted.

Formerly the mansion was more thickly surrounded with the wood, and an avenue led up to it from four directions, with the superstitious notion that if the plague came in from one quarter, like the famous Djinns in Victor Hugo's poem, it might escape in another. A curious feature of the house is a belvidere and dome at the top of the roof. This was made for a lantern, to guide wanderers over the hills by night—a very thoughtful provision, since there was formerly no regular road leading over the downs that way.

A hard road runs along the hollow underneath the steep down on the one hand, and a broad belt of rough pasture, thickly strewn with massive sarsen-stones, lies between the road and the wood on the other, now narrowing down, and again opening out to the end of the hollow, where other downs rise, and continue away to Lambourn, two miles off. These stones, from their light colour and general resemblance to sheep, are often called "grey-wethers"; they are very striking in appearance here, scattered so thickly along the hollow, as far as the eye can see. It is singular how the stones came to be at such an altitude upon the chalk, and one is tempted to associate them with the battle of the gods and giants in the far-off days of the world's history, though they are probably no more than the indurated remains of a stratum formerly overlying the chalk, which were left stranded there after the principal portion had been washed away. There was a vast number of smaller sarsen-stones in the hollow, which were gathered up and made into a loose wall extending over two miles around the wood; and a small *castellum*, called King Alfred's Camp, on the western side of the wood, was built of the same materials. At the end of the wood, in a charming site, are the remains of a Roman station; though the spot is calm and peaceful now, it was not always so; there was considerably more life and animation about the downs in the olden days than there is in our time.

The open spaces of the wood, and where the trees are not so dense, abound with many kinds of sweet wild flowers all through the spring and summer months; these also escape from the enclosure of the walls, and creep out some distance into the open, up to where the horses pass along on the turf and trample them underfoot. There are four main colour beauties, alternating in the wood, and extending through the months of March, April, and May, till the grasses come to such a height as to smother the ground plants, and conceal everything except the wild rose, the honeysuckle, and spindle-wood. First of all are the beautiful primrose and oxlip, covering the ground with their pale and deep rich yellow; then come the pure starry white or opal anemones, in countless myriads, dazzling in the bright sunshine, with the blue and white violet intermingled, lost amid the silver sheen of the other; next are the hyacinths or blue-bells, so dear to and beloved of all, covering the ground, and especially underneath the spreading boughs of the trees, with a luxuriant carpet of purple, and scenting the air; and, last of all, richer still in colour, and of a more overpowering sweetness than the rest, are the campions, which take possession of the spaces, and show a delightful soft red, glimmering against the dark background of the trees and hazel underwood. Here also are to be found the pretty yellow blossoming dead-nettle, the purple spotted orchis, and many others, nestling under the beautiful boughs, amid magnificent clumps of fern, while throughout the summer and autumn the bed of the hollow is ablaze with golden ragwort, growing to a height of four feet, and flourishing well in the thin layer of dry soil imposed upon the barren chalk beneath.

Half a mile from the village, on the eastern side, is a great coomb, carved out of the hill, the slopes of which are marked with a series of ridges running from top to bottom, as though they had been ploughed out by superhuman agency in days beyond the knowledge of man. Several large plantations of beech grow upon the slopes, and relieve the austerity of the outlines, and narrow terraces, no longer cultivated, wind here and there, rising and falling gracefully, following the disposition of the slopes at their bases.

Half-way down the hill, where the road crosses, the coomb narrows down to a considerable gorge, where fifty or a hundred springs burst out, the waters of which, dammed back some distance below, form a lake, clear as crystal, of about an acre and a half in extent, and supply two mills, the Upper and Lower, of Kingstone Winslow, a small hamlet adjoining Ashbury. The gorge is the most charming of all along the down-side, and is possessed of great beauty. At the lower end, where the water is bayed back, stands the Upper Mill house, facing the silver sheet and the green downs; each slope is adorned with tall, graceful elms, of exquisite shape, which tower to a great height, half shading the pool, and, with their bright foliage outlined against the delicate blue of the down sky, form a picture of rare sweet loveliness.

The mill-pool is not very deep—about a foot and a half at normal—but the supply of water, is well maintained from the springs, which ooze out of the green sand underneath the chalk all the year, and only flag during the autumn, if the summer has been very hot and dry. On one side, at the bottom, is a hatch to carry off the overflow; here the water continues to roar through, leaping down a well-like place, and flowing underneath the road, even when the mill-wheel is turning: it is estimated that fully 15,000 gallons of water pour out of the hill-side here every minute while the springs are high. In the autumn, when the springs are low, the hatch for the overplus is shut down; then it is usual for the miller to empty the pool by day, and, by keeping the wooden gate firmly shut, to fill it by night, ready to operate his machinery in the morning.

A number of ducks and moorhens inhabit the lake, and are fed daily by the miller. Sometimes he has as many as a hundred white ducks at once, which swim and paddle about with the wild fowl, and give animation to the scene. These are kept in the pool for a purpose, which is, to break up the weeds, and prevent them from thriving, otherwise they would soon cover the whole face of the water. In olden days a part of the hollow contained a fish-pond, for the use of the people at the manor, and trout have been introduced in recent times, but they require a bed of sand or gravel, and do not thrive above the soft bottom of the almost stagnant mill-pool. As the chalk dissolves in the water it forms a kind of slimy paste, degenerating into a white mud; it is well known that trout cannot thrive under such conditions as those.

The mill is separated from the pool by a road that winds round into the hollow and climbs steeply up on the other side. Above the door leading within is a tablet infixed in the wall, bearing the figures 1797—the date of the last restoration of the walls—and two sets of initials, which, curiously enough, are not the owner's, but the builder's, which was usual in those times. The water that turns the mill is conducted beneath the road inside the building, where it fills a large iron tank, and is always ready to flow out at the desire of the miller. Immediately beneath the tank is the huge wheel, fixed in a bed of masonry, the under-part out of sight low down in the brickwork, which is built so as just to contain the circle. The wheel is over-shot, made of iron, built in sections, and is of massive proportions. Its diameter is 18 feet, and width 4 feet, and it contains about 80 pockets, each capable of holding 10 or 12 gallons of water; the weight of the wheel alone, uncharged, is 15 tons. The cost of the iron wheel was £100, as against £20 for one of wood; but whereas a wooden wheel will not run above twelve or fourteen years, the iron one will easily last a century and a half, with the exception of the pockets, which will need renewing from time to time. The maximum capacity of the wheel—with the supply of water at hand—is 15 h.p.; its average rate of motion is 6½ revolutions per minute. The least power is required for wheat, which is the softest of all cereals; from 3 h.p. to 4 h.p. is all that is needed for that; barley requires 6 h.p., and maize most of all, from 7 h.p. to 8 h.p. If the corn in the feeder becomes obstructed and stops the supply to the stones, the pace of the wheel is immediately increased, and it will gain several revolutions extra per minute in a short time, otherwise the rate is even and regular; there is nothing steadier than water in mechanical operation.

To start the mill, the miller turns a screw lever, and, after applying the water for the space of half a minute, shuts it off again. This he calls "flushing the wheel." By checking the water he allows the wheel to start off steadily, otherwise it would rush off swiftly, which, though it might harm nothing, is not to be desired from the miller's point of view. The noise of the falling water, and the sish, sish, of the wheel are delightful to hear; the walls inside the house are covered with luxuriant ivy of a deep green.

The power of the wheel is conducted within by means of an iron shaft, and is afterwards transmitted to the stones through the medium of a system of huge wooden cogs and spindles, which revolve almost noiselessly, unless the cogs are worn with years of use. There are three sets of stones within, two for wheat or barley, and one for maize. The top stone alone revolves; this is called the "runner," and the other is named the "bed-stone." There are few solid English mill-stones in use; the majority are built up in sections, and are of a composition, of flint and concrete, and are usually obtained from France. English stones are not of the same consistency throughout, but are soft in places; consequently they do not wear evenly, while the composition stones may always be relied upon for uniformity in this respect. In grinding wheat the French stones are always used, as English ones are too sharp, and cut up too much bran with the flour. They are set according to the grain to be ground, and may be tightened or lobsened with a simple operation of the adjusting screws.

With continual grinding the stones soon become very warm, which would interfere with the dressing of the meal, and cause much waste, since the flour coheres when it is heated, and will not pass through the silks properly. To obviate this, there is a small fan close at hand, which forces cold air between the stones, and conducts the heat through a wooden, boxlike tube out into the open by the wall. By the old-fashioned method the miller had to grind the wheat, and then put it into sacks or bins, and allow it to cool before he could dress it, or he would not obtain a sufficient percentage of flour. So great is the amount of moisture in English wheat, and especially in that grown in a wet season that the vapour, blown from the stones with the current from the fan, condenses and drips through the joints and seams of the conductor. On the other hand, some Russian wheat is so dry and brittle that millers frequently damp it before admitting it to the stones; it is as much too hard as the other is too soft. All millers like fine weather for grinding; they obtain, on an average, 1 per cent more flour on a dry day than on a wet one.

The grain is fed to the stones automatically by the primitive but effective method of oscillation of the conductor, and is admitted through an aperture in the centre of the runner stone. The crushed grain—called the "meal"—falls below, and is raised by an elevator to the top of the building, and there received into the silks, and sifted out according to the fineness of the flour. The silks are hexagon in shape, being merely lengths of best Swiss silk fixed on a wooden frame, which revolves around a spindle. There are four grades of silk, from superfine to coarse, arranged along the frame, which is inclined, so as to insure the travel of the meal from end to end. A long steel worm, at the bottom of the trough, beneath the silks, forces the sifted flour along to the apertures, where it falls into the mouths of the sacks. The meal enters the silks at the highest end; as they revolve it is carried up and then falls "flap" on to the bottom, beating the fine flour through, while the coarser stuff is worked gradually along to the other end, and continues to sift, till there is nothing but the bran left to fall through. The order of produce from the silks is: firsts, seconds, pollards, and bran. The seconds and pollards, mixed, form toppings, and are used for pigs' food, though they contain the most nutritious parts of the wheat berry. A set of stones produce one sack of flour in forty minutes; the average weekly yield of the mill—day and night shifts—is 200 sacks. There is less waste in grinding with stones than in the case of a mill with rollers; these only convert 68 per cent. of the berry into flour, while the water-mill with stones converts from 75 per cent. to 80 per cent.

The sacks of corn are hoisted up to the top floor of the mill, and the flour lowered, by means of a pulley operated with a loose belt, which tightens with the weight of the sack and hoists in the case of the one, and acts as a brake to lower down in the case of the other. The greatest part of the wheat passes through a cleaner machine, to remove the seeds and dirt, before it goes to the stones. Formerly English farmers used to re-winnow their wheat after threshing, but they adopt the foreign method now, and send it along to the mill just as it is. What they extract from the quantity in the sacks is loss to them, and they receive no more than the current market-price for their corn, whether it is cleaned or not. Sometimes nails and iron nuts arrive in the foreign corn, and occasionally find their way into the mill, and cause considerable damage, cutting great grooves and rings in the stones.

The miller does his own repairs to the machinery, re-chipping the stones, when necessary, and sawing out his own cogs from apple-wood with a small band-saw, driven from the water-wheel. Fitting a cog requires great skill and exactness to insure smooth running; one old miller, by the fixing of a single new cog, broke all the others on his wheel. Though a great part of the mill fixings are home made, and of simple structure, they are highly valuable; the entire machinery of Kingstone Mill, if it were destroyed, could not be replaced under £900 or £1,000.

About a hundred yards farther down the hollow the water is bayed back again into another smaller pool, where a second wheel, that of the Lower Mill, is waiting to turn. The slopes of the hollow, between the mills, are covered with gardens and orchards; the purling stream, escaping from the upper wheel, hurries down the centre, tumbling over the stones, between banks yellow with primrose and celandine. In the bed of the hollow are a score of magnificent black poplars, 120 feet high, with trunks 15 feet in circumference, the leaves of which are nearly always rustling, like spirits in mid-air. In some parts the bark of the black poplar is used for tanning purposes, and the natives of India pollard the trees and fodder their cattle with the foliage. Though the custom of leasing in the fields is extinct in many quarters, it survives in the neighbourhood of Ashbury; in the autumn of 1911—the hottest and driest season for a century—no less than fifty sacks of leased corn found their way to the mill, to be ground into flour for the cottagers.

XIV

EVERY VILLAGE OF THE DOWN-SIDE has one or more large chalk-pits situated upon the open hill, from which material is obtained for building, or for rubble to make up the roads and farmyards. In some localities the chalk is worthless for building, being rotten and crumbling for many yards deep below the surface, but here and there good consistent stuff is quarried, which, when dried, is useful and durable. The chalk strata, as discovered by digging the pits, are very uneven and confusing. Here and there, they are regular, but frequently the chalk is piled up in almost vertical slabs, or the layers are thrown one against the other at sharp angles, or are cylindrical in shape: once a quarry is opened you may easily remove the different layers with the hands, until you come to more consistent material. Where the chalk is firmer, it is obtained in huge blocks at a depth of 20 feet, though the bed will be cracked and cleft into many sections.

There are traces of iron ore everywhere through the chalk strata. This has generally become converted into a red powder, causing deep stains where the water has soaked through and come into contact with it. It is astonishing how the roots of the down grasses and creepers penetrate through almost solid masses of chalk to such incredible depths; they force a way downwards for quite 15 feet, and often farther. The roots of wheat also descend to a great depth; they have been found to penetrate 10 feet below the surface through the cloven chalk.

About halfway between Ashbury and White Horse Hill, close beside the Ridgeway, in a large, oval enclosure, surrounded with beech-trees, is the far-famed Wayland Smith's Cave, with which is associated a time-honoured legend, firmly believed in by the villagers at the present time. The story goes that an invisible smith named Wayland, or Weland, dwelt in the cave, and had his forge hidden far under the earth, out of sight of all that passed that way. When any traveller wanted his horse shod, or arms repaired, he brought them and left them at the entrance to the cave, depositing the money for the fee at the same time, and then retired afar off. After a short while he came back and found the work done, and the money removed, but no one could catch sight of old Wayland. If one brought his horse and waited outside, though he stayed all day, and night too, no one came to see what his need might be, and he dared not venture inside the cave for deadly fear; but as soon as he departed from the entrance, the horse disappeared, and was soon restored again, newly shod. The great mystery was, there was no noise and no smoke; whatever assistants the smith had were invisible, too.

One day old Wayland lost his temper, and gave a thrilling proof of his mighty strength, striking fear into the folks of the country-side round about. Running short of nails, he sent his favourite imp, Flibbertigibbet, down into the valley to obtain some from the other blacksmiths, and bade him make haste about it, as a horse was standing outside to be shod. After waiting several hours he looked out from the cave, and saw the imp had yielded to the temptations of a mortal, and gone bird's-nesting in the fields, forgetful of the nails. Thereupon Wayland, falling into a passion, snatched up a big round stone, used as an anvil, and threw it at the loiterer, two miles off; the stone shot through the air with a loud whizzing noise, and, falling short of the mark, nevertheless slid along the ground, and struck the imp on the foot, retaining the mark of his heel on one side. Thereupon the imp appeared to the astonished rustics, limping and snivelling, and rubbing his eyes with his fist, so they called the spot Snivelling Corner, and the name remains to this day.

Strawberry Baxter, the old-time village cobbler, declares that there was a huge cavern in the earth there, and also a subterranean way, which had its egress in the coombs at Ashbury; while others imagine the place to be a cromlech, the burial-place of some famous Briton, or, perhaps, of a Danish Prince slain at Ashdown. Others think it was a small Druidical temple and altar, and the mark of the "heel" on the stone at Snivelling Corner may be a clue to its true significance as a "heol stone," or sun stone, from "heelios," Greek for sun, which is certainly in agreement with Druidical custom and tradition. The huge stones still remain, piled upon each other, and deeply embedded in the earth, while over them towers a big beech-tree, the trunk of which is engraven with hundreds of names and initials of those who have paid a visit to the spot in the hope of seeing or hearing something or other concerning old Wayland, his workshop and staff.

About a mile to the east of Wayland Smith's Cave, on a high ridge of the downs running back from the White Horse, is a knoll, bearing the singular name of Idle Tump, to which is attached an amusing story, characteristic of pastoral life on the uplands. One summer's day a traveller on horseback, lost on the downs, and desiring to come to the small town of Lambourn, was riding along the ridge, and chanced upon a shepherd lying on the turf, looking up at the heavens, and asked him the way; he merely nodded his head in a certain direction, and paid no further attention to the wayfarer. Proceeding a little farther, the traveller happened upon another shepherd, lying down like the first, half asleep in the warm sunshine, and asked him the way; he languidly raised a hand a few inches, and pointed with his finger, and went on with his dozing. Immediately afterwards the traveller came to a third, in the same state of delicious rest and ease, and again asked the way to Lambourn; this time the shepherd merely raised his foot indolently from the ground and indicated the direction, but vouchsafed never a word to the stranger. Then the traveller, amused with the unconcern of the shepherds, and the humour of the encounter, face-tiously named the spot Idle Tump, and such it is called to-day by the ploughmen and others. Down to the seventeenth century the shepherds of the Wiltshire and Berkshire uplands used to invoke the aid of Saint Oswald in the care of their flocks, and

> Did pray to God, and St. Oswold,
> To bring the sheep safe to the fold,

as the old rhyme quaintly puts it.

Past Wayland Smith's Cave the downs rise gradually till they reach their highest point at this end of the range in the noble hill of White Horse, nearly 1,000 feet above sea-level. The view of the slopes, taken from the vale opposite Compton Beauchamp, is very striking; the progress is from beauty to beauty all along the line of the hills. The bases of the downs, where they skirt the valley, and halfway up the first slope, are covered with avenues and clusters of elms 100 feet high, completely concealing the tiny village there; above these show the near hills, of a soft delicate green, and, after them, a long blue-black wood of fir, stretching obliquely, and nar-rowing to a point at the top, the whole crowned with the imposing heights of the huge hill and the rugged walls of the fortifications, frowning defiance over the valley and downs. The gradation of colour, from the deep green of the bottom woods to the lighter shade of the near hill, the dark sombre hue of the fir-belt, and the pale yellowish tint of the higher slopes and earthworks farther back, are quite remarkable, and especially in the afternoon and evening. In fine weather in autumn, on a dreamy, hazy day, the downs seem to melt into the sky at the distance of a mile or so; it will be difficult to distinguish the outlines from the purplish grey of the heavens a short distance off.

There were formerly two hamlets nestling under the hill, amid the trees and woods—Compton Beauchamp, and Knighton—but the first of these has long ago disappeared, except for the pretty church, and a romantic old moated Grange: the site of the defunct village is indicated by the unevenness of the ground, and a few stones scattered about the meadows. The hamlet of Knighton is perched upon the hillside, and is invisible until you drop down the steep road and find yourself in the very centre of it, with the geese running behind with outstretched necks nibbling at your legs, and the sound of the thresher in the farmyard opposite. The quaint old thatched dwellings are grouped around the farm buildings; it is a charming medley of rose and creeper-covered cottages, beehives, plum and apple trees, beeches and elms. "Stocks' tree"—the dis-membered trunk of a huge elm, underneath which the wooden posts of the stocks stood till recently—occupies a position in the centre of the place; the small school has lately been closed; in order to obtain their daily instruction the children must walk to Ashbury, two miles off.

The pretty chalk-built church stands below, a short distance from the village, alongside the old Grange, and is reached by a road lead-ing under an avenue of elms, and between farm buildings. Fixed on the trunks of the trees, at intervals, are oil lamps to light the way for worshippers on the dark winter evenings; several springs of water, leaping down from the hill above, tinkle in the shade of the elms and laurels, and plunge beneath the road, afterwards to hurry off down the fields in the sunlight. Near the church, at the foot of a mighty elm, the top of which was blown off by a tempest, is a huge excrescence, a yard high, and twenty feet in circumference, of nearly a ton in weight, growing out of the tree. This represents the energy of the root system; when the top was carried away, the sap, unable to be contained, burst out lower down and formed the growth.

The little church is ancient, and exceedingly picturesque. There is a tiny tower scarcely higher than the roof of the nave, at one end, leaning slightly against the body of the church, as though it was too puny to stand by itself, and containing a small bell. A large wood of elm and oak is situated beyond a green sloping meadow; here the doves and pigeons perch in the trees and utter their soft, dreamlike complaints, shedding an air of exquisite peace and calm over the scene. The little churchyard, half full of mounds, is yellow with primrose and daffodil in the springtime; and the peahen has her nest among the tall grasses underneath the spreading yew-tree. The interior of the building is sweetly graceful. The entire walls of the chancel are painted with grape vines and wood hyacinths, and the nave is adorned with several rarely beautiful monuments. One of these, erected to the memory of daughter of Sir Edmund Warneford, the old hunting squire, whose spirit haunted the village of Sevenhampton for a century and more before it was laid, with much ceremony, in the dark waters of the fish-pond, sets out the lady's virtues at some length, and, though many, perhaps, will be sceptical, I myself do most certainly believe the account to be true. Here we learn that—

> She was devout without Superftition, Serious without Morosenefs, regular without Affectation, perfectly eafy to Herfelf, and the delight of all that knew Her. In a word, She was a good Chriftian, a good Wife, a tender Mother, a kind Miftrefs, an agreeable Companion, and a fincere Friend. Go, Reader—says the inscription—and do honour to Her memory, by making Her Character still live in thy Life and Actions.

The moated Grange is near the church, hidden among the stately elms, that rear their crowns up 100 feet and more, above the roads and lawns. Half of the original building, many centuries old, still stands, facing a series of beautiful terraced walks and gardens, and surrounded with magnificent timber. Around the head of the spring, where it bubbles from the hillside, in the shade of the trees, are banks of primrose and violet, with forget-me-not and cresses: the stream, after nourishing these, runs down and fills the moat with water of crystal clearness, upon the surface of which the pure white lilies expand their exquisite cuplike blooms in the summer months. The grey old walls and shade of aged trees, densely overgrown with ivy nearly to the tops, and mysterious moat, have a weird influence upon the imaginative mind; the air seems full of faery shapes, ghosts and goblins, the disembodied souls of those who dwelled at the Grange in times past.

Leading up to the mansion, between high elm-trees, is a broad walk, called Wig Avenue, so named because it was here the young beaux used to stop to adjust their wigs before entering to pay their court to a certain marriageable lady who once occupied the Grange. Large numbers of jackdaws frequent the trees, and play merry games of hide-and-seek in the cavities, where the limbs have been torn away; thrushes and nightingales are plentiful in the woods and copses round about.

In the farmyard, halfway up the hill by the road side, the engine and machine are standing between the sheds engaged in threshing out sanfoin from the rick. The farmer and his men are working the machine, and a crowd of children, small boys and girls, home from school, smothered with dust and grass seeds, their hair full of white particles, and their faces grimy with smoke and dust from the engine fires, are helping, or hindering, carrying away the chaff and chaving, in baskets, and by lapfuls. An elevator is attached to the rear part of the thresher; as the sanfoin leaves the drum it is shaken out into the box of this and raised high on to the rick. The engine is a small light portable, of 5 h.p, with tall chimney and bonnet on the top to prevent the sparks from flying out; the words "PRIZE THRASHER" are painted, in large letters, all along the end of the machine nearest the engine. The tackle is the property of the farmer, and is worked by the regular farm staff, who get extra money for "dreshin'," how ever; when this is at an end they stow the engine and machine in the big shed, and go on ploughing and drilling.

Not many farmers harvest sanfoin for seed. Where they do so, they watch the crop in the summer, and apportion off the best lot, to save for the autumn. When this is well ripe and dry, they cut it and stack it, and, after allowing it to stand a little while, thresh it out. In about five minutes the sack will be full of the seed, which rains down from the fans at a quick rate, though more slowly than wheat and barley. Oats fall most quickly from the thresher; with an extra good crop, a sackful of these will be run out in the space of a minute. A hundredweight of sanfoin is counted a sack, and is valued at 30s. Only one sack receives the sanfoin as it falls; the others catch the husks and grass seeds, which are called "lops," and which are promptly burned up out of the way. The word "sanfoin" is seldom correctly articulated by the carters and rustics; they call it by a multitude of names, such as sankfoy, sinkfy, senkfay, sinfy, senfine, sinfine, sanfin, sinfin, and so on.

Though the farmer works with his men all day on the ricks, they take but very little notice of his presence, and jog along at a comfortable rate, chatting to each other, and gossiping about the everyday affairs of the village. The hours of work are from 7 a.m. till 5 p.m., with an hour out for dinner, and generally a short spell in the morning and afternoon. The time soon slips by out in the open with the downs and valley in view, and there is a lack of that high tension which is so distressful a feature of the manufactory. It is not unusual, indeed, for the farmer and his men to disagree, and I have known them even to indulge in a hand-to-hand fight, and go on working as though nothing had happened; but there is never the dreadful hatred and long-pent-up smouldering passion about the farms as there is in the factory sheds; it is altogether unnatural and dehumanizing there. If the rustic has troubles, domestic or otherwise, he usually unburdens himself to the farmer and his wife, and obtains their sympathy, and is happy in their friendship; but in the factories this is impossible; a man cannot even make a confidant of his nearest workmate; everyone there is too much concerned with himself to trouble about other people.

Hardwell Wood, so conspicuous from the valley, slopes down and borders the road running along the hillside to the White Horse. The entrance to the wood is through a large gate, and a notice-board, nailed to a tree, informs passers-by that "Trespassers will be prosecuted," though the warning is often disregarded by children and young people, who enter to pluck the beautiful primrose, violet, and hyacinth, growing on the slopes of a pretty dell higher up within. The lower part of the wood is of magnificent spruce, which has grown so thickly together as to shut out the light, and to make the entrance look dark and fearsome, like those woods veiling the approach to the awful caverns of Dis. The trunks of the trees, seen through the aisles, reflecting the light, look like spectres in the gloom: the ground beneath is destitute of herbage, but is covered with a thick soft carpet of the minute dead leaves which have fallen from the lower branches of the trees. The air within the wood, on the bleakest day, is calm and warm; and the sound of the wind in the tree-tops is ravishing to the ear, as the Greek Theocritus knew, and testified in the poem on Thyrsis:

Αδν τι τὸ ψιφύριομα καί ά πίτνς αίπόλε τήνα ά ποτί παγαίσί μελίοδταί.
[Sweet is the music of the pine, whispering beside the fountains].

Higher up inside is an open space, and, beyond that, a series of gullies, all densely covered with spruce and elder—the last-named grown from seeds dropped by the starlings—and the home of dozens of badgers and foxes, which inhabit the same earths, and fraternize one with another. Here the badgers are protected, owing to their cleanliness of habit, and usefulness in clearing out the earths where the foxes lie. This they do effectively, and with great regularity, during the hunting season; as fast as the buries are stopped up to keep out the foxes by day, the badgers perform the kindly office of opening them at night, and so afford a refuge for the foxes. Every few days the badgers make themselves clean warm beds of dry down-grass, often carrying it a great distance; when this is become stale they scratch it all out and obtain new material. It is not an uncommon thing to dig a badger and a fox out of the same earth; at a wood near by the keeper and his men recently unearthed a fox, a badger, and a live rabbit from the same bury.

The English spruce is a noble tree, attaining to a great size and beauty where it has sufficient room to thrive and expand its graceful drooping limbs and dark green foliage. Some of the trees on the estate are 70 feet high, with trunks 3 feet in diameter, and foliage covering a space of ground 66 yards in circumference. Besides English spruce there is also the Japanese kind, smaller and inferior in value, as the wood is more brittle—"frummer," to use the woodman's parlance. Larch is superior to spruce, and is nearly as durable as oak, standing well in out-of-doors work, while spruce is softer, and better fitted for interiors. Elm is always used for the beds of carts, because, when anything is thrown upon it, such as heavy, sharp stones, the wood "duffs"—dents—whereas other kinds would crack and split. The rich brown fir-cones, often 9 inches long, suspended from the outer points of the green boughs, are very striking in the autumn and winter; when they fall and become dry they are in great request by the housewives to kindle their fires, by reason of the gluey inflam-mable liquid they hold. The fir-cones contain from 100 to 200 dark seeds, similar to those of the onion, from which the trees are raised. Pheasants and squirrels are fond of these seeds, and practically live upon them in the hard winter weather. The woodman is employed with the trees all the year round, and, though he has no mate or companion, he is seldom lonely. Sometimes, however, he "feels a bit downy like"; then he walks out of the wood into the open light of day and revives his spirits by chatting with the shepherd or ploughman.

Hare-hunting on horse-back with hounds is indulged in twice a week in the valley immediately under the hill-line. A full pack is led out to chase the hare, which usually gives the dogs an all-day run, and perhaps eludes them in the end, doubling this way and that, and practicing many ruses to baffle them and throw them off the scent. Hares seldom make away in one direction, but travel to and fro, in zigzag fashion, and work around the same locality. Lately, however, the hares are getting more wary of the hunt; as soon as the hounds start one up, it makes straight for the hill and the open downs, where it is almost sure to escape its pursuers. If the dogs follow it to the open fields above, they generally start several others, and become confused in the chase; while they are in this perplexity, scattered here and there, the hare takes the opportunity of flying off, and vanishes into the first cover, out of sight amid the dense hazel and long "rowatty" grass.

Underneath the figure of the White Horse, carved high upon the hillside, is a mighty coomb several hundred feet deep, narrowing down to a gorge, a quarter of a mile long, which contains a wood of spruce, larch, birch, and beech, and through which flows the water of half a hundred springs, that bubble out some distance beneath the Horse's hoofs, and are first of all collected into a fish-pond, and afterwards released to turn the wheel of Woolstone Mill, situated below, on the border of the Vale. The slopes of the coomb—which is called the Horse's Manger—are rugged and wild, and of true grandeur. On the western side of the Manger are a series of huge banks called the Giant's Stairs, with smaller ridges running horizontally, looking, from a distance, like ramparts, but which are no more than a freak formation, wrought by the water in geological times. High above, a narrow road winds dizzily round the coomb's side, and climbs steeply up towards the fortifications; on the opposite side, detached from the rest, is a small round natural hill, called Dragon Hill, where Saint George is said to have slain the fiery beast, and ridden the land of the troublesome pest. On the top of the knoll is a barren patch of gleaming chalk, where the blood of the Dragon flowed out of the deadly wound; no grass or flower has grown there since, and never will; the poisonous stream soaked deep into the ground and destroyed all possibility of life there.

The little village of Woolstone lies below the hill, out of sight of the coomb, nestling among tall trees of elm and beech, shut away from the outer world, undisturbed with the fierce controversies of the hour, and the burning passions that unsettle and sway the rest of mankind. The cottages are quaint and ancient—of the Elizabethan period, and earlier—with walls of brick and timber interbuilt, and thatched roofs, picturesquely set amid gardens looking out from underneath green spreading boughs. Halfway down is the romantic White Horse Inn; a short way below this the waters of the spring—now the River Oak—emerge from the neighbouring grounds and plunge down beneath the road amid large moss-covered stones, as did the beautiful Arethusa to escape the embraces of the passionate river god Alpheus in the mountains of Acroceraunia.

The old mill stands farther down, a short distance from the road, at the head of a large pool well stocked with trout. It is not often in requisition now, though it is used for gristing occasionally. The great wheel is contained in a shed—to protect it from the wet, as is jocularly said; the floors and beams within the mill are mouldering away to dust. Once upon a time, at a small mill on a stream in the valley, the wheel was considerably out of repair; the oscillation was so great that it shook the crockery off the kitchen shelves in the miller's cottage adjoining. So the mill-wrights came to renovate the wood-work and bearings; after three days of hard labour all was well again, and the machinery was started, unknown to the miller's wife. She, good soul, came out in the afternoon to call the workmen to tea.

"Come an in an' hae a cup o' tea, then you can finish un better," said she.

"Bless ee, mother, 'e's finished now, an' a runnin' too, this long time," they replied.

"Is the mill a-gwain ?" she inquired, with astonishment.

"Gwain, aa! We ground dree sacks an' moore a'ready," they answered.

"An' I 'ent a yerd a sound o' nothin'!" the miller's wife regretfully responded.

One dry summer, when water was very scarce, at the same mill, the miller's son crept up a long culvert and blocked up the hatch-door with a stone, where the watet was bayed back into a fish-pond of five or six acres, and drained the whole lot for grinding before the ruse was discovered by the gamekeepers whose duty it was to attend to the pool.

The village church stands in a small field lying off the road, and is chalk-made, with bare walls within, and little ornamentation. The tiny building has no tower—the only church lacking this throughout the down-side—the small bell is hung at one end of the roof outside. There is no vicarage in the place, and no priest; he dwells at the small village of Baulking, below Uffington, and makes periodical visits to Woolstone. Strange use has been made of village churches before now, in the time of the wars, and during the plague, as places of refuge and safety, and they are still turned into conveniences, for someone or other who chances to be in need. A short while ago the caretaker of the tiny church, going to renovate the fires between services one Sunday, surprised a tramp in the act of cooking his dinner on the grating above the heat pipes; there were the fat rashers of bacon frizzling and spluttering; the building was filled with the savoury odour of hog's flesh.

The old White Horse Inn stands in the centre of the village, at an angle of the road, a short way down from the hill. The building is of the fifteenth or sixteenth century, rambling in structure, with flattish roof, large bay windows fitted with quaint panes of glass, and spacious rooms within, which have sheltered many a weary traveller from the bitter blasts that rage along the hill and over the graven figure of the Horse in the solitary winter nights. Around the entrance are piled up large sarsen-stones, gathered about the high downs, and each with an history, which seem to emphasize the great age of the inn; while inside are to be seen the antique oak panelling, old-fashioned settees, and a splendid specimen of the ancient "ingle nook"—a survival of other days—around which the old folks sat and drank from the loving cup, toasting each other in the ruddy firelight, and telling tales of adventures on the downs with robbers, poachers, and sheep-stealers, with which the region of the White Horse was formerly infested. All that is at an end now, though there is no lack of tourists and visitors at the inn, who come to walk upon the steep hill, or view the White Horse, and lounge on the worm-eaten settees, sipping ale or coffee, charmed with the pleasant air of antiquity that prevails about the place.

The names of the inns about the downs and valley are usually local in origin and relation: the references are easily understood, though here and there you meet with one that is more difficult of construction, which may be symbolical, as The Shears, or The Cross Keys; or suggestive of medieval times and the Crusades, as, The Saracen's Head, at Highworth; The Crown, The Rose and Crown, and The Sun, are common names everywhere. One of the quaintest hereabout is The Jacob's Ladder, at Stratton St. Margaret; though the common theory is that you would never reach Heaven through the medium of a public-house. Characteristic names of local inns are: The White Horse, The Black Horse, The Running Horse, The Shepherd's Rest, The Woodman, The True Heart, The Fox and Hounds, The Cow, The Elm Tree, The Plough, The Harrow, The Blue Lion, The Boar, and Trip the Daisy.

Small beer or "swanky," was sold at the cottages, in times past, at 1½d. a quart. Then tea was practically unknown to the labourers; they had ale for breakfast, dinner, and supper. The landlords of the village inns still keep the shoe-like tin vessels for warming the beers for their customers in the winter; these they thrust into the coals "to take the jaa (jaw) off"—to remove the cold snack from the liquor—as they say. Straw-plaiting, and weaving, too, was carried on in the cottages under the White Horse, in earlier times, but the industry has died out now, and the village is much smaller and poorer than it used to be.

Dad Eldridge, the hearty old carter, whose whole life was spent on the downs around the White Horse, has left the farm now, and lives with his daughter at the tiny Post Office of Sevenhampton, next door to the aged shepherd, with whom much of his day, and night, too, is spent, conversing of old times, and relating of divers experiences, the joys and sorrows, the pleasures and misfortunes of life. Here they indulge in many quaint expressions, bits of wit and lore, uncanny and weird beliefs, and repetitions of things, which at length become wearisome to the young people, who admonish them to "dry up," and "get off up the wooden hill," or pass mildly sarcastic remarks, as: "How many more times for that un?" and: "That's a tall un, I know;" but dad and shepherd continue to ramble on, squinting and nodding in the chimney corner, and, taking forty winks, soon to start off again, with another item newly remembered.

Sometimes the talk is of the wonderful golden coffin, full of treasure, buried on the downs between the White Horse and Wayland Smith's Cave; at another time it is of the famous Horn of Pusey, or the phantom coach and horses on the highway, the haunted well at Kingstone Warren, that utters a roar like thunder; or again it is of old Molly Jones, the cripple, who drove plough, hopping on one toe; honest Farmer Brooks, of Stanford-in-the-Vale, who always felt miserable and ill when one of his men was about to leave him; the White Horse Revels of 1857, when it took all the horses in Woolstone to draw the wild beasts up the hill; the old-time ballad-singers, ducking the pick-pockets in the pond at Wadley Fair, the jolly harvest-homes, sowing, reaping, threshing, and many other matters. "Tha tells I as we be ignerant, an nat much good fer anything, but jest let thaay come an' listen to I an' my owl' shepherd, we'll soon let thaay know whether we be ignerant or nat; we'll show thaay as 'tis thaay as be ignerant, an' nat we, right anuf." Here the old carter draws himself up with great self-respect, and speaks in tones of fine contempt, while his grey eyes flash with scorn and pride, but the shepherd smiles kindly and merely shakes his head in response; he is too philosophic and satisfied to care about what other people may think of him; the only anxiety he has is that his faithful old black-and-white dog may be kindly cared for if anything shall suddenly happen to him and carry him out of the world.

A great many of the down-side cottages and farm houses are full of curious odds and ends, and contain numerous quaint bits of furniture, beautiful old-fashioned chinaware, coloured prints, ancient guns and implements, cups, utensils, and every description of ornament. These are often met with in the most unlooked-for places, and always give greater pleasure when you happen upon them unaware, poked away in some dark corner of the cottage room, or smothered in the dust of the mantelpiece, than when they are arranged in collections, and ostentatiously paraded before the visitor. Some of the cottagers set great store on the dainty little china services, which have been handed down from mother to daughter for generations, and love them both for their parents' sake, and for art's sake too, and are not at all deficient in the quality called taste; while others, if they do not value them as highly, still guard them jealously, and soon indicate to you that they are not for disposal. "Aa, you be ogglin' round, you be. You'd like to get yer fingers on that, I warn, but you can set yer mind at rest now at once, you wunt 'ev it. That warmin'-pan belonged to my grandmother's grandmother, an' I don' know 'ow many 'ad un afore her, an' this yer skimmer's older than he. I 'oodn't sell none an't for a 'underd pound, no, that I 'oodn't." As a matter of fact, one old lady, in a small cottage, possessed of a fine collection of family chinaware, though very poor, and offered £50 for her treasures, would not part with them.

Some of the coloured prints met with in the cottages, where they have been kept clean, are very beautiful, and may be of high value. Others are distinguished by their primitiveness and simplicity of subject, such as those entitled The Mower, The Reaper, The Ploughman, The Haymaker, and another kind, containing personifications of things, as: Europe and Asia, Peace and Plenty, and so on. But the kind most usually met with is a very good print, in colours, of Scriptural subjects, and Continental wars of the latter half of the eighteenth century, such as the Battle of Wissemburg, the Battle of Thiers, and others, which are a German production and contain titles printed in four languages, e.g., German, French, Spanish, and English. Some of the subjects are boldly conceived, as, for instance, the picture of The Trinity, with God the Father— like a representation of ancient Zeus or Jupiter—on the right, God the Son on the left, and The Holy Spirit in the form of a dove, between the two. Occasionally, though not often, you meet with old paintings, quaint woodcuts, and prints of parliamentary riots; books also are rare, except for the great old leather-bound Bible and Prayer-Book.

Figures and ornaments are plentifully found, ranging from the old common chalk images of cocks, dogs, cats, and other animals, introduced from abroad, and sold by Italian hawkers a century and a half ago, to highly artistic groups in coloured stoneware—things of beauty that will not fade—purchased by our grandmothers, and eagerly sought after by collectors and dealers in antique things. Even the stone jars containing potted meats and pickled herring were artistically made and coloured in the early half of the nineteenth century; you occasionally meet with some of these on the cottage mantelpiece containing pictures of notable events—of famous battles, and so on—worthy ornaments with the rest, and dearly prized by their owners.

At the farmhouses, too, many curios and works of art are to be found, together with household utensils, old-fashioned ware, jugs, mugs, and implements, all held in high esteem, and treasured with great pride and care by the farmers' wives. At one place, a happy dame almost dragged me inside the kitchen to see a famous warming-pan, a family heirloom, of polished brass, bearing the date 1630, with the inscription SAVE KING CHARLES around the cover; here it was an old metal mortar, sets of brass ladles and table tackle, or a fine earthenware jug, 200 years old, painted with the "Farmer's Creed" in symbols: a hatchet and bilihook (crossed), a harrow, a plough, a wooden beer flagon, a beetle and rake (crossed), a sheaf of corn, a prong, a reap-hook, and a set of flails. The "Farmer's Creed," in rhyme, dating from about 1780, is also met with on two-handled mugs, and is as follows:

> Let the Wealthy and Great
> Roll in Splendour and State,
> I envy them not, I declare it,
> I eat my own Lamb,
> My Chickens and Ham,
> I shear my own Fleece, and I wear it;
> I have Lawns, I have Bowers,
> I have Fruits, I have Flowers,
> The Lark is my morning alarmer,

So jolly Boys now,
Here's God-speed the Plough,
Long Life and Success to the Farmer.

Freaks of Nature, such as a white blackbird, or a white stoat, stuffed, and in glass cases, are sometimes found, together with owls and foxes; and here and there, though not commonly, the one and only cottage hen is discovered perched upon the back of the couch, or between the chair legs, while the happy family gathers around the fireside, gaily laughing and chatting the hours away before bedtime.

XV

White Horse Hill—Storms in the Vale—The old
"Revels"—Uffington Village—Tom Brown's School—
Clouds on the hill—The Blowing Stone—Around the
fire at the inn—Poaching and sheep-stealing

From Uffington the glaring road leading up to the famous
White Horse passes between level fields for a mile to the base
of the hill, with the mighty chalk down, lying like huge Tityon,
the giant whose body covered eleven acres in Tartarus, straight in
front, showing greater and grander the nearer you approach to it.
A short way up the slope a narrow road crosses, leading along to
the Blowing Stone at Kingstone Lisle; that from the valley continues straight up, winding round the Horse's Manger, and emerges
on top, passing underneath the walls of the *castellum*, afterwards
degenerating into a rough track, full of deep ruts, used only by the
farm-carts and waggons. On the left-hand side of the road is a deep
coomb, and, beyond that, a large wood of ash and hazel, suspended
beneath the hill, and teeming with primrose, violet, anemone, hyacinth, and bell-flowers in the season. Adown the slope of the hill,
at the coomb's head, long whitish marks are visible some distance
off. These are shining tracks, where the young people and holiday-
makers slide down from top to bottom on the long slippery grass.
Here the declivity is very steep, and the fine down-grass, once it
is traversed over, is as sleek as ice; a great speed is attained soon
after the start and continued right down into the hollow. On the
opposite side of the road is the mysterious Dragon Hill; the old
White Horse sprawls his huge length on the slope high above,

though its shape is undistinguishable till you are removed a mile or more off in a north-westerly direction.

The view from the top of the down, above the Horse's Head, is truly magnificent. It is claimed that eleven counties are visible from the hill; but that is probably an exaggeration, though the eye can penetrate forty or fifty miles, until it is baffled by the faint blue haze along the horizon, where the far end of the exquisite down-line fades and melts insensibly into the soft azure sky. The spacious Vale—"The Garden of the Lord," as Tom Hughes called it—is extended below in all its beauty and loveliness, dotted with numerous villages and dark blue woods, stretching away to the Thames and Cotswolds on the one hand, and over towards the city of Oxford on the other. Back from the valley lie the downs, green or golden, yellowish-white, or light brown, now enclosing a level plain in an amphitheatre, with a few plantations and farms, now rising into ridges and lines, running and leaping, twisting, curving, and winding like living things, the whole strangely and deeply impressive, silent, lonely, and solitary, yet acting powerfully on the mind and soul, and awaking immortal feelings and desires, which are mollified and diminished when you turn round and contemplate the milder and more human scenery of the valley.

The wind, during an ordinary storm or gale, rages along over the hill-top with terrific fury, dashing fiercely against the steep western walls of the *castellum*, and roaring with the noise and din of ten thousand cataracts, whirling you back from the parapet as though you were no more than a dry leaf, and chilling you through and through with intense cold and numbness. It would have been a comparatively easy matter to storm the camp under such conditions; the mighty gale behind lifts you up the steep slope with the lightness of a cork, and dashes you headlong down from the naked walls above.

During stormy weather you may stand on the hill and watch the isolated showers in their birth, progress, decline, and death, all over the valley. These first of all show in a thin, white, pillar-like mist, growing rapidly into the density of a large cloud trailing a mile long, or more; as the moisture is spent the phantom-like shape gradually dissolves and presently vanishes from view, and another appears and takes its place in mid-air. Snowstorms often travel at a great rate across the Vale and dash straight upon the hill, though only a few flakes may whirl around the earthworks: the body of the storm was lower down, and was spent against the slopes, or round the Horse's Manger.

The long dry grass around the White Horse is fired every year, in January or February; the flames sweep along and rise to a great height, and are visible for thirty miles across the valley. This allows the young grass to shoot up and nourish the sheep and lambs, while the ashes of the burnt stuff serves to fertilize the chalk soil. The slender paths, made by the hares, plunging straight down, or sweeping gracefully round, still show after the fire; the grass, trodden hard down, does not catch; the flames leap over the tracks, and travel rapidly along the surface of the ground.

The thin layer of soil over the chalk is perforated with innumerable small round holes, the haunts of field-mice and humble bees, which have their home on the hill. Inside the camp the soil is much deeper, and of a rich brown colour—an evidence of the former occupation; here the busy moles tunnel and bore, and raise countless small mounds of earth, holding supreme sway in the lonely deserted fortress.

The scouring of the Horse, which used to be the occasion of much festivity and mirth, proceeds on different lines nowadays; there has been no great celebration of sports and games in connection with the event since the year 1857. Whatever cleansing and renovation is needed now is carried out privately by the workmen of the estate; they merely cut out the weeds from time to time that encroach upon the graven figure, remove the discoloured chalk, and fill up the cavities with fresh bright material obtained from the pits. A few years only will suffice to discolour the chalk, and render the outline of the Horse invisible at a distance of several miles; and when the heavy and violent rain-storms sweep over the hill they wash the chalk out of the body and limbs of the

Horse and swill it down the hillside for twenty yards and more, where it accumulates in small white heaps. When the Horse's figure has been renewed with fresh bright chalk, it is visible eighteen or twenty miles off, with the naked eye; it will scarcely be seen at a third of that distance when the material is dull and discoloured with the changes of atmosphere, the alternations of heat and cold, the rain and frost of winter.

Nearly all those who took part in the famous games of 1857, the back-swording, wrestling and racing, recorded in "The Scouring of the White Horse," are dead now, though here and there you meet with one who entered the lists with the champions as a young gamester, and bore off the trophy of a broken head, or administered the same to his opponent. It is a remarkable thing, and significant of human nature, that out of all the great epoch-making events that have happened in England and about the world in the second half of the nineteenth century, there is none that is so well and fondly remembered for miles about the Vale as are the great "Revels" of 1857. Of wars and coronations, and mighty scientific achievements, the villagers speak scantily, and with little real interest, but for the "revels an tha owl' White 'Oss" they evince a boundless enthusiasm: whoever is so fortunate as to have taken part in them, or even to have been present at the time, is looked upon as a real hero, and is shown superior respect.

Old William Reeves, of Shrivenham, who is nearly ninety, is one of the most interesting of the last "Revels"; he, with Henry Cook, of Uffington, and John Breakspear of Woolstone, can relate the most of what happened there, and they were personally acquainted with many of the competitors mentioned by Judge Hughes in his book: as Harry Seely, of Shrivenham; Gregory, of Stratton; the Hedges' and Slades, of Purton; Joe Giles; Simon Stone, the Beckinghams, of Baydon; and Mapson, the Somersetshire champion. Old William, with his picturesque red woollen waistcoat, red knitted cuffs, and head slightly inclined, is delighted to talk about the Revels, though he admits there was a little "blaggardness" sometimes, and sundry small accidents; as when, in the cart-horse race, a big mare stumbled and fell on her rider, killing him on the spot; and again, after the pig hunt, how five competitors claimed the prize, and killed the poor pig in contending as to which should have it; and how thieves broke into the booths and carried off all the takings, and other suchlike happenings. The wheel used in the race down the Manger was a solid one specially made by Henry Jones, the old carpenter of Ashbury. This was the size of a cart wheel, and had a stout pole, 10 feet long, passed through the hub, to prevent it from tipping, though it generally came to grief against the hard road leading round the Manger. The side of the hill is almost as steep as the wall of a house; the wheel, if it struck the road there, usually smashed all to pieces, though sometimes it might leap over, and continue its headlong flight down to the bottom of the hollow.

At the foot of the slope, bare and naked above the roadside, is a house, no bigger than a cottage, with a barn and buildings, and half a hundred acres of land attached, the whole comprising a holding called Sour Hill, occupied by a former carter at the farm, who, by dint of hard labour and sacrifice, has attained to a state of comparative independence in his old age; it is common talk with the neighbours round about that "Owld Goodenough 'ev saved un a thousan' er two out of 'is veow cows 'an things, an' 'is bit o' carn land." The old fellow is assisted by a son, and his wife, who weans the calves, sees to the milk and butter, and works outside, when necessary.

The interior of the cottage is plain and bare, with little ornamentation, in keeping with the severity of the occupants; a table, and several chairs, a dresser containing the crockery ware, an old clock, a fox's head, and a brass cornet, standing on a small sideboard, are about the only furniture. The old carter had two more sons, but they were killed in the war, and though he has not been at the farm many years, he is thinking of retiring. This he confides to you with a broad smile, and a knowing look, and adds, furthermore, that he will "nat be fooast to apply for the howid age pinchin, thenk God." Starting with one cow, he now has thirteen, which yield 40 pounds of butter a week; then there are the hens, which add a good sum to the revenue. Though dwelling in a charming spot, the good-wife does not think it pretty, and is absolutely unmoved with the scenery of the hill. "Lar, 'tis a huncid[1] place to be in, an' cowld anuf to vrizz the nose off an e in the winter, an' martal lonely. I don' envy nobody under this hill, awhever."

The village of Uffington lies down in the Vale, about a mile from the base of the hill, and is separated from the downs by a tract of level land which was formerly all cornfields, but which is now turned into meadows. The red tiled roofs and white walls of the houses, nestling amid the trees, with the grand old church tower rising over all, make a charming picture seen from the hill; standing over beyond, four or five miles away, is Faringdon Folley, a tall clump of trees on an eminence, visible for many miles up and down the valley.

The village is large and straggling, with a population entirely agricultural, and very poor, considering the great riches and fertility of the country round about. The majority of the cottages are ancient, and are chiefly chalk-made, with thatched roofs; the walls of many are crumbling away, though some have stood for centuries, and are still in excellent condition. The chalk stands better in some localities than in others, and it makes a great difference as to how the blocks are laid in the walls. If the grain of the chalk is laid horizontally, the blocks will last almost any length of time, but if it is placed perpendicularly, the outside part soon crumbles away, and falls off in flakes. A feature noticeable in the village is the large number of windows that have been stopped up in the cottages. This took place at the time of the introduction of the window tax, which was from 2d. to 2s. per window, according to the number in each house; the owners stopped the lights to avoid paying the impost.

The famous old church, with its stately roof and lofty octagonal tower, grey and sombre in outline, stands on the western side of the village, overlooking a small field that slopes down to the swift-flowing River Ock, near which the old-time village feast and sports were held, and where little Tom Brown rode on old Benjy's shoulders, with a bright new two-shilling piece in his pocket, to see the back-swording and wrestling, three quarters of a century ago. Facing the church, on the opposite side, is the mill house, shorn of its machinery, and now used as cottages for farm labourers, and an old inn, the Craven Arms, situated a short way down the Longcott road. The brook has been cut off, and diverted from the mill; several large poplar trees, with the tops blown away, stand around, and add to the dilapidation of the scene. The paddock, through which the water ran from the mill-wheel, has been turned into an orchard; there is no grinding here now, and never will be any more.

Near the church is a small building, used as a reading-room, but which was formerly a school, whereat the youthful Tom Brown, with others of his age, attended to learn the elements of education, and receive the severe attentions of the pedagogue. The little place stands high up above the road, and is entered by a low stone arched door round the corner at the back. The foundations are of large rough sarsens, which stand a couple of feet above the ground, and the walls are of native stone, gleaming white in the sunshine. Over the door is engraved the date 1617, and near by is another inscription, in bad Latin, which expressed the hope that "nothing troublesome or annoying would assail the walls within which the boys were having lessons," which was flagrantly disregarded by young Tom and Jacob Doodle-calf, who wilfully invaded the school one afternoon, and brought the day's lessons to an abrupt end with their brazen interruption. A copy of the original deed and constitution of the school, hanging upon the wall inside, expresses the opinion that it is not comely or decent for girls and boys to be taught together, but times have changed since then; there is not now the old objection to boys and girls commingling in the village school.

There is a brass band in the village, the members of which are farm workmen—ploughmen and foggers—and the conductor is carter at a farm under the downs. These hold their practices at the school in the evening, but call themselves "The Kingstone Lisle

Band," because, as the old carter says: "Ther's nob'dy yer to sup-poort a band, the fawks got nothin' to gie, tha be too poor; us wants gentry to kip us agwain." In addition to the band of music, the schoolmaster has taught the children pretty morris dances, and Maypole games. These the fathers and mothers, with granny and "granfer," attend, full of pride and wonder at the dainty graceful motions of the morris, and the fairy-like children tripping among the buttercups.

In rainy weather clouds sometimes cover the White Horse, hanging motionless over the crown of the hill, or hurrying along, rasing the summit, and passing off into the open again. The dense volumes of mist, meeting the hill, do not break up, but conform to the oval shape of it, and cover it like an envelope, as though the earth attracted the vapour; the fringe of the cloud descends halfway down the slope of the hill, but is drawn up again when it nears the other end, and vanishes into the upper air. At such times Dragon Hill is strongly silhouetted against the main body of the down, though the space intervening, by the Horse's Manger, is no more than thirty yards. Upon the hill, near the earthworks, the mist is so dense you cannot see many feet before you, or, if the cloud is moving, it rolls and sweeps along like smoke, affording momen-tary glimpses of the vale, and immediately obscuring everything from view again. The appearance of clouds upon the hill is usually before, or after rain, and in mild weather. When the heavy show-ers pelt down in earnest, the rain is nowhere so thick as upon the downs; the water seems to fall in solid sheets, so that you might imagine yourself to be in the midst of the sea waves.

The downs and top of the hill are strewn with small marine shells, thousands of years old, some of which crumble into dust between the thumb and finger, while others are in a good state of preservation. These testify to the former submersion of the downs, and afford a topic for the villagers, who imagine the Flood to have been the cause of their presence there. Here and there green sand is dug from pits beneath the downs, and used for various purposes. The sides of the pits are interesting, as showing the interdepositing of chalk and sand; the thin layers and perpendicular veins of chalk show like the seams of mortar in a stone wall. Besides the sea-shells, the downs are strewn with brightly coloured snail-shells, too, of a delicate pink, or yellow, stained with purple, or adorned with rich brown stripes and rings. These the country children gather and thread on strings, and wear them around the neck as an ornament. The stems of some of the hawthorn bushes scattered about the hill are of a remarkable tint, ranging from deep orange to brilliant yellow, or peach; this is probably the result of growing upon the chalk. These thorn-bushes are common upon the open downs and along the Ridgeway, and live to a great age; the wood is much in request by the rustics during the winter months.

East of the White Horse is a small coomb, the slopes of which are covered with tall trees of elm, ash, and hazel underwood, with the gleaming trunk of a silver birch showing here and there, while the open spaces are beautiful with wild flowers, pink, white, opal, and purple, all through the spring and summer. At the bottom of the hollow are a farm house and buildings; an orchard runs up to the hill-slope behind, and a fold for the lambs is pitched underneath the spreading boughs of the tall wych elms. Beneath the road, on the other side, is the usual gorge, with springs, and watercress beds, thickly bordered with hawthorn, maple, and ivy-covered apple-trees. A sweet calm broods in the hollow, broken only by the liquid strains of the thrushes and blackbirds in the hawthorn, the doves in the wood, and the black-and-white magpies chattering around the ricks and ash-tree tops. Farther along is another huge gorge, rugged and wild in aspect, half full of hawthorn and crab boughs, running out into the valley; and a little way beyond this, underneath the magnificent plantations of Kingstone Lisle, are cross-roads, near to which is the famous Blowing Stone—King Alfred's Bugle—as the shepherds and ploughmen call it. The pretty village nestles at the foot of the hill, out of sight among the towering elms and firs; the road in front runs along under the downs beneath a splendid avenue of beech, half a mile long, towards Childrey and Wantage.

The Blowing Stone Inn has been done away with in late years, and the building turned into cottages, because it was thought to be a stronghold for poachers, and the landlord was furthermore accredited with selling his beer during prohibited hours; at any rate, the house fell into disrepute, and the order was given to close it forthwith; but there is another quaint old inn—The Plough—a little way below in the centre of the village. The queer-looking stone itself, perforated with many holes, still stands in its place underneath the dismembered elm-tree, and you may have the pleasure of blowing it, or of hearing the weird, hornlike sound—half moan and half roar—produced by the mouth of another, on application at the cottage, after which you may inscribe your name in a book and hand over a small fee to the fund for maintaining the village nurse, which is the latest use to which the old stone has been put. The road up the hill to the "Rudge" is quite as long and almost as bad as it was in Tom Brown's day, when he stopped to chat with mine host and take a "modest quencher," or helped the old dame to "scawt up" with her donkey and cart, full of nuts and gingerbreads, on her way to the "Revels," but once on top the labour of climbing is forgotten, and you are rewarded with the invariably fresh sweet air of the downs, and the incomparable view of the valley beneath.

As to what transpired at the old Blowing Stone Inn between the poachers, mine host, and the police, that is scarcely remembered, since the house has been closed, and that generation has passed sway; but there are those about Uffington still who are reminiscent of the old times, and who can entertain you with interesting tales and gossip, if you are not above sitting in the chimney-corner and conversing with them at one or other of the inns.

"Then you byent a gone to the P'int to P'int to day, Chaales," the shepherd remarks to the old carter, sitting beside the piled-up wood fire, and leaning heavily on his withered staff at the Baker's Arms, while the rain falls in a deluge without, dashing wildly against the window-panes, and the chalk-white water rushes in a torrent down the street, and leaps over the greensward into the meadow beyond.

"No, begad! 'Tis too many an one vor I.[2] Tha'll be like drownded rats, all an 'em, as be gone ther todaay. What do you saay, black-smith?" the carter replies.

"Gob-bless tha, that wun worry thaay, one mossel; nat if it raained 'achets," the sturdy blacksmith answers, taking his short clay pipe from his mouth, and knocking out the ashes against the brickwork.

"Tha'll never get awver Rosy Bruk to-daay, wi'out gwain into 't, I knows," the carter rejoins.

"Aa, Rosy Bruk, and round the Devil's Knowwl, an' varright Childrey. 'Tis the Devil's Knowwl, yen it, shepherd?"

"Yes, yes, yes, yes. The Devil's Knowwl, tha's it: Yes, yes, yes."

"I thawt 'twas. Yer, gie us up another o' thaay clefs. What is it, yelmin, or aishen? 'Tis main spealy[3],whatever 'tis."

"Ya wants a bit o' owld crab, or tharnin tackle. Begad! that ull make e draa back a bit, if nothin' else wunt," the carter says. Then he continues: "I minds one night at the Blawin Stwun, as used to be—"

"Thee shet up about the Blawin Stwun. We don' want to yer no moore about 'e, all tha's gone an' done wi', an' ther's moore pheasants an' 'ers about than ever. I counted vive in one leetle patch nabbut[4] 'isterday," the blacksmith replies.

"I knows all about that, but I was jest a-gwain to tell tha, look, about a bit o' fun as some an 'em 'ed a main veow years ago, when Jack Horton was tuk, an' got traanspoorted. 'Twas a cler night, an' a bit blake, an' tha'd all 'ed a drap to drenk, and was warmed up like. Tha know'd wher the owl' pheasants roosted, very well. About the turn tha crapes up an' acraas, an' into the ood, an' bang, bang, tha goes, an' vetches 'em out o' the tree an to the ground. But ther was a bit o' bad luck in stoore that time. Tha 'ed a party at the 'ouse, an' when tha yerd the guns a virin', out tha all runs, ilter-skilter, some yer an' some yander, a hull swarm an 'em. Off the chaps goes, an' got out o' the ood into the awpen, an' t'others aater 'em a hollain': ''Tis no good. We knows ya; we knows ya.' Some was well a'ed, but Prince an' Horton was laggin' be'ind, an' t'others was gainin' ground. Then Prince stopped shert an' shouted to Horton: "Shut the devuls! shut tha devuls," an' bang, bang, um lets dreeve, an' shut the 'at off o' one's 'ed, an' peppered one er two moore, an' terrified thaay, but tha 'ed Horton awright, an' traanspoorted 'e, an' Prince 'e clerd off, an' stopped away till the owl' squired was dead, an' then showed up, but tha nabbed un, an' sen' in acraass the water. Horton, 'e died abroad, but Prince come back wi' a bag vull o' suverins and spended 'em all a drenkin about from one place to t'other."

"Aa, thame times be over, begad! An' a good job, too. I'd soonder go a 'ongered than take the risk o' that for a bit o' dinner," the blacksmith remarked.

"The owl' Rooshan was one o' thaay, athout I mistakes, awhever. Dost mind owl' Charlotte, shepherd?"

"Yes, yes, yes, yes, to be sure. Owl' Charlotte an' Gabby. Yes, yes, yes."

"A used to call 'er 'usband 'my owl' Rooshan.' A met I at the bottom one night, an' a sed: 'Est thee seed my owl' Rooshan, Chaales?' an' the owl' man was clawss 'andy, an' a spakes up an' ses: 'Yer 's thy owl' Rooshan, if thees wants un, an I'll owl' Rooshan thee when I gets tha indoors tareckly.' 'Gad!' the owl' dooman sed, 'I didn' know e was ther, mun.' This ood milt the butter, oodn' it, owl' man? Aa, poor owl' Johnny Tarrant! I met 'e many a time a comin' out o' the whum ground, an' dursaay a 'ed it about un then, if I'd oni a know'd. A ust to do the churnin', an' crib the butter reg'ler, an 'ide it in 'is 'at. A good many werd the 'igh 'ats in thame times, work-vawk an' all. The owl' farmer 'ed s'picion an in at last, an' led a trap farn. A got un to do the churnin' at night, dost know. While a was at it a went indoors an' made up a girt vire, as med be this un, an' laays the supper an the table. When a'd a done churnin' a ses: 'Come along in ta supper, John.'

"'No, thenk e, maaster; I'll get along whum,' t'othern ses.

"You come along in an 'ae some supper now, do e,' the owl' man sed. So tha goes inside. Ther was a girt vire, anuf to roast a ox. The owl' man made un set right up bi tha chimbly. Johnny wanted to take 'is 'at off, but t'other oodn' let un. 'You kip yer 'at on. 'Tis draafty in yer,' a sed. The owl' man pawked the vire up all the time. By-'m-by the butter begun to milt, an run down 'is 'ed an' face.

"'Ow tha dost sweat, you!' the owl fella sed. 'Never sin a fella sweat so in mi life afoore.'

"''Tis sa 'ot in yer, maaster,' t'other sed. So tha made un stop ther till 'twas all run down 'is 'ed an' claws. A never cribbed the butter na moore, aater that. What! 'ev em gied tha owl' squired a snuff-box awver yander at Pusey, shepherd?"

"Tha do saay so, b'leeve," the shepherd answers. "E'll be put up a top o' the shilf, along wi' the owl' horn, right anuf."

"Yes, yes, yes, yes, to be sure; Yes, yes, yes."

"''Tis a strannge theng, ya know, but if thaay was to loose 'e tha'd loose the lot, the 'state an' all an't. Tha's what the owl' king sed. As long as thaay kipt the horn thaay should 'owld Pusey, an' no longer. The sowjers met the cowman, an gied e their horn to blow, when a went aater 'is cows in the marnin', an 'e blowed un, right anuf, but I warn a stood fer anuf back when the two lots an 'em come together."

"An I'd soonder a carred 'e about than the owl' Blowin' Stwun, that e ood," spoke the blacksmith. "Tha wanted a per o' oxen to lug 'e about. But ther's nob'dy as can blow 'e nowaday; tha aant a got anuf wind in ther billis. Wanted owl' Wayland Smith to cart 'e to an' agyen. Did'n the owl' shepherd fine in up a top ther, ayant the White 'Oss, in the fust place?"

"Yes, an' wherever 'e was found the golden coffin yent fer away, neether. A good many 'ev searched aater 'e, but tha could never come acraas un. Ther was 'e as was about yer a while back. 'E 'ed the ingine a pullin' an't about, for wiks an' wiks, an' a shiftin' thaay owl' saasens, an some an 'em tha couldn't mauve at all, an' 'ed to gie't out, but I be sartin sure I ploughed a top an in one daay, but I was afeared to stop an look at un, or saay anythenk about it. 'Tis a bit brighter out now, siminly, yen it, landlerd?"

"Aa, but 'tis no good for thee to caddie thiseif; t'ull be as bad as ever, dareckly, an' jest look awver Kingstone Lisle yander. Bad job fer the P'int to P'int. Oni the 'ed uns ool be ther to-day."

"Ed uns er no 'ed uns, I byent ashemmed o' myself, ef e be

a cyarter. My trade's as good as yer an' ther one, an' thine, too, shepherd, yen a?"

"Yes, yes, yes, yes. To be sure a is. Sixty years I've 'ed a back o' the White 'Oss, an' a raa cowld wind a bitin' an e in the winter, an' I bin that nummel e could n' veel nothin'; an' if e wanted a mou'ful o' bren cheese e 'ad to 'owld it wi' one 'and an' nibble't a bit, an' then channge it to t'other an' nibble a bit moore, an' stuff 'em in mi pocket to an' agyen, to warm 'em. Aa, thaay can zaay what tha be a mine t'oot about thaay 'ills, but 'tis a sight 'warmer down yer, in the winter, awhever."

"Dost mind when the owl' bwoy killed the devul, blacksmith? That was Aishbury way, was'n' it?" the carter interposes.

"Aa! Tha send un up aater the coulter, as we'd a mended, bi night, an' tried to vrighten in, but tha couldn' do that; 'e was too derrin'. A 'ed to come along the grounds ther to Odstone, an' one an 'em put a cow-skin awver is 'ed, 'arns an' all, an' set an the stile under the tharnin boughs. When the owl' bwoy come up an' sid un a top o' the stile, a sed: 'Out o' the rawd, an' let I get awver,' but t'other un set still, an' never squatched a word. 'Out o' the rawd, an' let I get awver'; the owl' bwoy sed agyen. No answer. Then a ses: 'If thee dossn't get out o' the rawd an' let I get awver, I'll fetch tha down wi' this coulter,' an' begad if a didn't, too, an' killed un, right anuf, an' went whum an' telled 'em all a'd bin an' killed the devul, an' thaay went along wi'n an' found matey dead, wi' the cow-skin wrapped all roun' in."

Then the carter began again: "Tha's like Bill Bunce an' Joe New, as stawl the ship down at Roves', but tha's a purty many years ago now. Tha'd bin a stwun deggin', an' tha sid the ship 'angin' up from the beamm, skinned an' dressed. Tha 'greed to hae'n that night. So tha crawp up the lane in the quiet, an' on'ooked un, an' awaay tha went, wi' ther 'ed inside an in, bi turns. When tha was aaf-way down the lane tha yerd somebidy a comin'. 'Chock un in the ditch, you !' Joe sed. 'No, that I wunt,' sed Bunce. Way goes Joe, droo the 'edge. Then Bunce 'e drowed the ship down in the middle o' the road, an' stroddled acraas 'is back. By-'m-by the strannger comes up an' stops. A didn' know what to make an't. Then Bill Bunce lifted the ship's 'ed up, and shouted: 'Barr-r-r.' 'Way goes matey, full ter, an' Willum went 'ome wi' the ship. A few days aater a met the maaster, look. 'Mister Bunce,' ses 'e, 'I hey a mind to hey you locked up. What did e steal my ship for?'

"'Cause I thawt a'd bide ther an' spile, maaster,' Bunce sed.

"'Ef e steals ar 'nother I shall hev e locked up, mind.'

"'I wun 'ae nar 'nother if ya don' skin 'is yed better.'

"'Good job I did n' ketch tha!'

"'Aa, you was abed an' asleep awright, maaster,' t'other answered un."

Presently the rain ceases to beat against the window, the clouds lift, and a patch of blue sky appears over the line of the high downs. Then the carter jumps up and prepares to leave, with: "Yellacks is the Dutchman's britches a top o' the chimmuck, an' bagger if owl' 'Enery Cook yent a bin to the P'int to P'int, an' back agyen. I must go an' ax 'e all about it, an' see who got the bit o' ribban, an' 'ow many fell into Rosy Bruk, an' all an't. Dwunt ferget thaay shet lenks, blacksmith; an' jest steck a bit o' sowlder roun' that kittle fer I, ef you plaase, awhever. The sun ull be a shinin' out an the owl' White 'Oss yander, tareckly."

1. Dismal.
2. Too many raindrops on one.
3. Full of sparks.
4. Not but.